WELCOME TO

Art Class

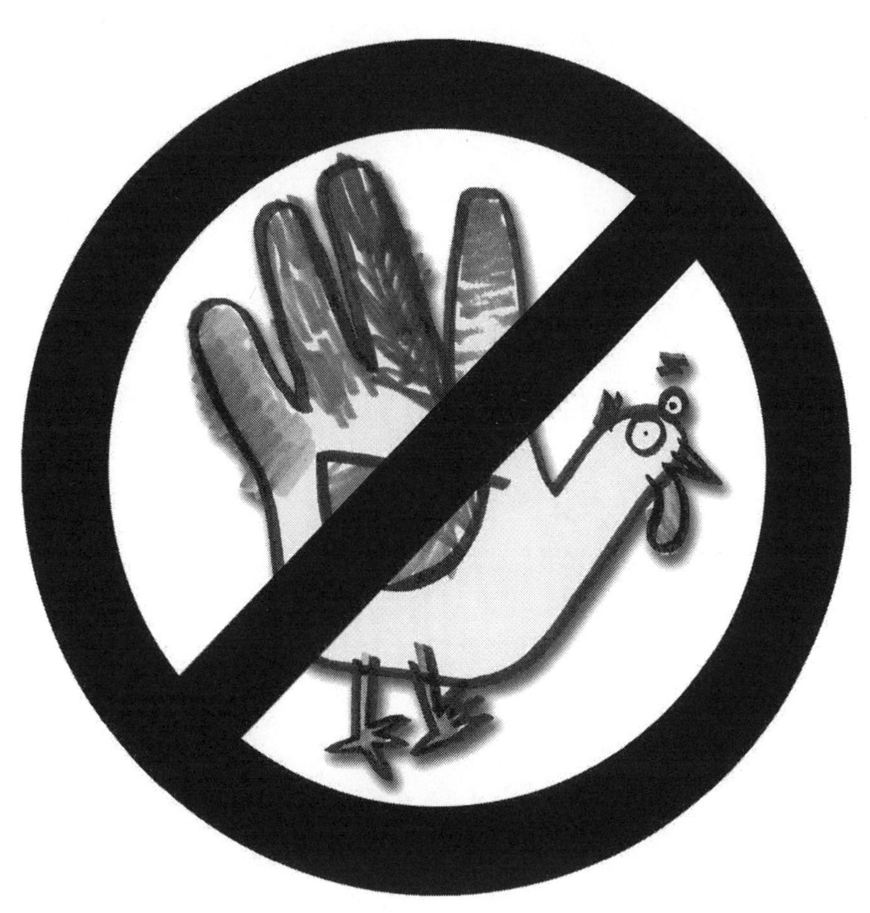

Your Name ________________________ Period _____

Class: ________________________ Homeroom _____

> You will use this ALL year!
> # DO NOT LOSE IT

Teacher Edition

Elementary Art Explorations

A Classroom Companion for Painting, Drawing, and Sculpture

Teacher Edition

ISBN 13: 978-0-9838622-7-7
ISBN 10: 0983862273

Printer: Createspace
Publisher: Firehouse Publishing, www.firehousepublications.com

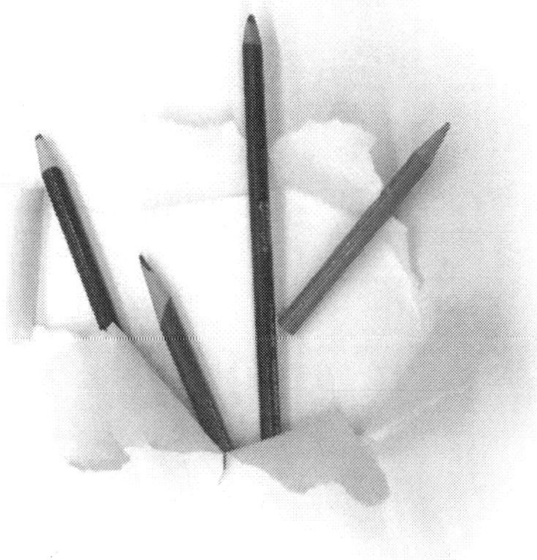

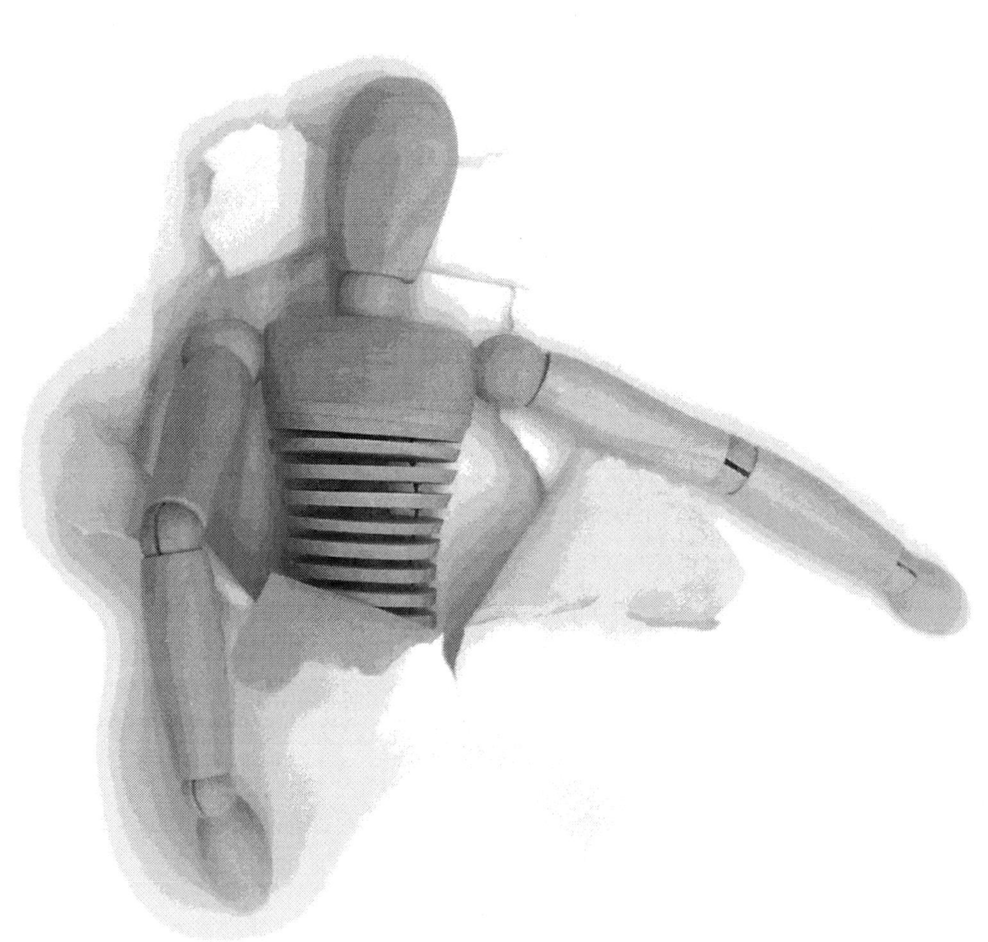

Student Achievement & Relevance

In a time when the economy is strained and schools must choose to make cuts, it is often the art department that is the first to suffer as it is considered peripheral "fluff" or a dumping-ground.

There is a wealth of evidence that a rigorous arts program benefits students. It may be the problem solving methods we use daily, or our natural "backwards design" approach that helps our students succeed. Art teachers know that these same concepts are what we already do, but they are only recently coming into the light as the new "cutting edge" of education. I think it is this and more.

Informal evidence from my school's guidance department indicates that students who take my course are 50% LESS likely to fail standardized testing. (high school) This is information that can grab the attention of your administration and Board of Education.

Art is the one class where the concepts of math, science, history, language, and writing can converge in a well-orchestrated, rigorous, and relevant program. We not only come to understand the concepts but we use them and manipulate them for deeper understanding on multiple sensory levels of thinking. I have divided this workbook by multicurricula units so that this concrete connection to academic core courses is more easily seen.

Does an art class lose its creative edge by incorporating other subjects? All my experience tells me that this integration enhances it. Students have a deeper understanding of the work; they come to see the relevance, and are more likely to "buy into" the concepts. When students ask, "Why do we have to know this stuff?" the answer becomes relevant through our daily approach, process, and end products.

ALL projects herein are designed to have successful divergent results, incorporate creative problem solving, and bring relevant connections to students' lives. This book, targeting grades four through eight, is built for student success on many levels from gifted to challenged. This in turn is helpful in fulfilling mandated state and federal accommodations so that *no child is left behind.*

This elementary edition is based on my previous book focusing on middle and high school populations. Mush is the same here though often simplified for the younger population.

~ Eric Gibbons

Teachers Please Note

Most of the following worksheets are repeated in the back of the book with answers filled in. This is true in the student edition as well so that those with incomplete answers can have complete information for exams and tests.

This is helpful too for students with special needs that you are required to provide additional study guides and information for. In this way their families may help them study.

Though the answers are in the back, I would not share that with the students until right before a test. Most do not explore their workbooks enough to know that many answers are there.

> **Please tell students to write their name on the inside cover,**
> **spine, and on all "pass-points" at the rear of their books**
> **with a color permanent marker.**
> **This will help avoid loss or theft.**

Student Workbooks DO NOT include lessons or as many samples.

Teacher Workbook Contents

Rules & Expectations	8
Elements of Art	10/133
Principles of Art	12/135
Color Vocabulary	16/138
Color & Shape Feelings	30/140
Material, Care, & Safety	27, 38
Self Expression	34, 43
Math & Geometry in Art	63/200
Shading & Forms	83
Perspective	76/139
Face Proportions	88
Science Concepts & Art	90
World Cultures & Diversity	96
Service Learning	106
English & Literature	116
Composition & Writing	124
Vocabulary & Reference	133
History & Research	125
Visual Review	135

---- Teacher Edition Only ----

Video Resources	167
Intercurricular Lessons	171
Sketchbook Concepts	178
The Tao of Teaching Art	183
Project Rubrics	184
Supplies List & Suggestions	187
Critique (*For photo copies*)	190
Sub Plans	191
Math Answers	

Student Workbook Contents

Rules	6
Elements of Art	8
Principles of Art	10
Color Vocabulary	18
Color & Shape Feelings	32
Material, Care, & Safety	29, 41
Self Expression	34, 45
Math & Geometry in Art	64
Perspective	74
Shading & Forms	79
Face Proportions	84
Science Concepts & Art	86
World Cultures & Diversity	92
Service Learning	100
English & Literature	109
Composition & Writing	116
Vocabulary & Reference	125
History & Research	133
Visual Review	151
Project Notes	163
Project Sketch Pages	169
Video Notes	179
Sketch Ideas	188
Project Rubrics	193
Pass Points (4 per year)	198

Welcome to Art Class

My name is _______________________________

My Teacher's name is _______________________________

The rules of the classroom are:

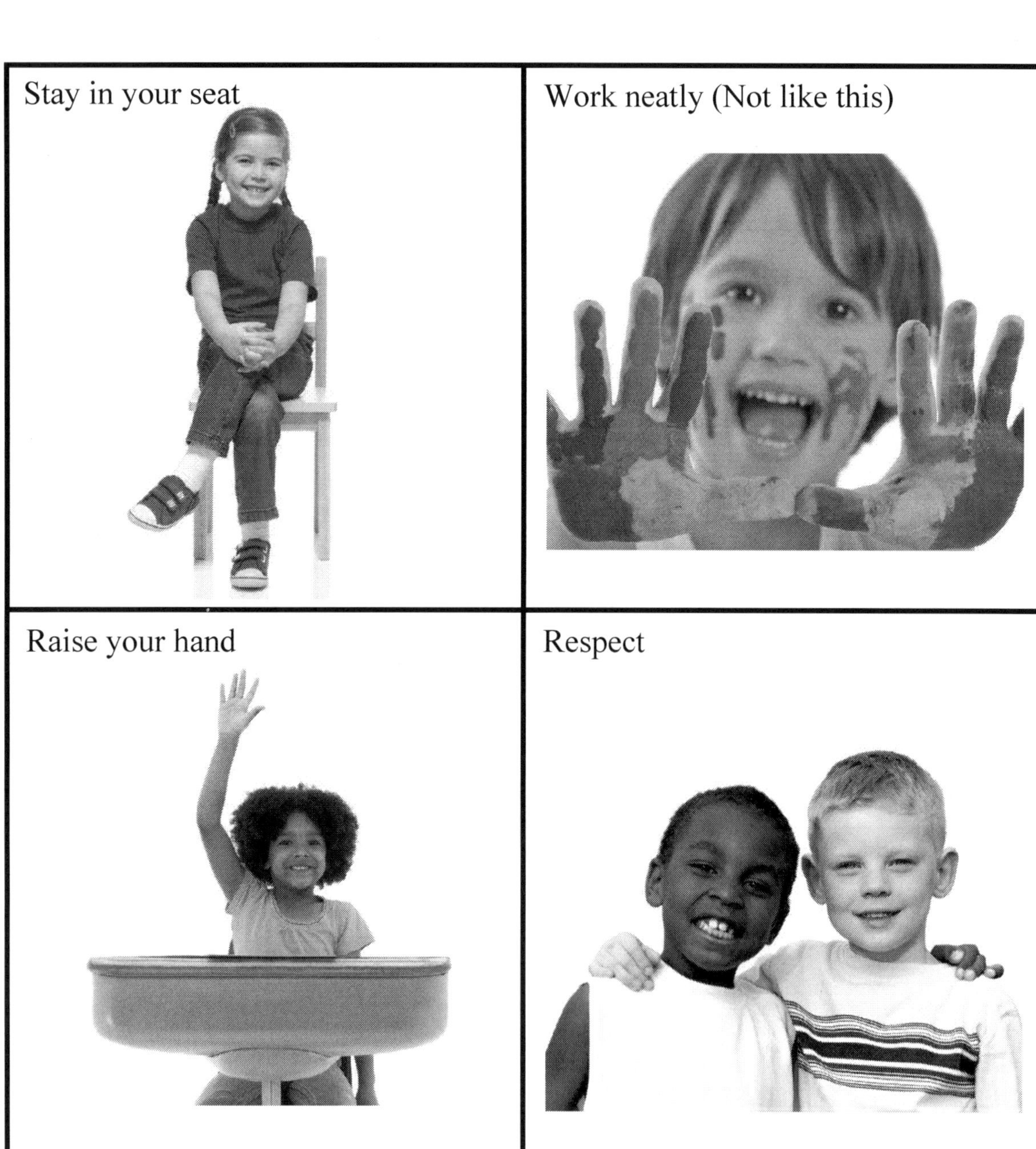

The rules in this room are about… **RESPECT**

...**For the teacher,** when you raise your hand and stay in your seat.
...**For each other,** when you treat each other with kindness.
...**For our projects** when you keep things neat and follow directions.
...**For the stuff that we use** so it is not wasted or ruined.

_____% of your grade is your art projects
_____% is written work like tests
_____% is video notes or homework
_____% _________________________
_____% _________________________

<u>Your art projects are graded on an average of the following 5 things:</u>

Neatness: NOT folded, ripped, no smudges, not rushed or messy.
Completeness: No empty areas, filled in, well done, has everything we asked for.
Originality: Not copied, 100% your own idea. BONUS for new ideas!
Following Directions: Going step by step, not skipping steps.
Conduct: Were you helpful, or did you stop others from working?

Your artwork does not have to be "pretty" or somehow a great work of art. NOT everyone is an ARTIST. If you are neat, complete, original, follow directions, and are respectful, you will pass.

<u>ANYTHING</u> is better than a ZERO. Even an "F" is _______ points. A zero is nothing. If you are missing just one project, passing is very hard. <u>If you work on your projects every day, your projects will not fail.</u>

Remember:
— Be ready and on time every day
— IF you MIGHT be late, get a pass!
— Have a pencil EVERY DAY.

The rule about phones and i-pods is: _________________________________

ALSO: ____

It is ALWAYS your job to make up any missing work. You need to see your teacher when you return from a vacation or sickness and make up missing work.

The 8 Art Elements

A line is the most simple thing in art. We call it an art element. You need lines to draw anything. What can you measure about a line? ___________________________
What are some lines you see around you?

Draw 3 different kinds of lines here:

<table>
<tr><td>1</td><td>2</td><td>3</td></tr>
</table>

A line that touches itself makes a shape. A shape is _____ -D because we can measure the __________ and __________ of it. "D" is short for Dimension. There are # _____ basic shapes. Draw the basic shapes below:

__________ put together can create a form. A box is a form made from 6 square shapes. In art we call a box a special name. Think of the ice in your freezer at home. You don't call them *ice boxes*, you call them ice ___________. You eat ice cream in a __________, that's another basic form. What are the other two basic forms? ______________ and ______________.
Can you draw all the forms below?

Color is sometimes the first thing we see. Most colors we see are mixed from just #_____ basic colors. These colors are ___________, _________, ___________. The other name for basic colors is ______________ colors. When basic colors mix, they make new colors. We call them ________________ colors. Try mixing the basic colors below to see what colors they make. (Use marker, crayon, or color pencil)

<table>
<tr><td>Red and blue</td><td>Red and yellow</td><td>Yellow and blue</td></tr>
</table>

All things, art and not-art, take up ________________. It comes in two kinds, ______________ where the thing is, and ________________ which is the empty area around it. When you swim in a pool, you are in the _____________ __________ of the water. When you are in school, you are in the _____________ __________ of the building.

Everything around us we can see has weight. Even air has weight! What is another word for weight? _______________ . Sometimes things look heavier or lighter than they really are. Metal and rocks are things we think of when we see dark colors. Cotton and clouds are things we think of when we see light colors. ________________ colors often look heavier than _______________ colors.

Everything you touch has a feeling; smooth, rough, wet, dry, etc. This is the art element of ____________________ .

Draw 3 examples below:

<table>
<tr><td>1</td><td>2</td><td>3</td></tr>
</table>

The last art element might be the most important. Without it we cannot even see any of the rest. What can it be? _______________ . When we draw, we sometimes add shadows, which are the opposite of this art element.

Principles of Art & Design

1. What does **balance** mean?

2. Draw two things balanced below:

3. Can you draw one thing balanced by many smaller ones below?

4. Try drawing something that is moving. How do you make it look like its moving? **Movement** is an art principal.

5. What is **contrast**? ____
Can you draw two opposite objects below?

6. What is **unity**? ____
Can you draw some things in unity below?

7. What is **emphasis**? (*em-fa-sis*) _______________________________

8. Draw sometime below and make one thing stand out with emphasis.

9. What is **pattern**? ____
Please draw 3 patterns below.

1	2	3

10. Draw two kinds of patterns below: a planned pattern and an organic pattern.

Planned/Mechanical   Organic/Natural

1	2

11. What is **variety**?

12. How is variety different from **contrast**?

13. Do a drawing of your shoe on the next page. Label three or more of the art principals you can see in your drawing. (Student book has sketch page here →)

Art Principles Worksheet   *(Student Workbook has 4 pages like this)*   (tiny sketch below)
(TEACHER: Put up a poster from art history and have students complete this form)

The artwork sample is called:

____

by _________________________________.

_______________________ is the style of art.

Where do you see unity?

Where do you see variety?

Where do you see contrast or opposites?

What is emphasized in the art? What is the main important part?

Where do you see movement?

How does the artist balance the picture?

What kinds of patterns can you see?

Let's Learn About Color

Shade is the opposite of ___________. Without shadow we would all look flat like a cartoon picture. In art we draw shadows to show that things take up space. They usually have one side in light, and another side that is shaded. Sometimes people draw shadows with black or gray, but you can also use cool colors like green, purple, or blue. I drew a ball below with a shadow. You try and draw something with a shadow too.

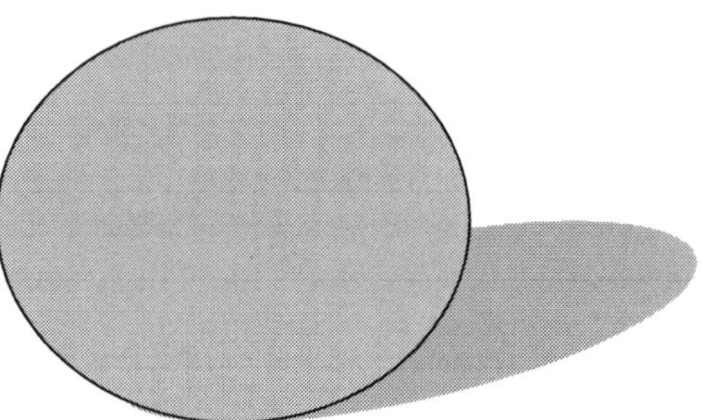

Primary Colors (Pry-mary) are sometimes called the basic colors. Primary means *first* or *the beginning*. Just like Primary school is for grades one through about six. There are #_______ primary colors. These colors are _____________, _____________, and _____________.

When you make a cake, you need to use eggs. If you don't have eggs, can you just use pickles or jelly instead? NO, you have to go out and get some eggs. Eggs are a primary ingredient. You cannot put things together to make an egg, you have to go and get it.

This is just like the primary colors. You cannot mix a primary color, you have to go get it. This is why they are so special. Almost every color you see around you is a primary color, or was made from mixing primary colors.

Use only your primary colors, and draw your shoe or bookbag below.

Secondary Colors are like the children of the primary colors. Secondary means the second layer of color, after primaries. Just like secondary school is after primary school. When two primary colors mix, they make a secondary color. Use crayons, pastels, or colored pencils to color in the circles below with primary colors. See what colors they make when they mix.

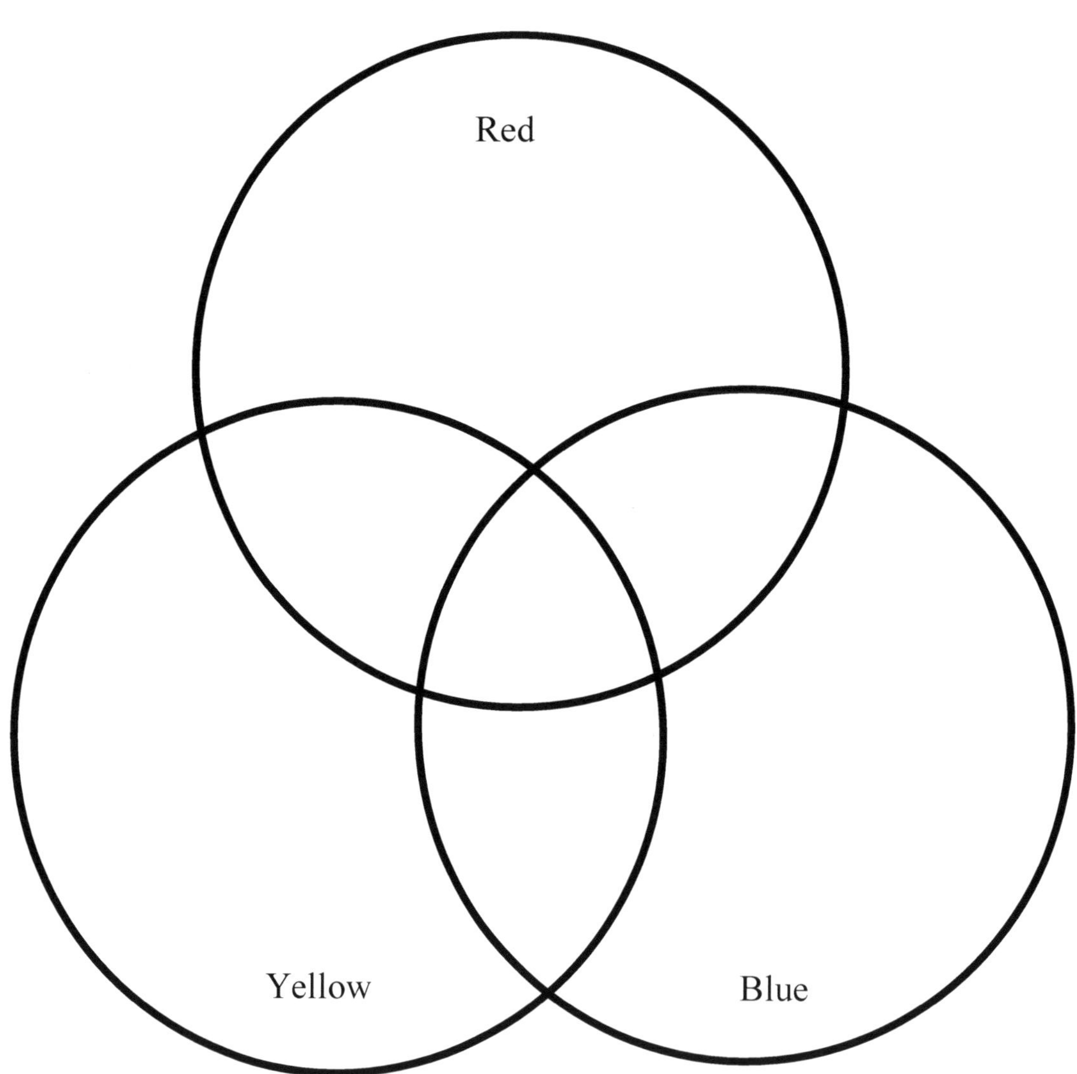

Want to know more? The color in the middle has a long and special name.

__________________________ ____________________.

Spectrum is the colors in a rainbow. A rainbow is made when the water drops in the air splits the white light from the sun into all the colors we can see in a rainbow. These colors are red, orange, yellow, green, blue, and purple. They are always in this order. These are also all the primary and secondary colors.

Please fill in the colors of the rainbow in the picture below, starting with red.

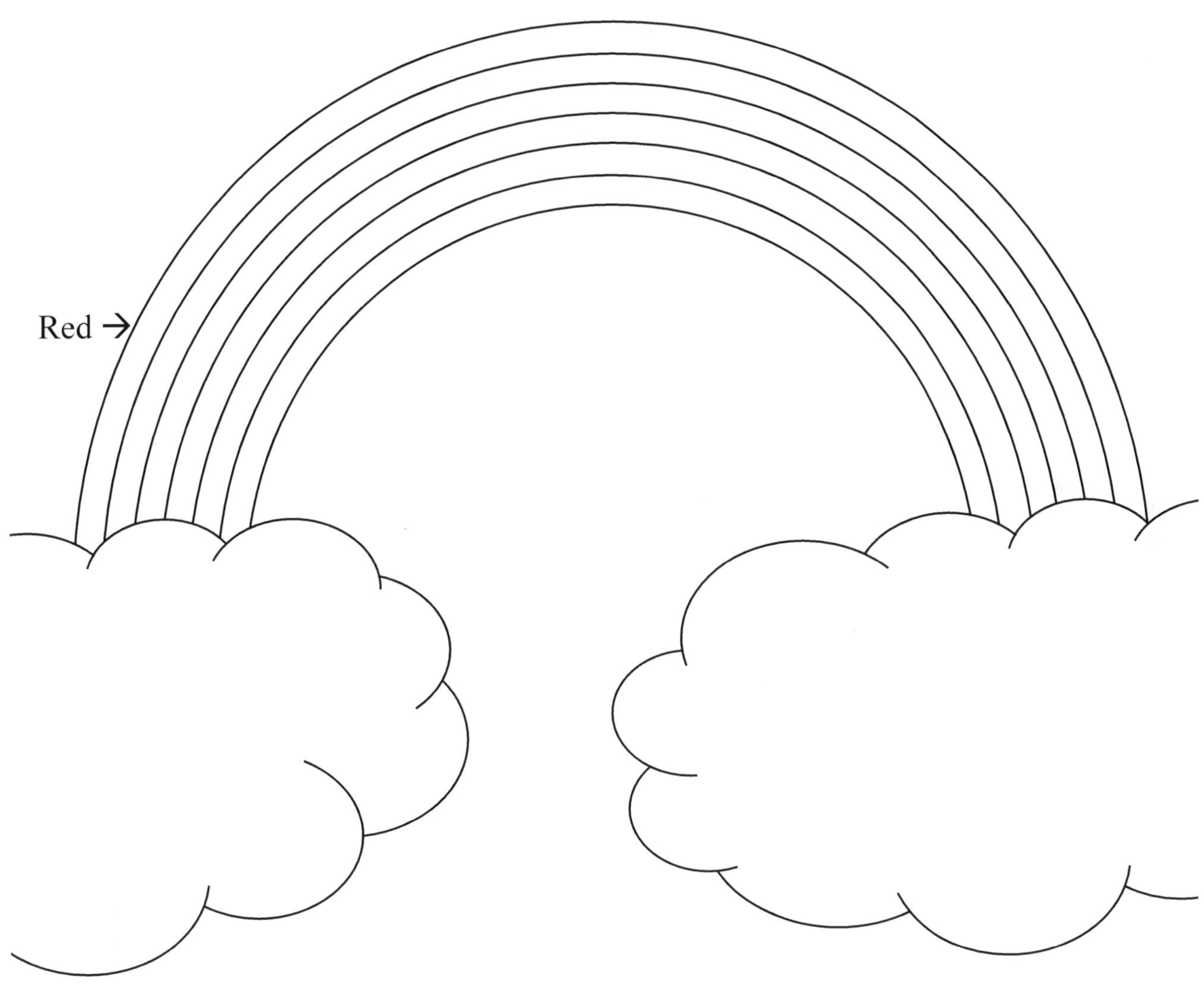

Analogous Colors (*Ah-nail-la-gus*) These are neighboring colors. When you look at the rainbow, red is next to orange, so they are analogous colors. The only strange one is red and purple. If a rainbow was in a circle, like the color wheel below, then you can see how they are neighboring colors too.

COLOR WHEEL →

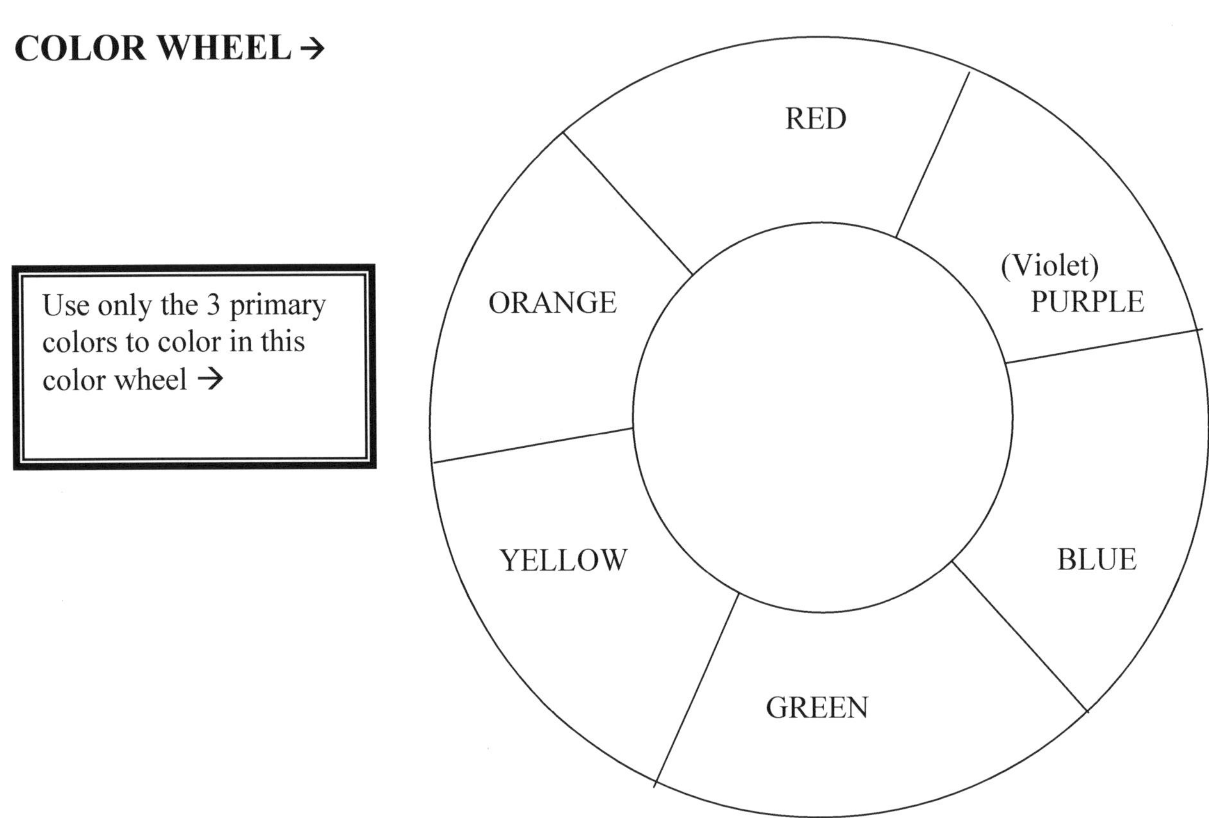

Use only the 3 primary colors to color in this color wheel →

How can you remember the colors of the spectrum? We know they are red, orange, yellow, green, blue, and purple. It might help to make a silly sentence to help you remember. What sentence can you make? The first word should start with an "R" for red. Then "O" for orange, and so on. Try to make a sentence below for you to remember your spectrum.

R________ O________ Y________ G________ B________ P________ .

Complementary Colors: (*Com-pla-men-tary*) These are colors that are on opposite sides of the color wheel. When you look back you will see that colors like blue and orange are on opposite sides. When you mix opposites, you get a really muddy or dirty looking color. This is called Chromatic Gray. (Kro-mat-tik) If colors were perfect, the gray would look like a real gray, but it just looks like brown to us.

Complimentary colors are often used for holidays. What holiday goes with each pair of colors? Can you draw a whole holiday scene with just 2 complimentary colors?

1. Red and green are used in this holiday: ________________________________

2. Blue and orange are used in this holiday: ________________________________

3. Purple and Yellow are used in this holiday: ________________________________

Mini-holiday picture below:

Monochromatic: (*ma-no-kro-ma-tic*) Mono = one, Chroma = color, so mochromatic means *of one color*. If you did a monochromatic picture in blue, you would do it in all kinds of blue; light blue, dark blue, medium blue. You could even add black or white. Many artists make colors lighter or darker by pressing harder or softer with their crayons or pencils. Can you use one color to create a picture of something below? What is your favorite color?

Warm Colors: Warm colors should remind you of warm things. Think of fire, the sun, a hot stove; what colors are these things?

________________, ________________, ________________.

Warm colors are active colors. They have lots of energy because they are so bright.

Draw something hot below and only use your warm colors OR draw yourself doing something very active, like a sport, and use just warm colors.

Cool Colors: cool colors should remind you of cool or cold things. Think water, the ocean, a river, grass, or the sky when it's getting dark; what colors are these?

______________, ______________, ______________.

Cool colors are calm colors. They are relaxing and have little energy.

Draw something peaceful below and only use your cool colors OR draw yourself doing something very relaxing, like taking a nap, relaxing with friends, or strolling through a park using only cool colors.

Coloring Neatly

Do not rush. When you rush things like coloring, it does not look neat

- — Never Scribble, it is messy
- — Color with small side-by-side marks. (Parallel Strokes)
- — Press light for light color, press harder for strong color
- — Try to stay in the lines you have made
- — Color in layers. Nothing is the same color as a crayon
- — Try shading with a neighboring or opposite color before using black
- — Be patient, good work takes time

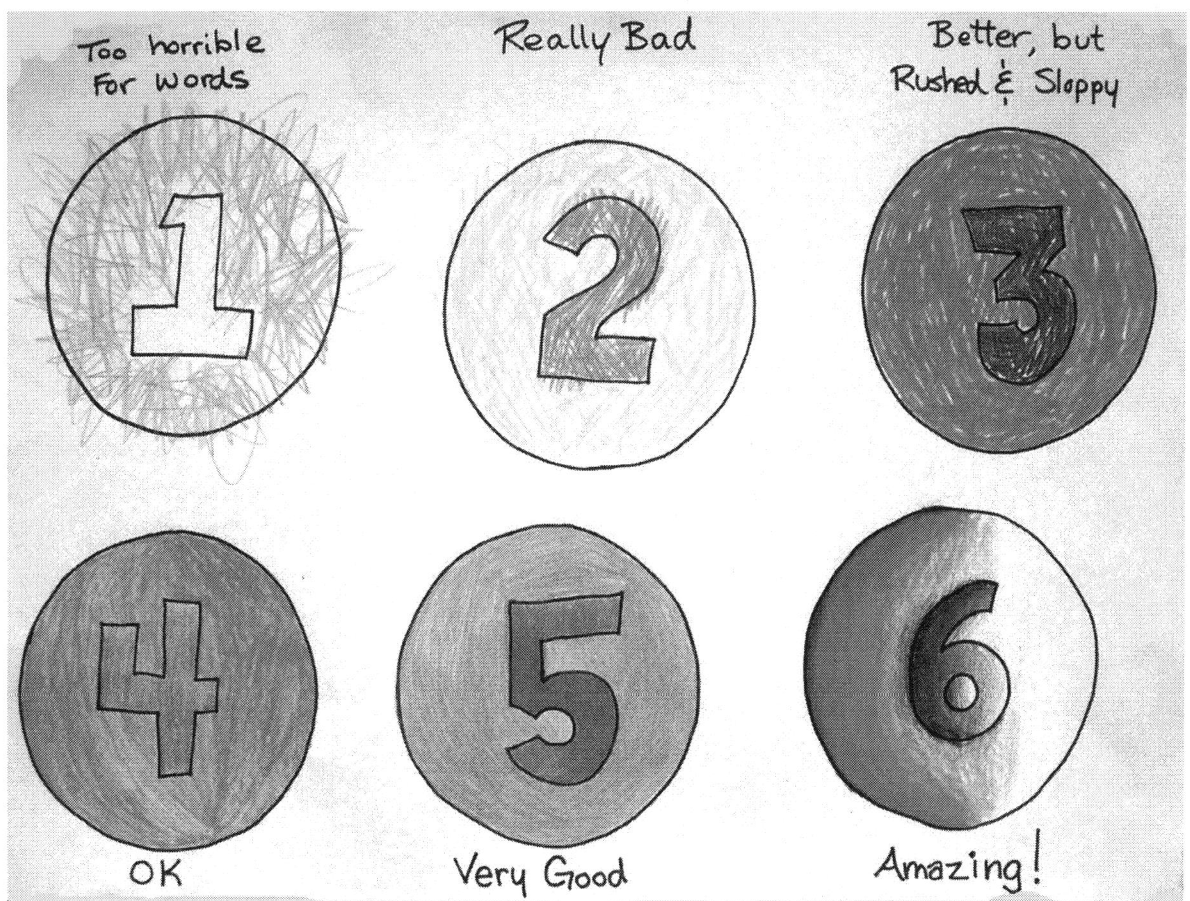

You do not have to be an artist to be neat!
Take your time, do your best.

Coloring Practice:

Start with shape number 1. Color it in neatly; try to stay in the lines. When you are done, show it to your teacher. They will tell you how you did, and what you can do to make it better. Then you can do the next one. Show your teacher after you finish each shape. This is a chance to show off your coloring skills.

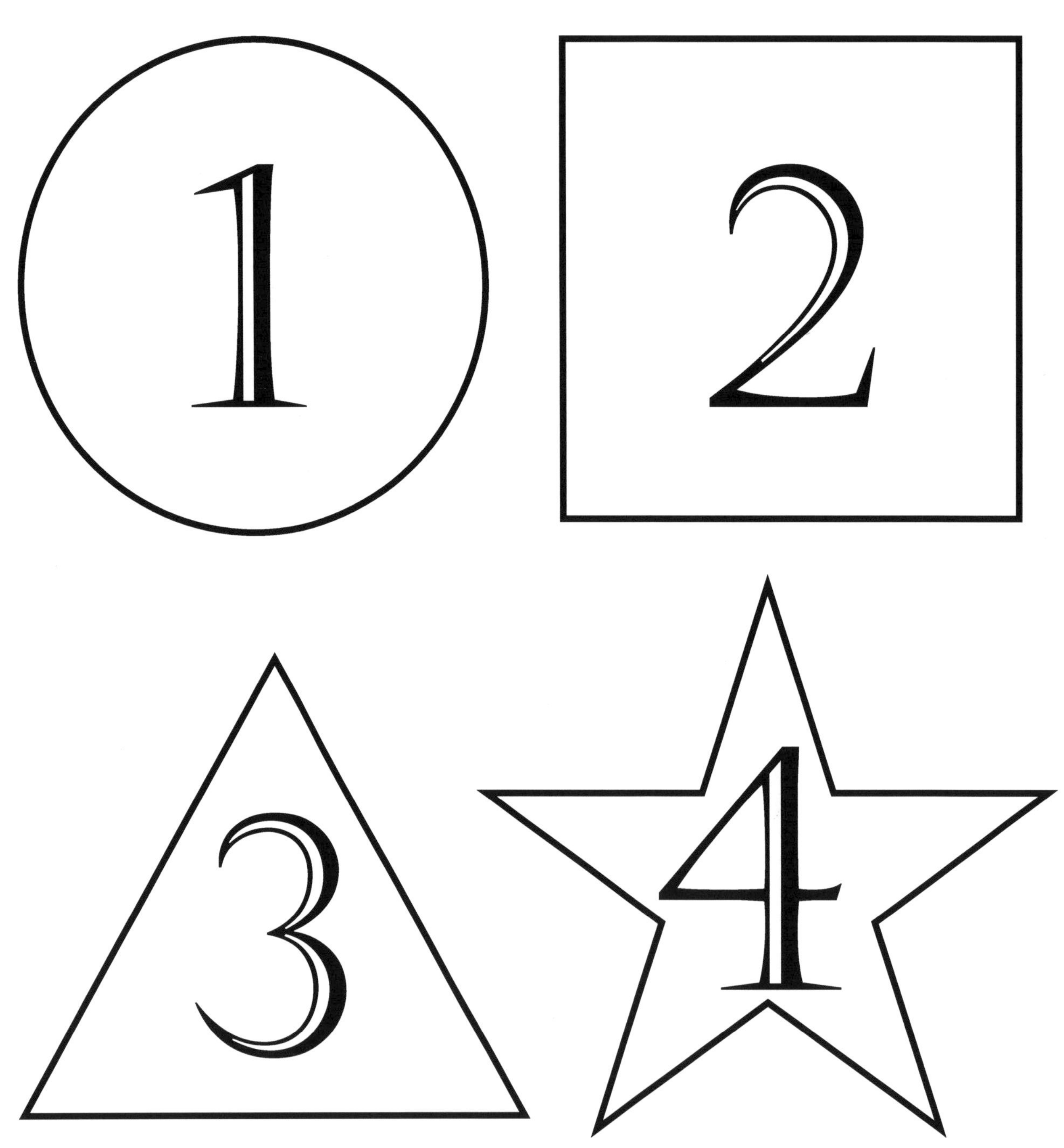

Paint Brush Care

Paint brushes are an important tool in art.
They are expensive and need to be cared for.
Some paints can ruin brushes,
if they are not cleaned right.

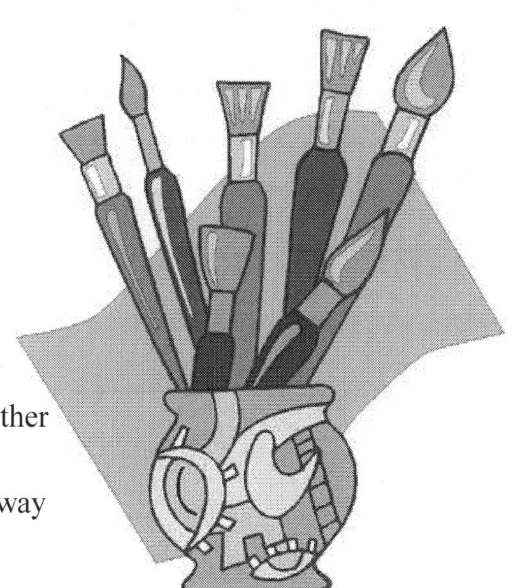

— Always use COLD water to clean a brush

— Hot water melts the glue that holds the brush together

— Wash the **collar** of the brush too

— Test your clean brush on paper before putting it away

— Put brushes in a cup or can with the brush-end-up

Wash all three parts of the brush

Symbols

Symbols are very important in art. We use symbols every day. If you had to make a symbol for a park, you could draw the whole park with trees, walking paths, animals, grass, and more, or you could use a leaf as a symbol for a park.

1. How does someone know to stop their car on a road? What symbol is at the corner to tell them they have to stop?

2. If you wanted to tell someone you loved them, you could draw a symbol and they would know right away what it meant. What is this symbol?

3. Even letters are symbols for sounds that we use to speak words. An "M" is just a line with two bumps like a mountain. But in English it is a symbol for the "M" sound. What popular restaurant has a giant "M" outside? (Hint: chicken nuggets)

4. When you go to the bathroom in school or in a restaurant, how do you know what door to go in? Usually there are at least two different doors to go in. What is the symbol of the door you use? Draw it here:

(*Answers*: 1. Stop light or stop sign, 2. Heart, 3. McDonald's, 4. Usually a boy or girl cartoon.)

On the next page draw a symbol in each box or the word in the box. Sometimes everyone will draw the same symbol, but sometimes people will draw different symbols. Draw a picture to be the symbol for that word.

Draw a symbol in each box:

<table>
<tr><td>Nature</td><td>People</td><td>Playground</td></tr>
<tr><td>Home</td><td>Computer</td><td>School</td></tr>
<tr><td>Ocean</td><td>Farm</td><td>Teacher</td></tr>
</table>

Colors and Shapes have feelings too!

Red is the color of blood, stop signs, and lava. How do these things make you feel?

Orange is the color of a hot stove burner, warning signs, and some spicy sauces. How do these things make people feel?

Yellow is the color of the sun, smiley faces, and many flowers. How do these things make people feel?

Green is the color of grass, healthy vegetables, and many things that grow. What feelings does this give people?

Blue is the color of the ocean and the sky. When you are relaxing at the beach or laying down looking up at the sky on a beautiful day, how do you feel?

Purple is the color of royalty, deep oceans, and starry nights. What kinds of feelings do these give you?

Triangles are sharp like broken glass, knives, and arrows. How would you feel if these were on the ground all around you?

Circles are soft like balloons, balls, bubbles, and hoopla-hoops. How do these things make you feel?

Squares are used to make bricks, boxes, buildings, and tables. Why do we not use circles to make bricks, boxes, and buildings? (*Because squares and boxes are…*)

Now that we see that colors and shapes can represent feelings, what shapes would you be most like? Are you mostly a square because you are strong, or would you say you are more playful like a circle? Can you be both? We can mix shapes together to make new shapes. If you have a bit of a temper, but most of the time you are a serious person, what shapes would you put together? _______________ and _______________ . Would that look like a house shape?

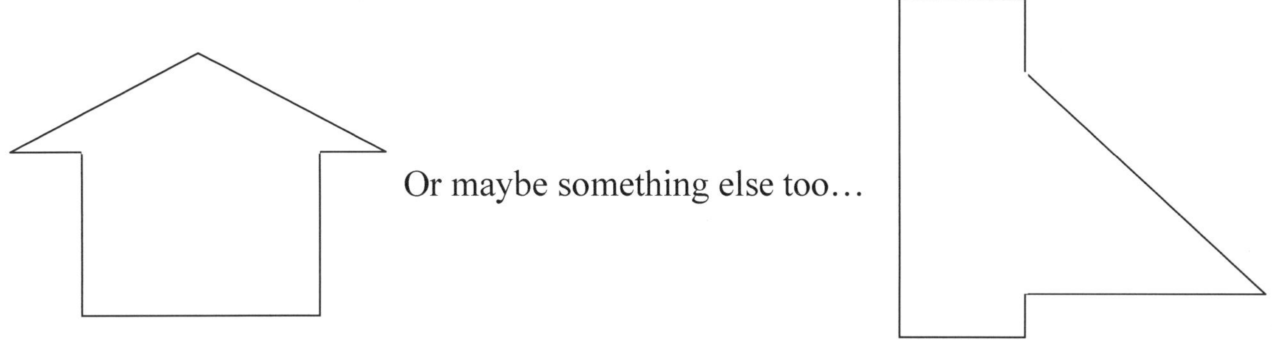

Or maybe something else too…

On the next page, draw a shape that is a mix of shapes as a symbol for you. Use colors and patterns too that help show your personality.

Draw a shape that is a mix of shapes as a symbol for you. Use colors and patterns too that help show your personality below.

Teacher: See rear cover of book for helpful "Emotional Color Wheel."

A Family can be made with symbols in 2-D or 3-D

The first sample is a watercolor painting where all family members are shown with shapes and color as symbols. Overlaps show the relationships between people. The second sample is a mobile of a family. The form and color symbolize each person in the family.

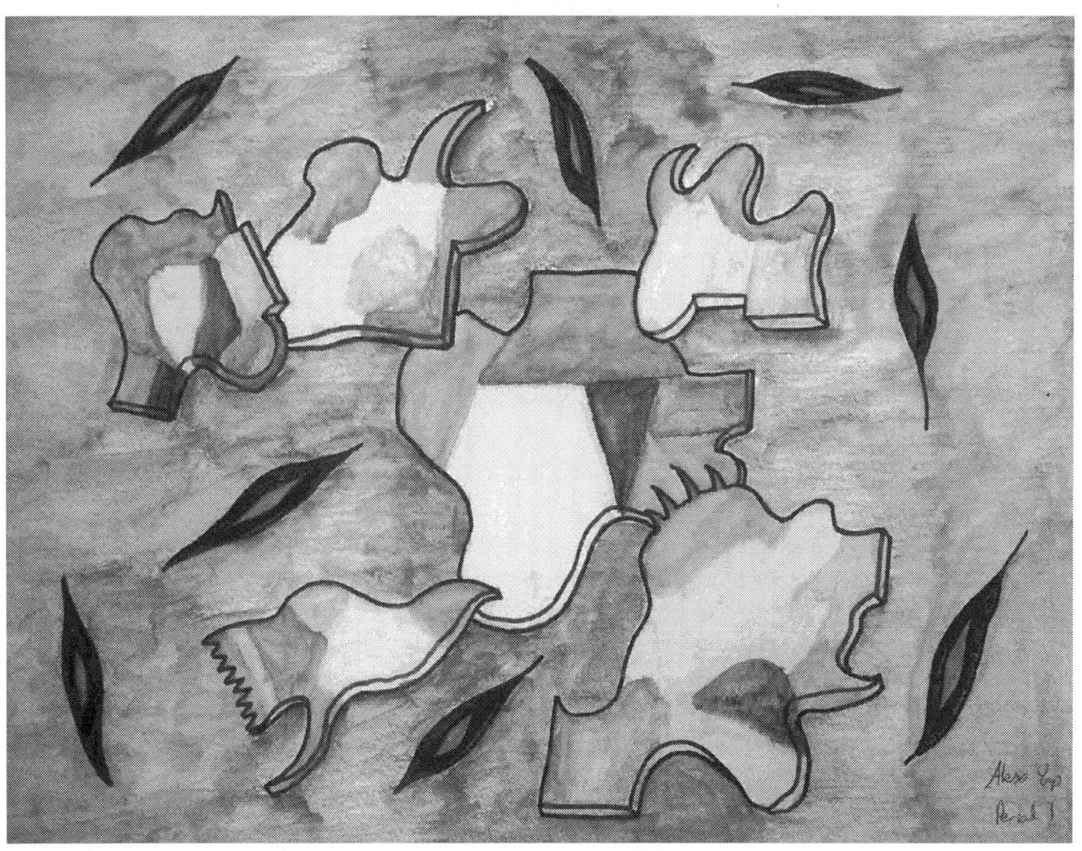

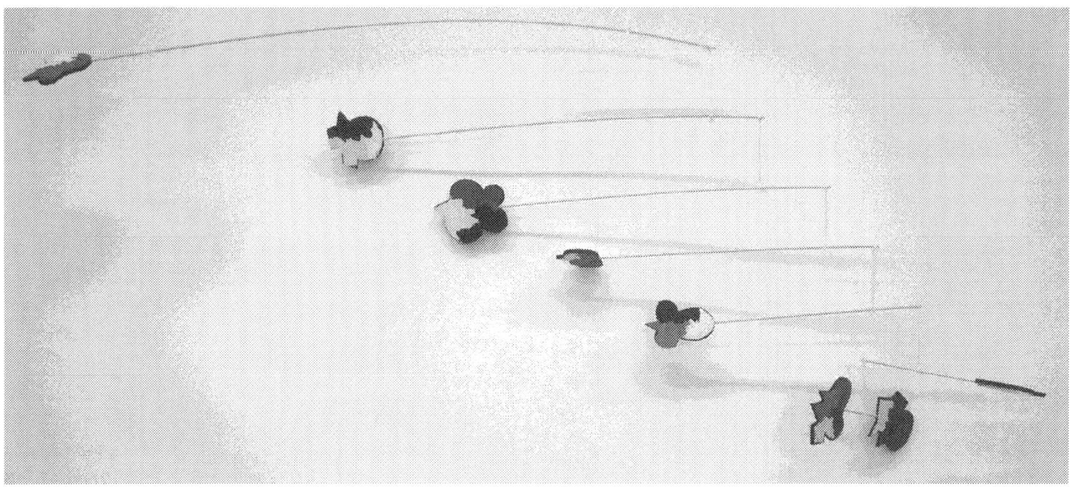

FAMILY

List 8 to 10 people in your family below. It is okay to use initials. Start with people who live with you, then add others. It is okay to include people who have moved away or died. After each name describe the person. **You can include up to ONE pet.**

Tiny Sketch Below

1. _____________ : _________________________

   ____

2. _____________ : _________________________

   ____

3. _____________ : _________________________

   ____

4. _____________ : _________________________

   ____

5. _____________ : _________________________

   ____

6. _____________ : _________________________

   ____

7. _____________ : _________________________

   ____

8. _____________ : _________________________

   ____

9. _____________ : _________________________

   ____

10. _____________ : _________________________

   ____

Put a shape and color in the margin to represent that person.

How would you put the shapes of your family to show who you are closest to, and who you do not get along with? What colors would you put between shapes to show how you feel about them? Sketch your idea below.

Expressive Art (x-press-siv) is art that shows feelings but not "stuff." We show how we feel with colors, shapes, and lines using the pages in this book that teaches you about what feelings go with colors and shapes.

Below is a list of expressive words. Can you create an artwork based on one of these words? Maybe your teacher will put them in a hat and you'll choose a word.

You can do this as a drawing, a painting, with cut outs of color paper, or even as a sculpture. When you have a word picked, write down the colors and shapes you should use to be a symbol for your work. Sketch out some ideas on the next page…

Love
Hate
Flight
Death
Burial
Crazy
Strong
Sad
Depressed
Hopeful
Grace
Dirty
Shy
Embarrassed
Shame
Pride
Hero
Sinful
Travel
Risk
Anger
Happiness
Lazy
Narcissism
Chaos
Heaven
Royal
Forever
Complex
Simplicity

Expressive Sketch Here

PLASTER STRIPS

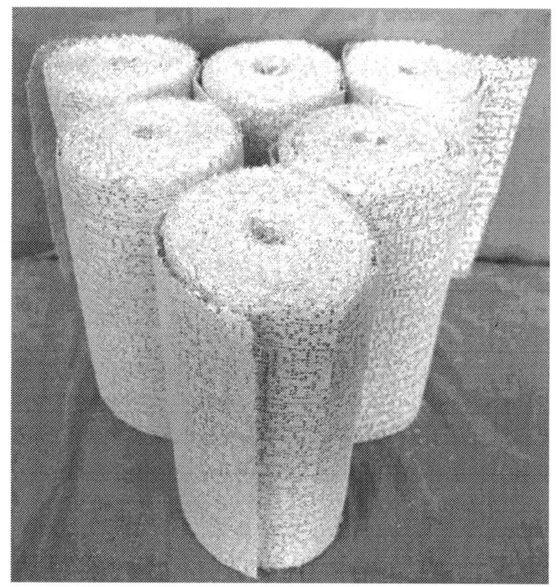

Plaster becomes hard after it touches water. It is very messy so we need to be sure to be neat when we use it.

1. Cover your table area with paper or plastic. Take off any jewelry.

2. Keep plaster and water far enough away that the water won't accidently splash, drip, or spill on the plaster.

3. Watch others so you do not have an accident or spill. Several people can work from one bucket.

When plaster has been dipped in water, it must be squeezed through the fingers and put on your project. Plaster will need to be 2 or 3 layers thick to be strong.

If you get water on a plaster strip, use it right away.

Plaster cannot be re-used once it has hardened.

Smooth strips with your hands as you add them. Without smoothing, one layer will not stick to the last and your art can fall apart.

NEVER put plaster water down a sink. Not from your hands, not from the bucket. It will make stones in the pipes and be VERY expensive to repair.
- Wash hands in plaster water first
- Stir plaster in bucket with hands and put it _________________________
- Let bucket dry and crack out the plaster into garbage

Plaster will come out of clothes, but wearing a smock is good protection.

LIQUID PLASTER

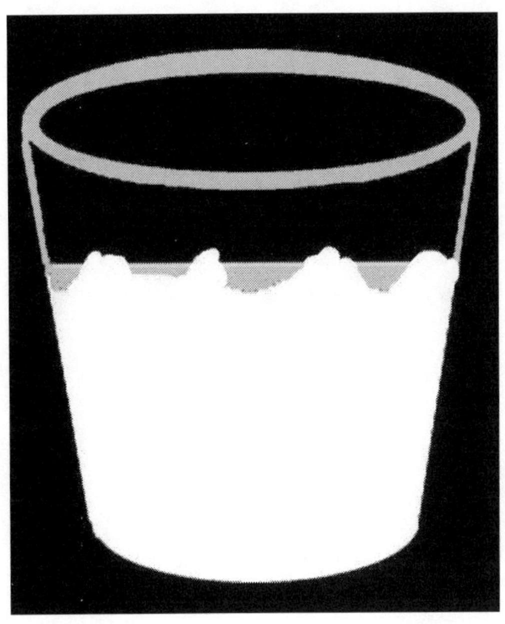

Plaster becomes hard after it touches water. It is very messy so we need to be sure to be neat when we use it.

1. Cover your table area with paper or plastic. Take off any jewelry.

2. Keep plaster and water far enough away that the water won't accidently splash, drip, or spill on the plaster.

3. Watch others so you do not have an accident or spill. Several people can work from one bucket.

Guess how much liquid plaster you need (cup or bucket). Start with LESS THAN HALF of that with water. Hot water hardens plaster faster than cold water; choose what you need.

Add dry plaster with a dry cup, scoop, or spoon by sprinkling a little at a time. . DO NOT STIR! Too much at once will ruin your plaster. DO NOT STIR! Be sure to sprinkle evenly all around your container so it fills evenly. **DO NOT STIR!**

Slowly add plaster until it makes islands in the water disappear in the water. See picture above. Once you have enough islands—about 50%—**you may stir**. The more you stir, the faster the plaster will harden. *Remember, Plaster heats as it dries; be careful if you put it on a person's skin. Thick plaster gets hotter than thin plaster.*

NEVER put plaster down a sink. Not from your hands, not from the bucket. It will form stones in the pipes and be VERY expensive to repair.
   — Wash hands in a bucket of water first
   — Let bucket dry and crack plaster into the garbage. Toss cups.

Hint: *Acrylic paint or medium can be added to plaster. They make the plaster dry much more slowly. Add 1/10 of acrylic medium to the water **before** adding plaster. This can be a fun way to add plaster icing to food sculptures.*

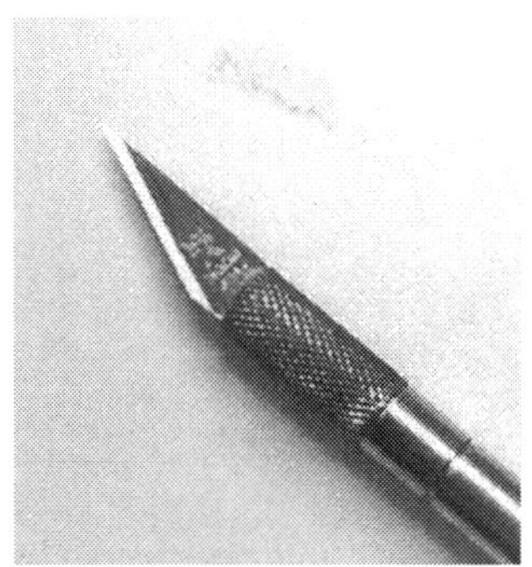

Razor Blades
SAFETY

ALWAYS get permission to use any sharp tools.
- — NEVER play with these tools.
- — Taking one out of the classroom is ILLEGAL and considered a weapon in school.
- — Check that the blade is secure and tight.
- — Keep it capped when not in use.
- — Protect table when cutting.
- — ALWAYS cut away from fingers or body.
- — Hold like a pencil for best control.

IF YOU GET A CUT…
- — Hold cut tightly closed.
- — Tell teacher immediately.
- — Wash with running water.
- — Pinch closed with paper towel.
- — See teacher for band-aid or hall pass to the nurse.

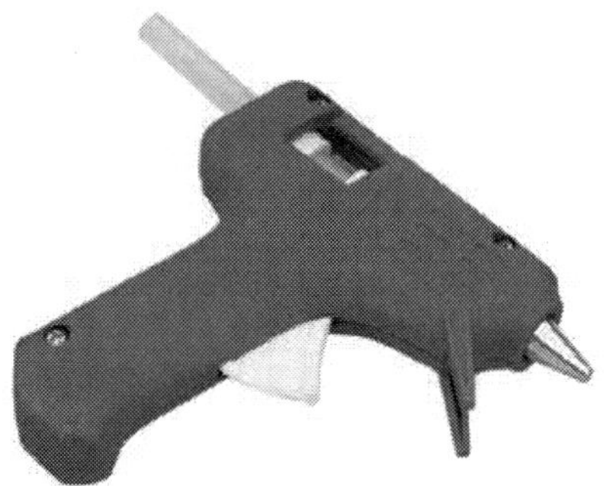

GLUE GUN
SAFETY

GLUE GUNS can heat up to about 400 degrees. They will burn deeply.
NEVER touch the tip of a glue gun. EVEN the glue that comes out can burn badly. Use a craft-stick to move the glue if you need to. Glue guns stay hot for a while after being unplugged! A glue gun is NOT A TOY!

IF YOU GET BURNED, go to a sink quickly and rinse with cool water. If you get a blister, get a pass to the nurse.

Scissor Safety

— Always ask before getting scissors
— Never run with scissors
— Never throw them, or slide them to someone.
— They are not a toy. Even scissors with rounded tips can still cut skin.

Scissors work best when one blade scrapes on the other. Pull a little with the fingers, and push a little with the thumb. Just opening and closing a scissor does not work well. It takes a little practice to use a scissor well.

Cut out this page and practice cutting out this curly line.

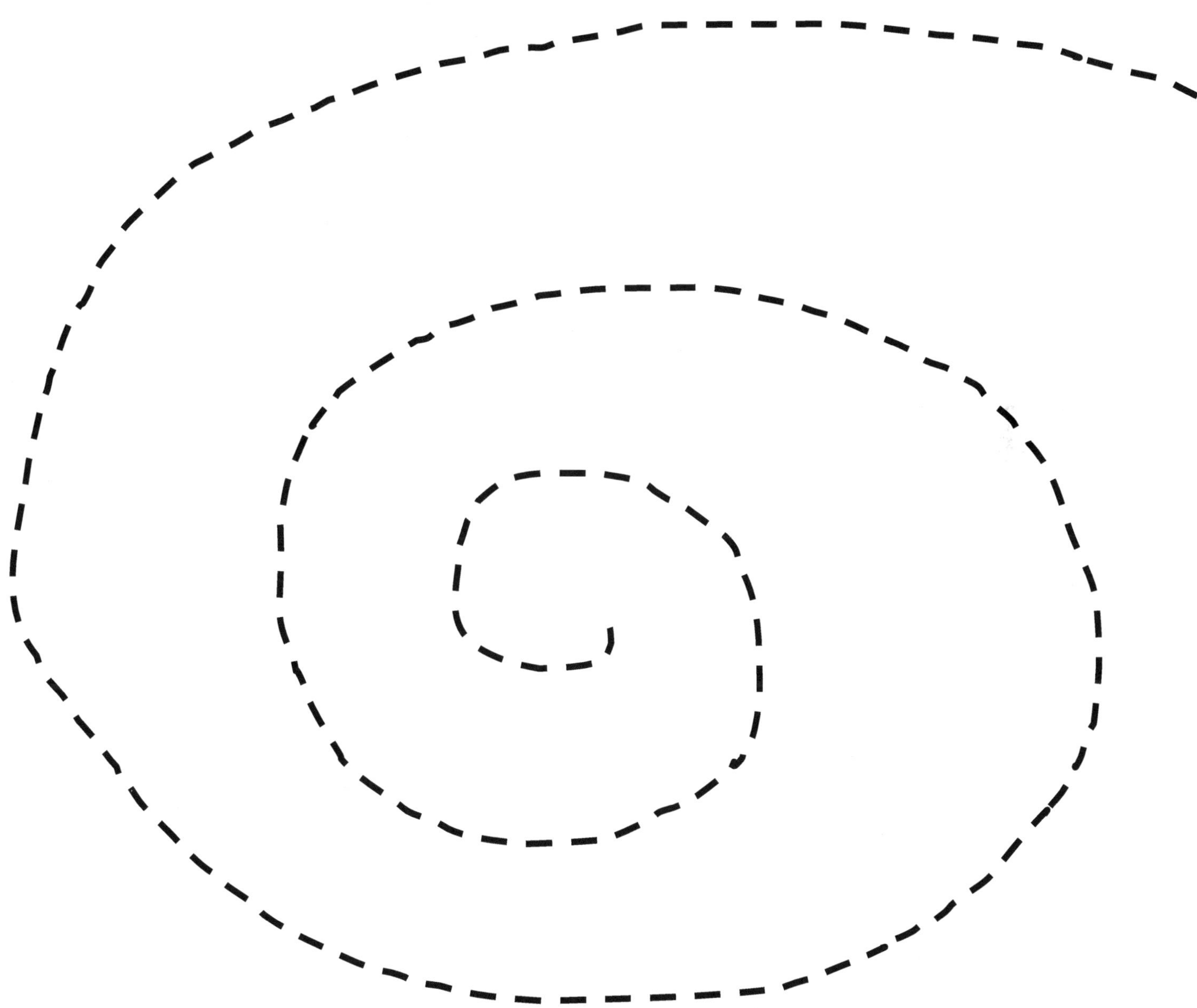

About Me

Art should tell people about who you are in a way they can see. Art can show your feelings.

What are things that people know about you:
(Talents, skills, personality, awards, hobbies, likes, or dislikes…)

List things that most people do not know about you:

List things people think about you that are NOT true:

On the next page, draw what you know about yourself on the inside of the rectangle, and what others think about you on the outside of the rectangle.

See the bottom of the previous page for directions.

Who Am I?

Make a list of what people think they know about you, and another list of what you know about yourself. These lists might be very different. Some people may know you like art, but may not know you traveled to Europe, OR people may not know you have a special talent. You can use codes to hide stuff you do not really want to share with the class.

What others think they know about you / **What you know about yourself**

1. _______________________   1. _______________________

2. _______________________   2. _______________________

3. _______________________   3. _______________________

4. _______________________   4. _______________________

5. _______________________   5. _______________________

6. _______________________   6. _______________________

7. _______________________   7. _______________________

8. _______________________   8. _______________________

9. _______________________   9. _______________________

10. _______________________   10. _______________________

11. _______________________   11. _______________________

12. _______________________   12. _______________________

Make a two-sided project. Do a collage or drawing on one side about what people know about you and the other side revealing what they do not know. You could also do this with a box or mask too, decorating differing parts inside and outside based on your lists.

Goals

What are some life goals you have? Things you hope to do in the future.

— In 5 years I hope I have :

— In 10 years I hope I have :

— In 20 or 30 years I hope I have :

— Before I die, I hope that I have :

What are some things that can hold you back from your goals:

1.

2.

3.

4.

5.

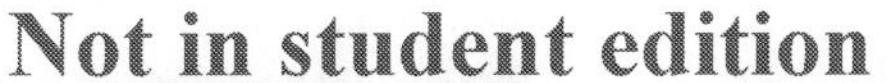

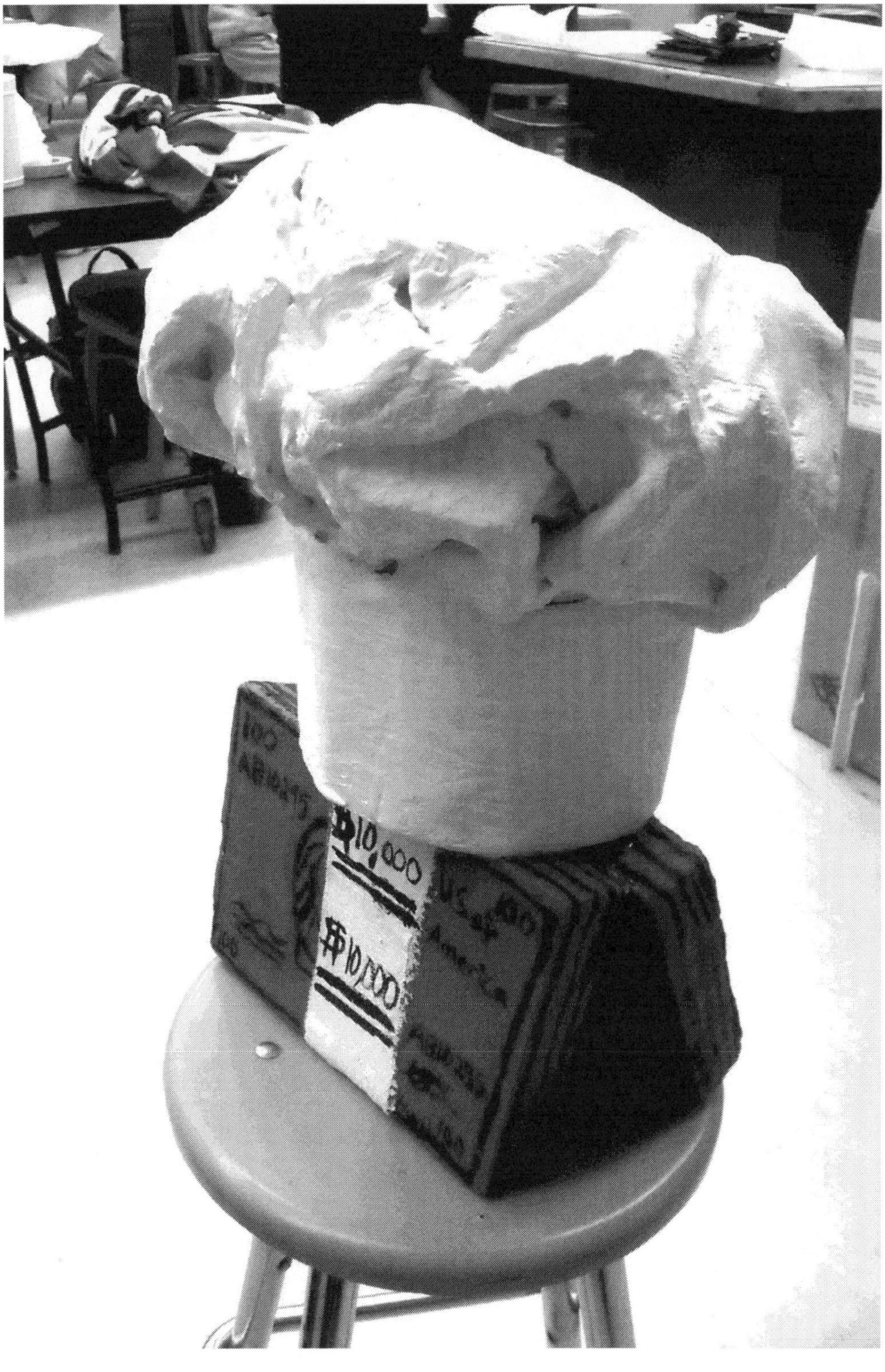

The student's sculpture shows his GOAL to be a great chef; the base is the thing that could hold him back. It is the money to go to a good school.

Fears

List 5 things you are afraid of.

1.

2.

3.

4.

5.

List 5 things others may fear but you do not.

1.

2.

3.

4.

5.

Make a little picture for each.

9 Important Things

What are the 9 most important things to you? They can be real things like a dog or
a person, or a feeling like love, or freedom. What are the 9 things you do not want
to live without? Write each one in a box below, and draw a simple symbol for
each. If nature was important to you, you could draw a leaf.

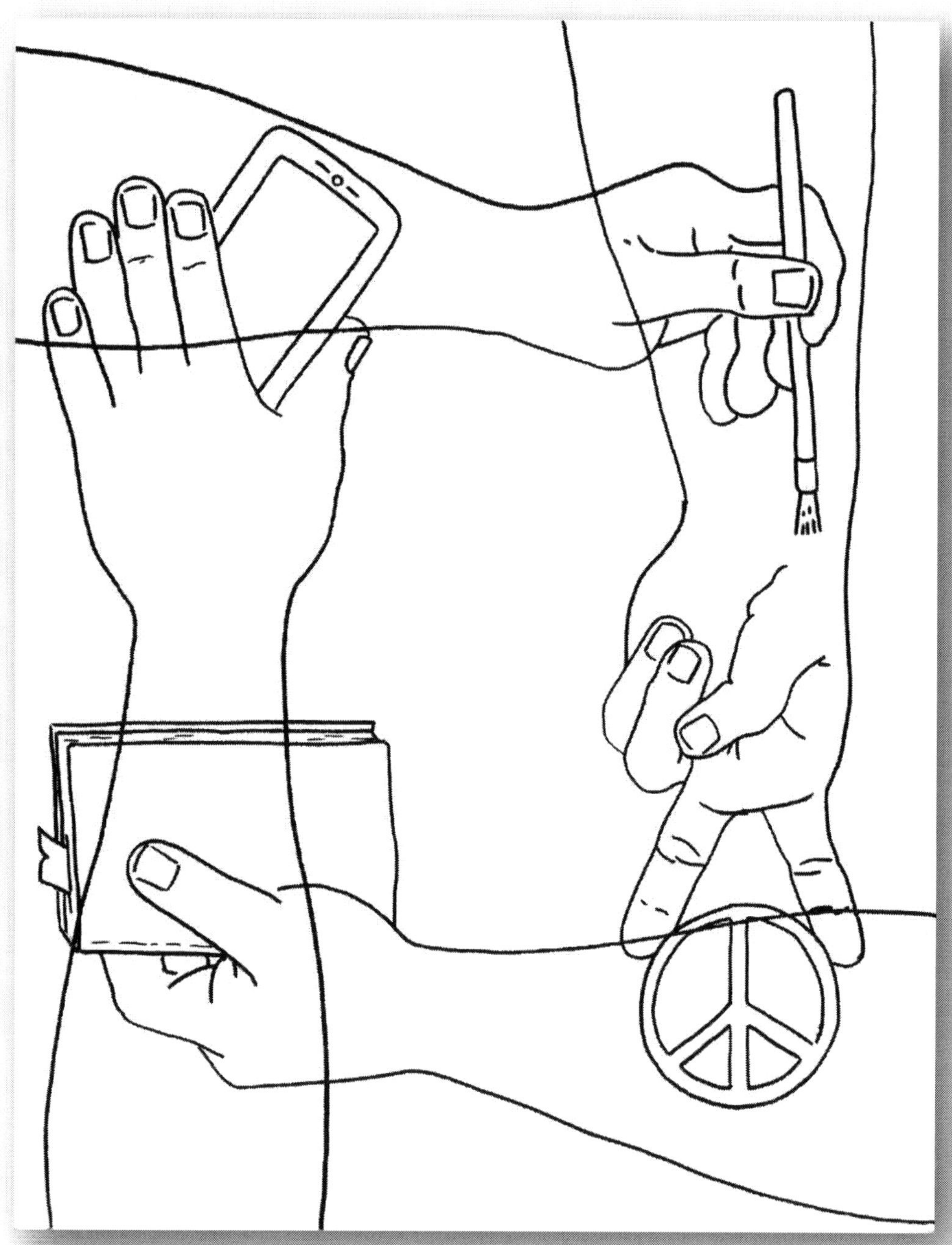

Hands: Trace your hands four times, overlapping, then go back in and fill in simple details like nails and main wrinkles. Add four important symbols that are important to you.

Think about what you will put in the middle. Will you overlap letters of your name, make a single important symbol, or do a picture of your own face? It's up to you.

When lines overlap making new shapes, color in each shape a different color. This is a great time to learn to blend colors. Try using only primary colors and have white available as a bonus color. Because our lines are black, black color is not an option for this project. You can also do this with all warm colors or all cool colors too.

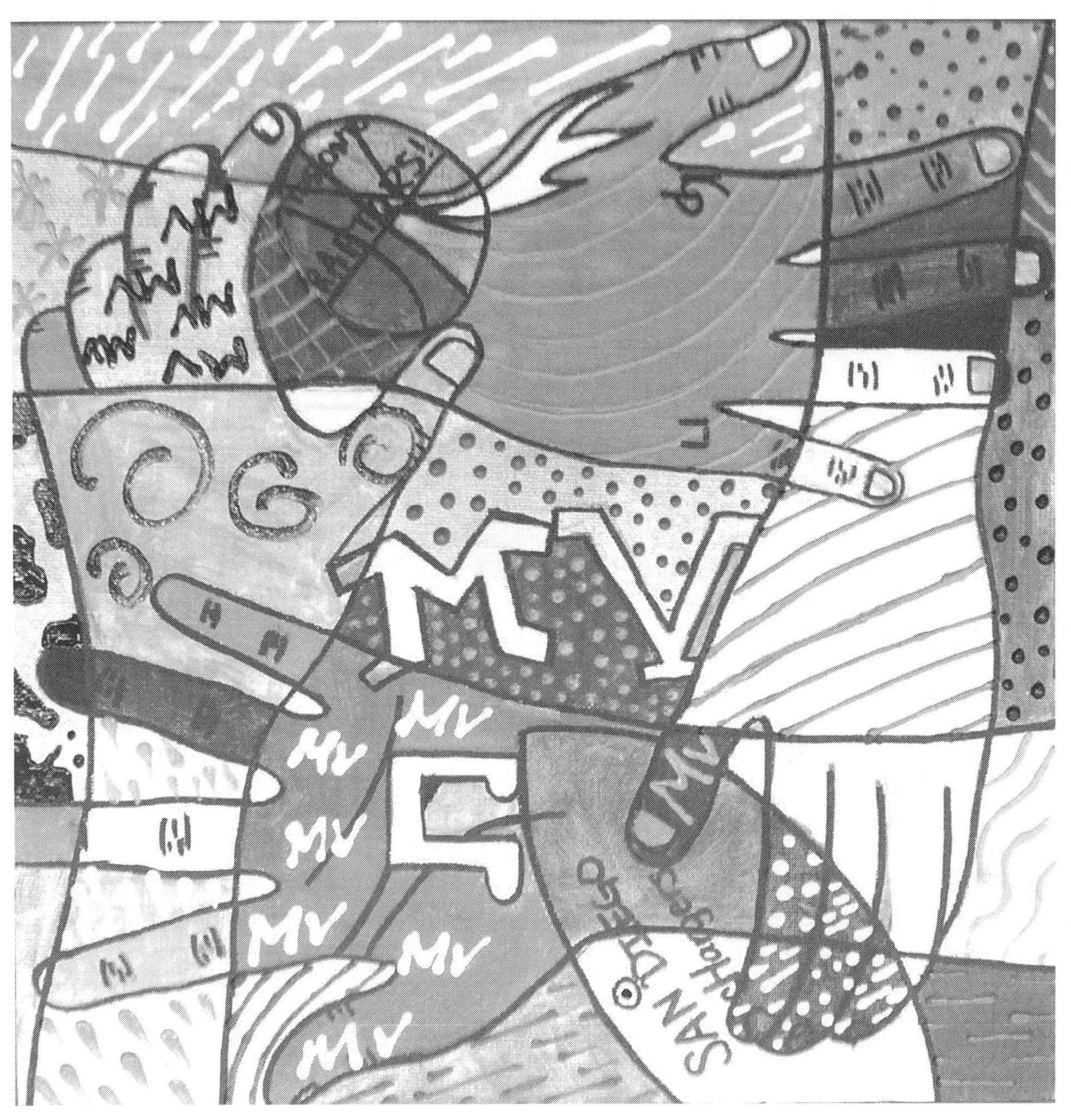

Not in student edition

Masks

Masks are usually used to hide your face. In this project, we are going to design a mask that will show others a side of you that you normally keep secret from others, or something people don't normally know about you. This can be done by using symbols and shapes that you can either paint on the mask, or shape the mask to look like. So, if people think you are kind of silly but you're really smart, you can shape the mask into the shape of an owl to represent how smart you really are.

1. Sketch out how you want your mask to look. Use symbols that you might paint on to the mask. Write down the meaning of your symbols to remember later.

REMEMBER: This can be a mask that can be worn OR a mask that is simply decoration on a wall. You should decide what kind it will be before you begin, so you'll know how to build it.

2. Your teacher will decide how to build the mask. Some people start with a balloon covered in plaster or paper mache'. Some put plaster right on top of a face. You can even make a mask on top of a paper plate, cardboard, or some aluminum foil pushed into shape.

3. Add shapes that will help show off your feelings.

4. Use the next page to sketch out your idea.

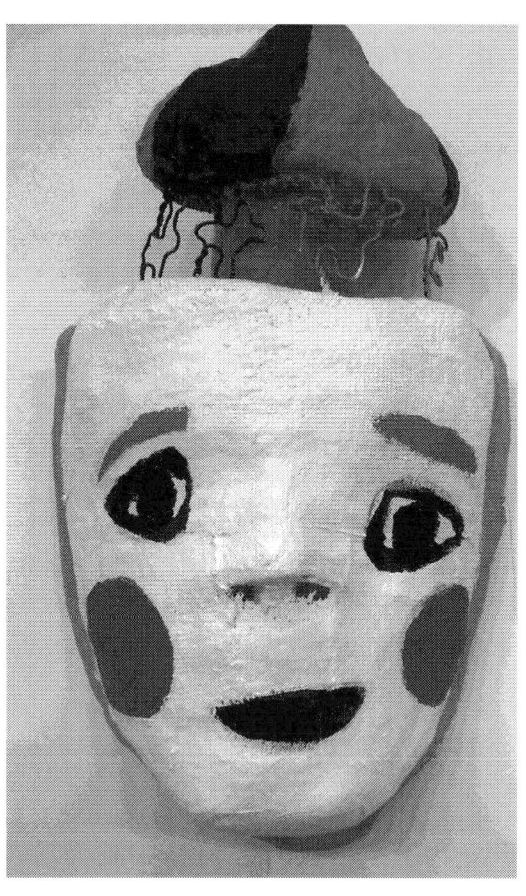
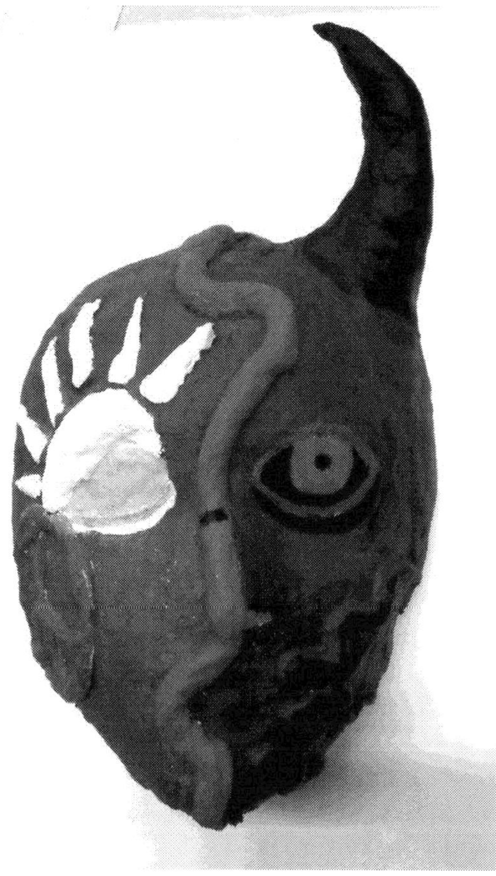

Mask Sketch

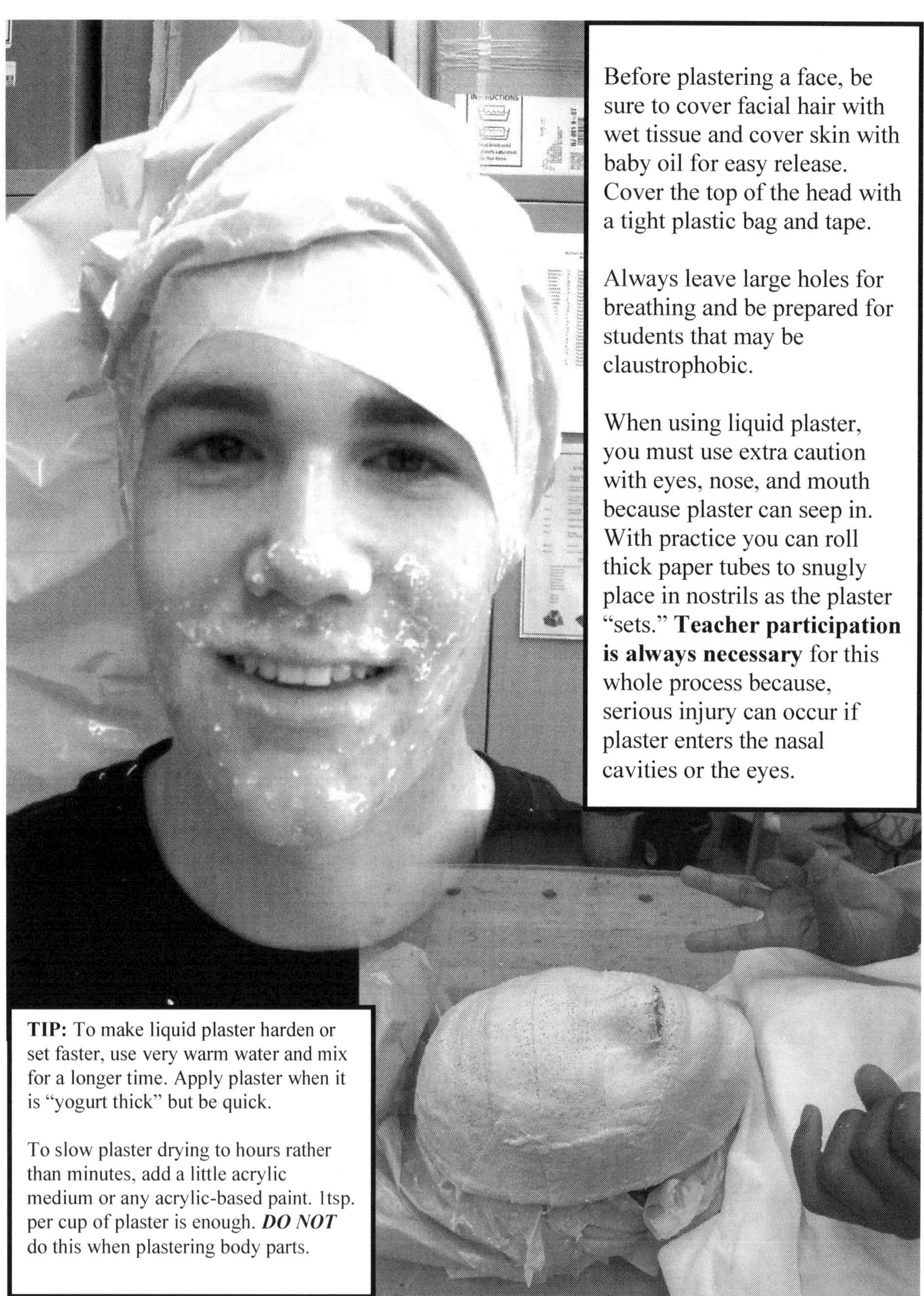

Before plastering a face, be sure to cover facial hair with wet tissue and cover skin with baby oil for easy release. Cover the top of the head with a tight plastic bag and tape.

Always leave large holes for breathing and be prepared for students that may be claustrophobic.

When using liquid plaster, you must use extra caution with eyes, nose, and mouth because plaster can seep in. With practice you can roll thick paper tubes to snugly place in nostrils as the plaster "sets." **Teacher participation is always necessary** for this whole process because, serious injury can occur if plaster enters the nasal cavities or the eyes.

TIP: To make liquid plaster harden or set faster, use very warm water and mix for a longer time. Apply plaster when it is "yogurt thick" but be quick.

To slow plaster drying to hours rather than minutes, add a little acrylic medium or any acrylic-based paint. 1tsp. per cup of plaster is enough. *DO NOT* do this when plastering body parts.

Life Changing Events

IF you do not want to write yours down, write in code so YOU know what the situation was.

- The time you won an award
- First time you were caught lying
- First time you went to a funeral
- When you did good when everyone thought you wouldn't
- New baby in the family
- First time you were tempted to do something wrong
- A time you saved someone's life, or someone saved yours
- A time you found money
- Your first time in an airplane, but, train, or boat
- A time you had to move to a new home or school

ANY big thing in your life, good or bad.

Your Event:

Symbols:

Make a list of things that help you remember the event. If it was a new baby in the family, maybe a baby bottle is a good symbol.

Memorial

We will be making an artwork for someone special to you who is *no longer with us*. If you have not lost someone in your life, please pick someone you admire who is not living. (It must be a real person)

You may use the person's initials to write below.

Their name is: _______________________________

Write about your memory of this person.

____
____
____
____

What about him or her changed your life?

____
____
____

If you could tell people only one thing about this person, what would you say?

____
____

Please write 5 positive words describing the person.

____

Was there anything you didn't like about this person?

____

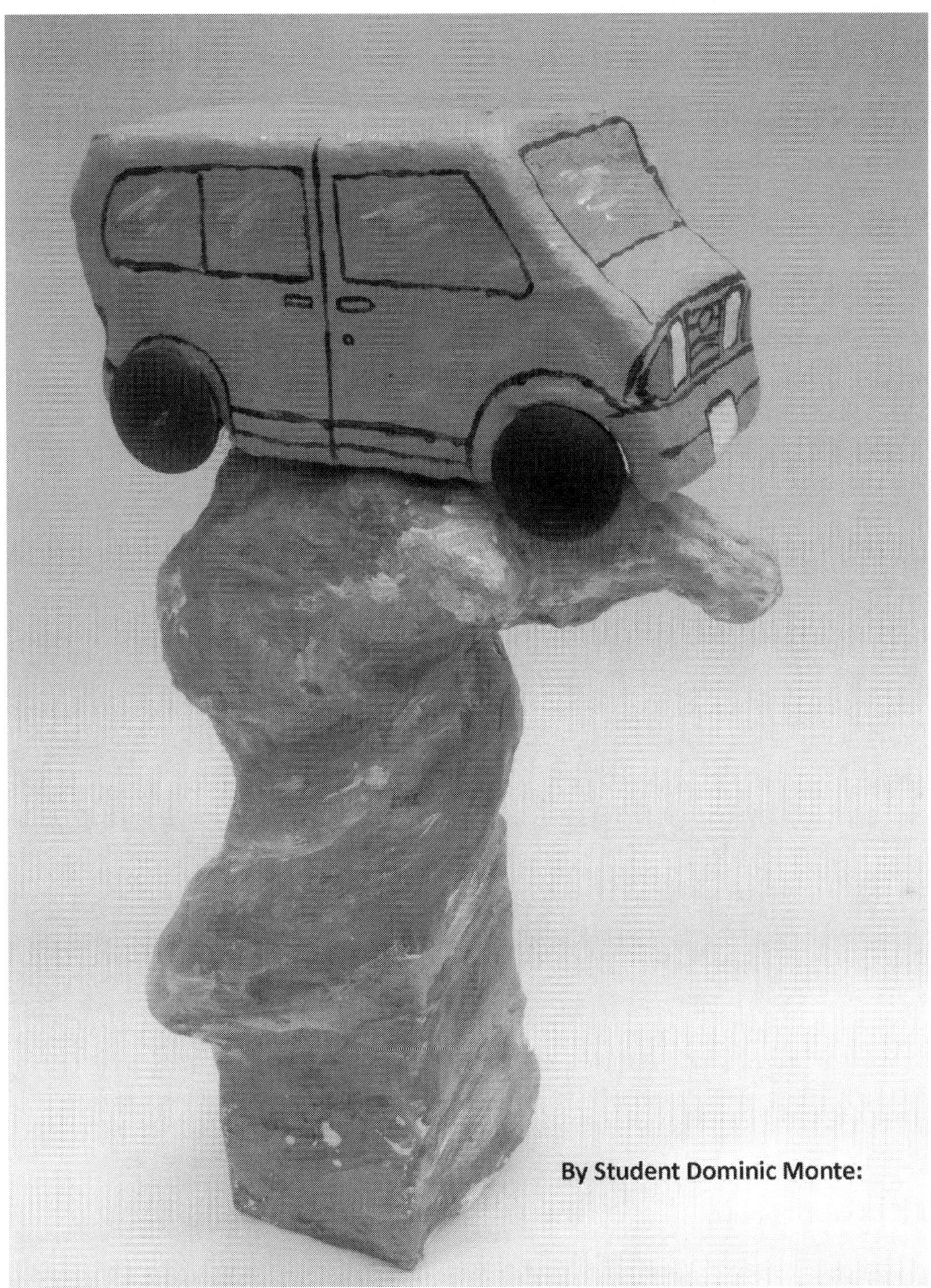

This memorial is about the student's grandfather. It shows symbols their long road trips to the ocean. This is their van riding a wave, symbolizing the fun of the experience.

Name Symbol

Write your first or last name to show the things that are important to you, or things that you like. Your name should be 6 letters or more. Use an initial after the first name for a short name.

DO NOT try to make an "A" an "A-Word" like <u>a</u>pple. Look at the shape of an "A" and see what it might look like? Do you like pie, pizza, Doritos? Thes would all make good "A" shapes. An "A" can be written in many ways… even a triangle looks like an "A."

It always looks better if the letter is made from one thing and not a bunch lined up to make the letter. Think about a bite in a cookie to make it look like a "C." It is okay to mix capital and small letters.

Start with the EASY letters like "O" or "A" and do the more difficult letters later. Write your name here in capital letters, small letters, and script if you know how… seeing them in front of you makes a BIG difference. It's okay to ask a friend for suggestions, but you need to do all your own work.

THE PROJECT:

Use a half sheet of drawing paper cut long-ways. Use a ruler on the top and bottom sides to make borders. Make the letters touch the top and bottom lines.

Draw in pencil first, LIGHTLY. Then draw the letters again in pen. Erase out the pencil and color in very neatly with small strokes no wider than your thumb. Be sure to add details. Can you mix colors to make them look more nice?

Alphabet Themes

LIST 5 ideas for yourself and 3 themes of someone close to you (Mom, Dad…)
BIG themes are easier to do. So if you pick a theme like *Field Hockey* it will be
really hard to make a whole alphabet out of that. But if you pick *Sports,* then you
would have tons of other stuff you can use.

     — Instead of Clothes, choose fashion (Then you can include Fashion Logos)
     — Instead of Vegetables, choose Foods
     — Instead of Rock and Roll, choose Music

There are 3 levels of difficulty to this project.

Level 1: A Single idea to create a whole alphabet, like the balloons below. If done
very well, It can still look pretty cool.

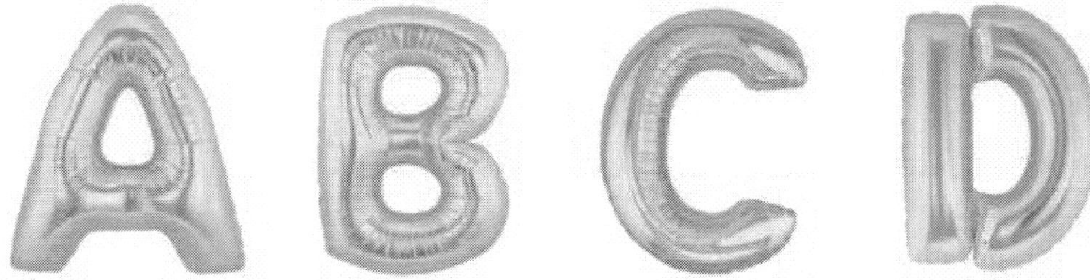

Level 2: A single idea with 30% to 60% of repeated pictures ideas like above.

Level 3: Every letter is a different idea in the theme. This is the most difficult but
is very professional. Below is an alphabet of logos. Each is different, but this is not
a very original idea.

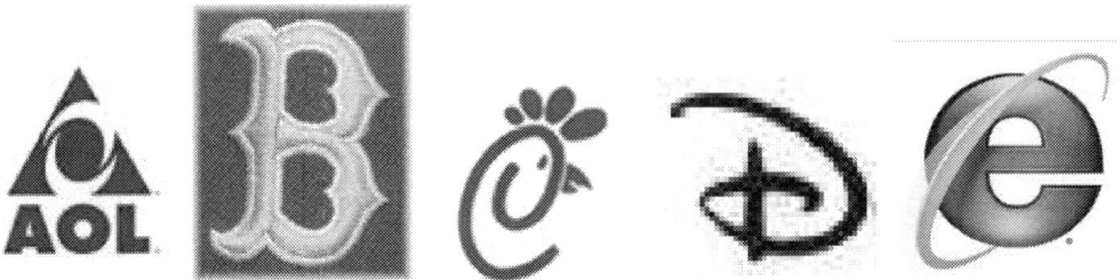

**Remember: The Letters do not have to sound like what it is. "A" does not
have to be "APPLE" the symbol just has to be an "A" SHAPE.**

Holiday Themed Alphabet Sample

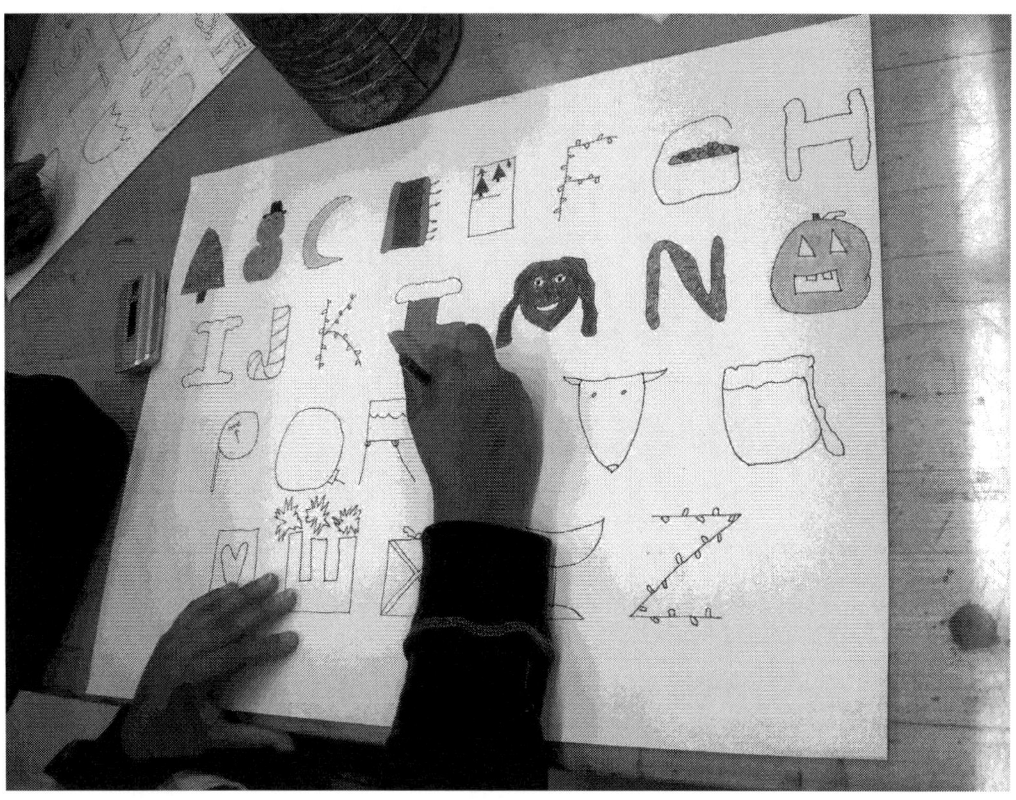

Note how each letter is different but still follows this student's theme of holidays. Only "F," "K," and "Z" repeat ideas, so this is almost the highest level of ideas for this project.

Students can even make sculpture words to show their meaning.

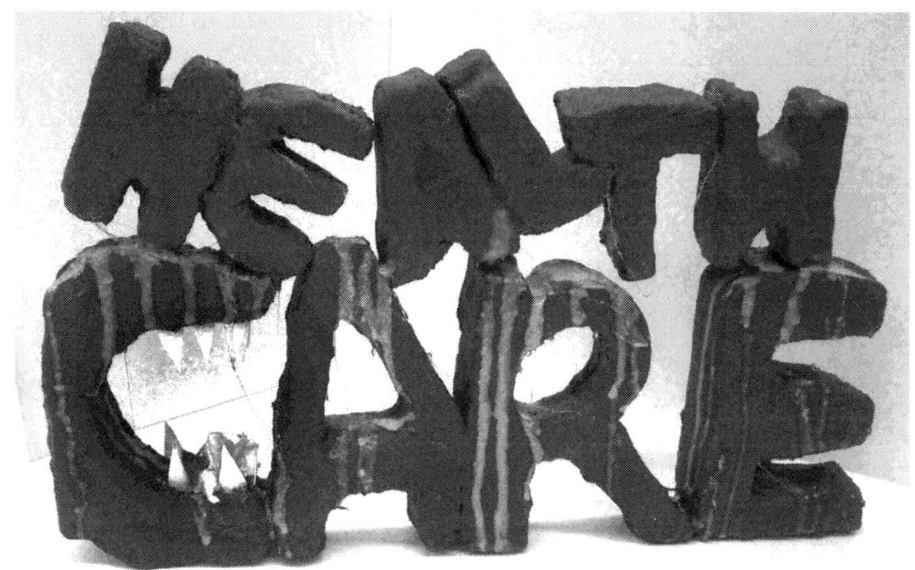

THIS PAGE IS NOT IN THE STUDENT EDITION

Helpful Hints

DO NOT START WITH "A"

Start with the easiest ideas and cross them off. If you chose SPORTS, make a ball and cross off the "O" first! Use the alphabet below to cross off what you have sketched.

REMEMBER! Letters can look many different ways and still be that letter.

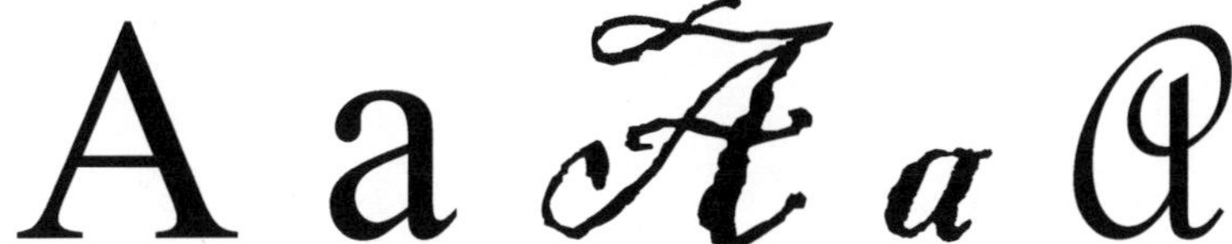

Cross off letters as you sketch them.

A B C D E F G H I

J K L M N O

P Q R S T U

V W X Y Z

Alphabet Sketch Page

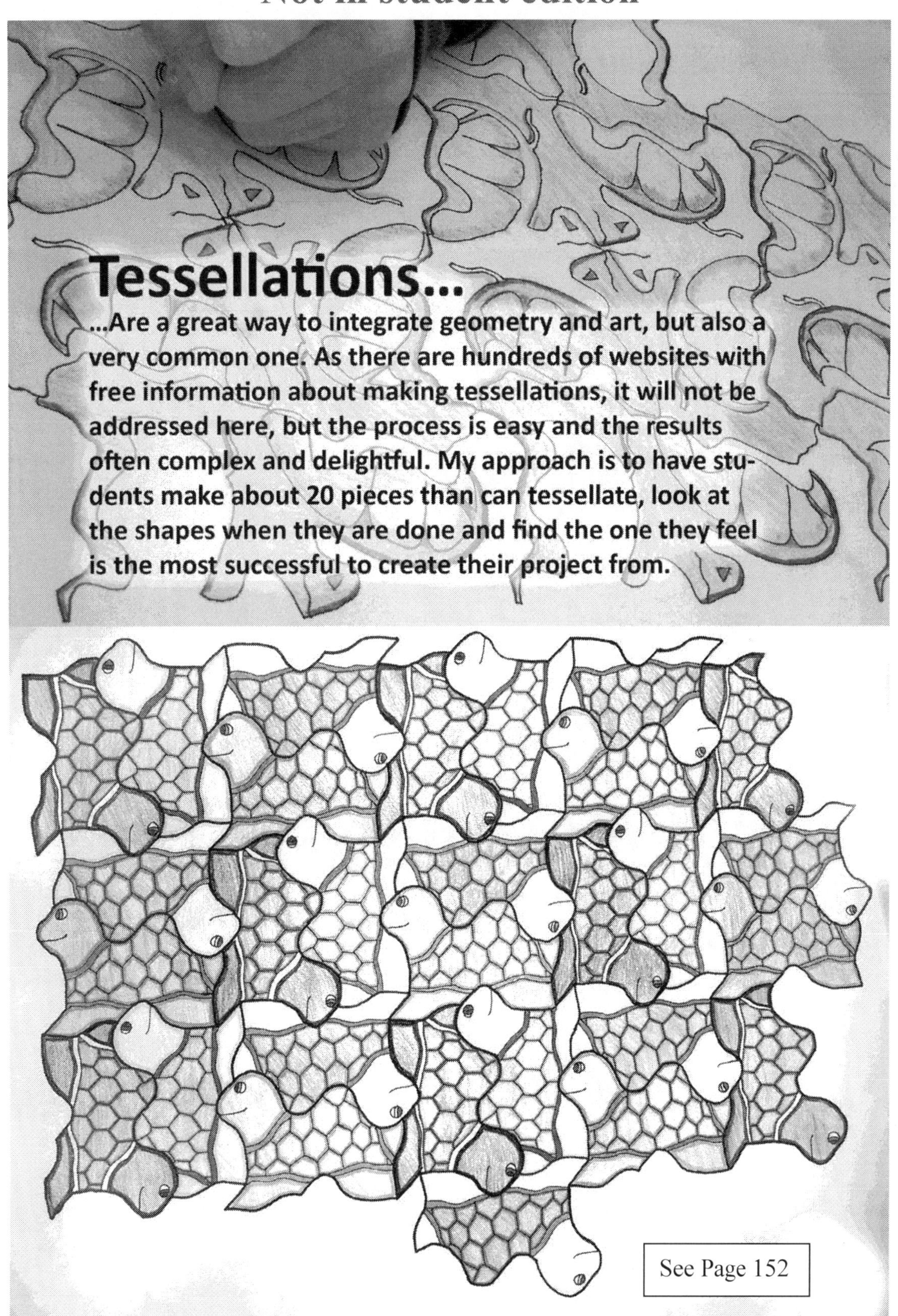
Tessellations...
...Are a great way to integrate geometry and art, but also a
very common one. As there are hundreds of websites with
free information about making tessellations, it will not be
addressed here, but the process is easy and the results
often complex and delightful. My approach is to have students make about 20 pieces than can tessellate, look at
the shapes when they are done and find the one they feel
is the most successful to create their project from.
See Page 152

Treasure Maps

Create a treasure map of an imaginary island. The island can take on the contour of an object, but break it into small pieces so it is not too obvious. Include the following: Detailed border, rose compass, longitude, latitude, 5 land feature symbols, key for symbols, 2 landmarks, 2 water symbols in the water, 1 sea monster, and 1 ship. Maps can be aged by wrinkling and soaking in watered down acrylic paint, coffee, or strong tea. Include geology & cartography elements.

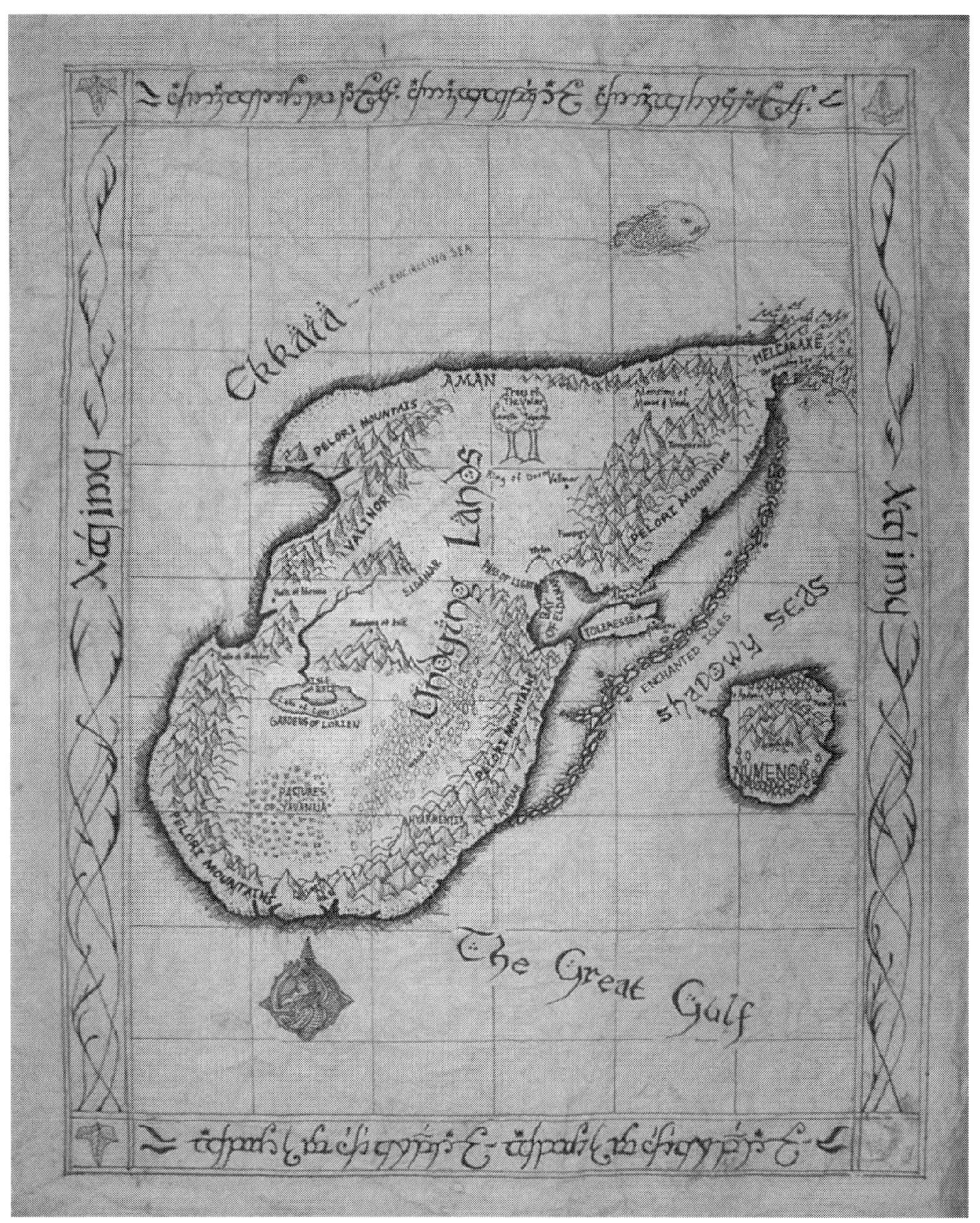

This page is not in the student edition

Grids

Grids can be a great way to transform a design, enlarge or reduce a drawing. They are often used to make murals. A grid is a great tool in making a difficult drawing more easy by breaking it up into smaller parts. The gridding technique is very old and we know it was used by many Renaissance artists like Leonardo da Vinci.

The following pages have 3 grids of different scale. You can place a piece of plastic, acetate, or overhead sheet on top of the grid and trace the lines using a ruler and sharpie marker to have your own grid. It can be placed over a photograph, magazine image, etc, and transferred to a similar grid on another paper.

Gridding is a skill that most 4th graders can handle, some younger kids too. Some will struggle, but trying is always a good way to find out. If gridding does not work for some students, have them try, and then do a regular drawing after that.

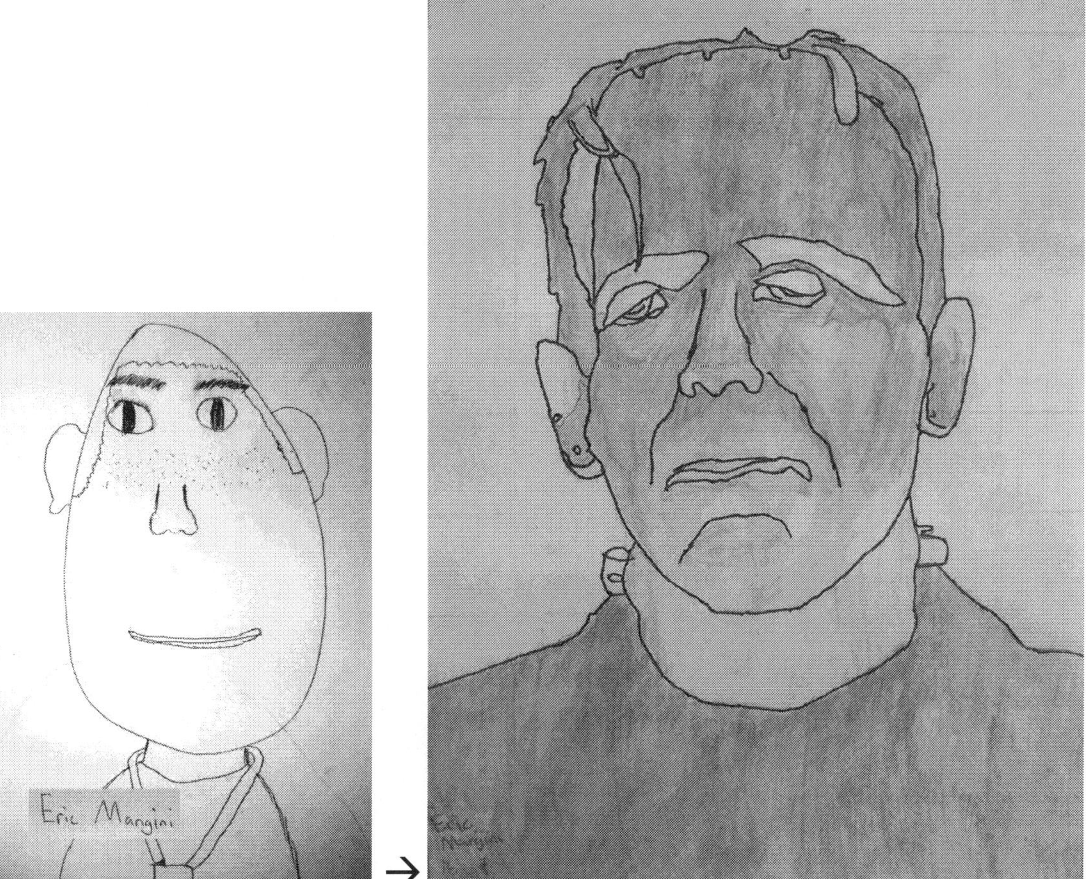

Grids can be a great way to improve drawing skills.

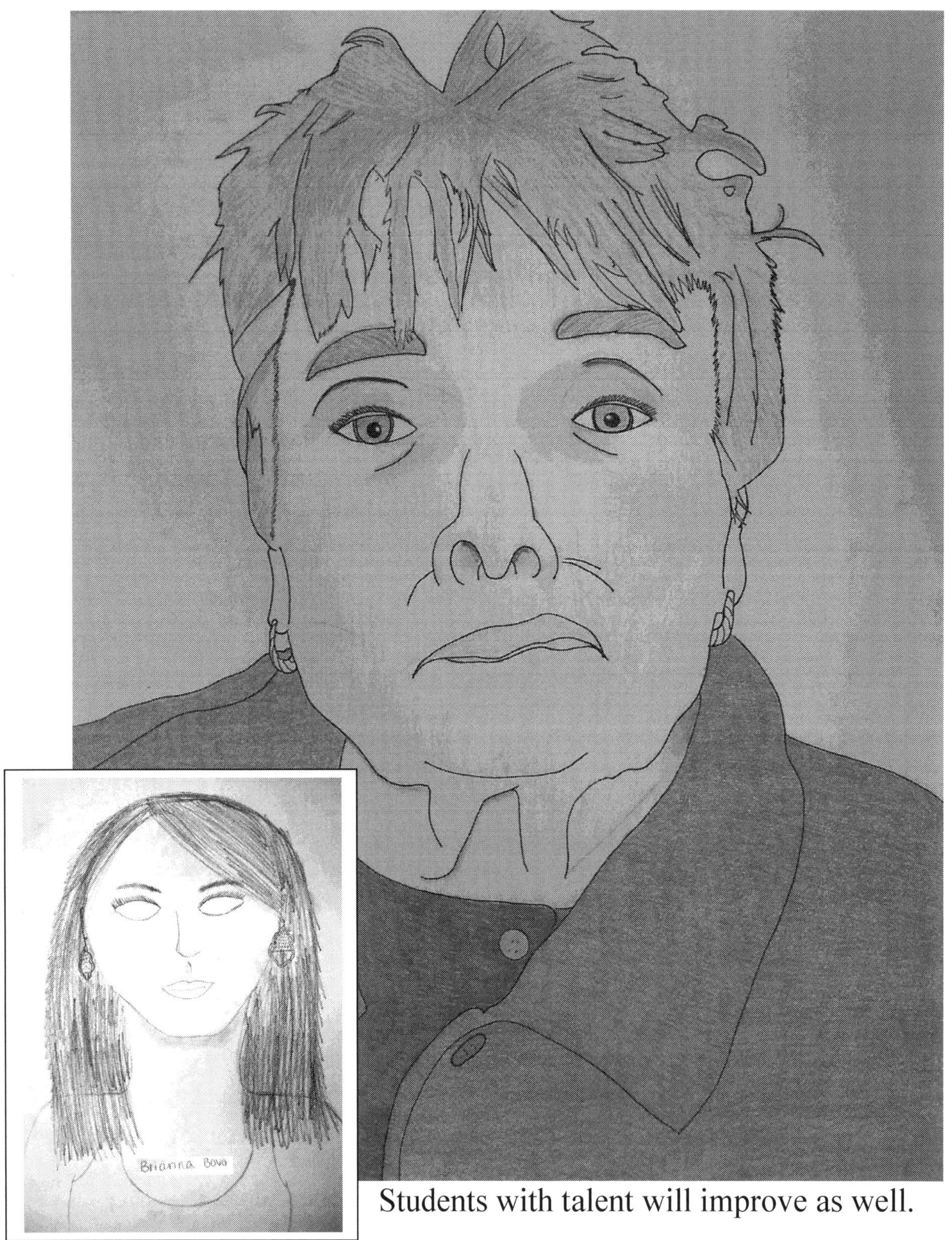

Students with talent will improve as well.

68

Art and MATH?!?   *(You do not have to do all of these in one day, try one per week)*

1. In every state, you need to pay sales tax on a sale, but this is added on after the purchase. What is the sales tax in your state? ______ % . So you sell your last project for $100.00, how much is the tax?

2. From questions #1, what is the price the customer has to pay for your artwork?

$_________ Show your work below:

3. Most New York galleries will keep 50% of the sale price from the art they sell. This is called a commission. So if you want $100.00 for your artwork, and the gallery will take 50%, what is the final* price of the art?
(*This is called the retail price)

$_________ Show your work below:

4. There are some grids in this workbook. How can you know the number of squares without counting each and every square? Write out how to find the answer.

____

____

5. There are three grids in this book. How many squares are in each?

A (big squares) _______, B (medium squares) _______, C (little squares) _______ .

Show your work here:

6. If you have a drawing that is 10 x 8 inches, and you frame it with a wood that is 3 inches wide, how large will the whole thing be with the frame?

_______ x _______ inches.

Show work here:

7. If you have a present to wrap and the box is a cube with 6 inches on each side. How many square inches of wrapping do you need to cover the whole box without wasting any paper?

____

Show work here:

8. If you need exact measurements, why should you never measure from the end of a ruler?

____

____

9. Let us say your class is going to paint some art on one wall of your classroom, and it will be so large it will take up the whole wall. One gallon of paint will cover 300 square feet of wall. How many gallons of paint do you need to buy?

_____________ gallons.

Show work here:

10. A gallon of paint may cost $15.00 each. So how much is the paint for your mural in number 9.

$____________.

Show work here:

11. Putting questions #9 and #10 together, how much money does your class have to get to buy all the paint for your mural in questions #9? (From #1 use the tax rate of your state, and figure out how much the price will be for 1 gallon with tax)

$___________

Show work here:

12. Look back at question #3. If you did the math right, you will have earned $100.00 for the sale of your artwork. Does this mean you have a profit of $100.00?

YES _____ / NO _____

Write why you said yes or no:

13. Question #3 says that a New York art gallery will keep 50% of the money from your art that sells. This is a lot of money. Why would a gallery take 50%?
(Do not say, "they want money," what is the *reason* why they need 50%?)

____

____

____

____

14. If your art room was an art gallery and the monthly rent is $5 per square foot, how much is it to rent the room?

How wide and long is the room? _______ x _______ feet.

Square footage of room is _______ feet squared.

The rent is $_____________

Show work here:

15. If it takes 30 seconds for each student to wash his brush in a sink, (one at a time) how many minutes need to be allowed for clean-up in the classroom?

__________ minutes.

Show work here:

16. If your friend gave you a picture from a magazine that measured 8 x 10 inches, and they wanted you to do a drawing of it that was 50% bigger, how big would the paper for your drawing have to be?

__________ x ____________ inches.

Show your work here:

Perspective

Vocabulary:

— Perspective (Per-spec-tiv)

— Horizon (Ho-rie-zon)

— Vanishing Point (Va-nish-ing)

— Parallel (Pare-ra-lel)

— Converging (Kon-ver-jing)

— Vertical (Ver-ti-kul)

— Eye Level

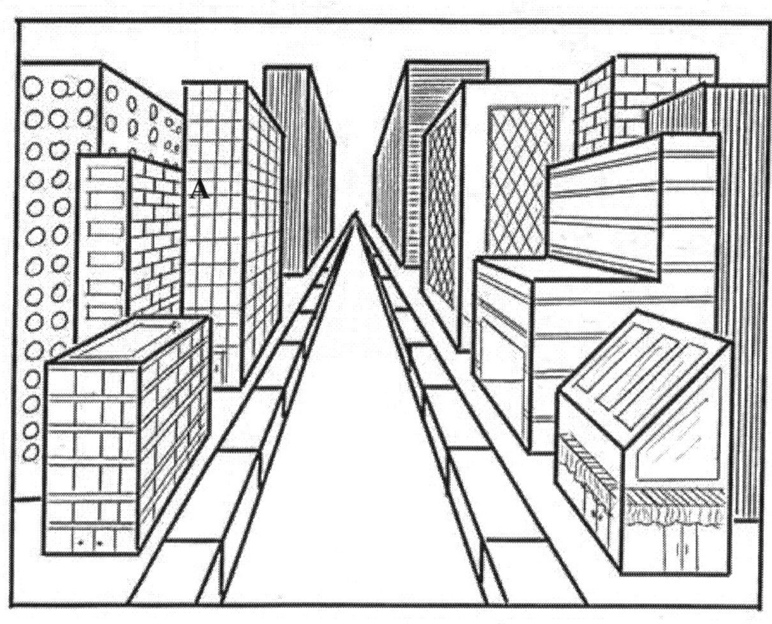

This is 1 Point Perspective. Everything seems to be going to one point "A".

Your Name in 1 Point Perspective

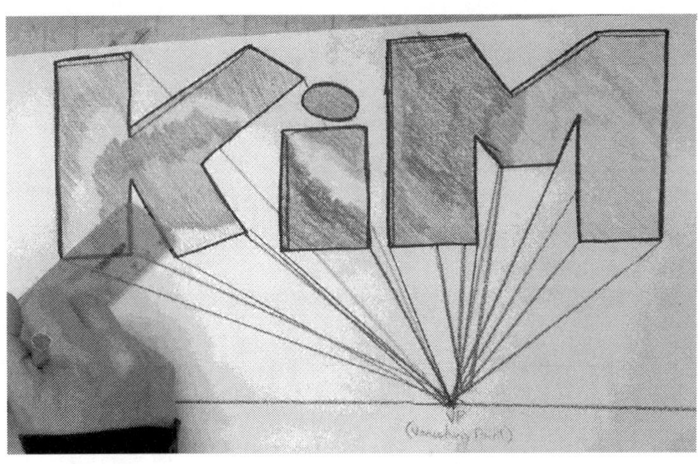

1. Can you draw your name with block letters? Do it below.
2. Create a horizon and vanishing point.
3. Make all corners of your name go to that vanishing point.
4. DO NOT draw lines that overlap the letters of your name.

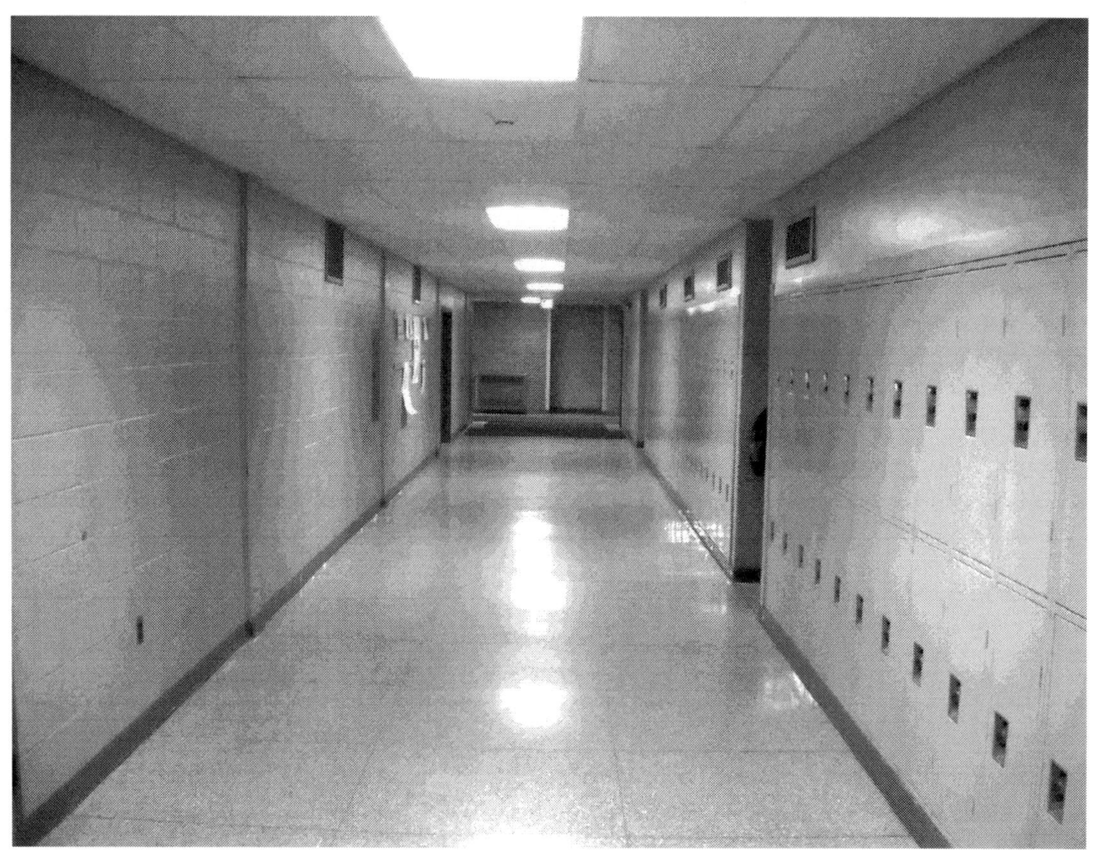

Use a ruler and draw along all the edges that go into the background. Where do they meet? What do we call this point? Is it the same for the image below?

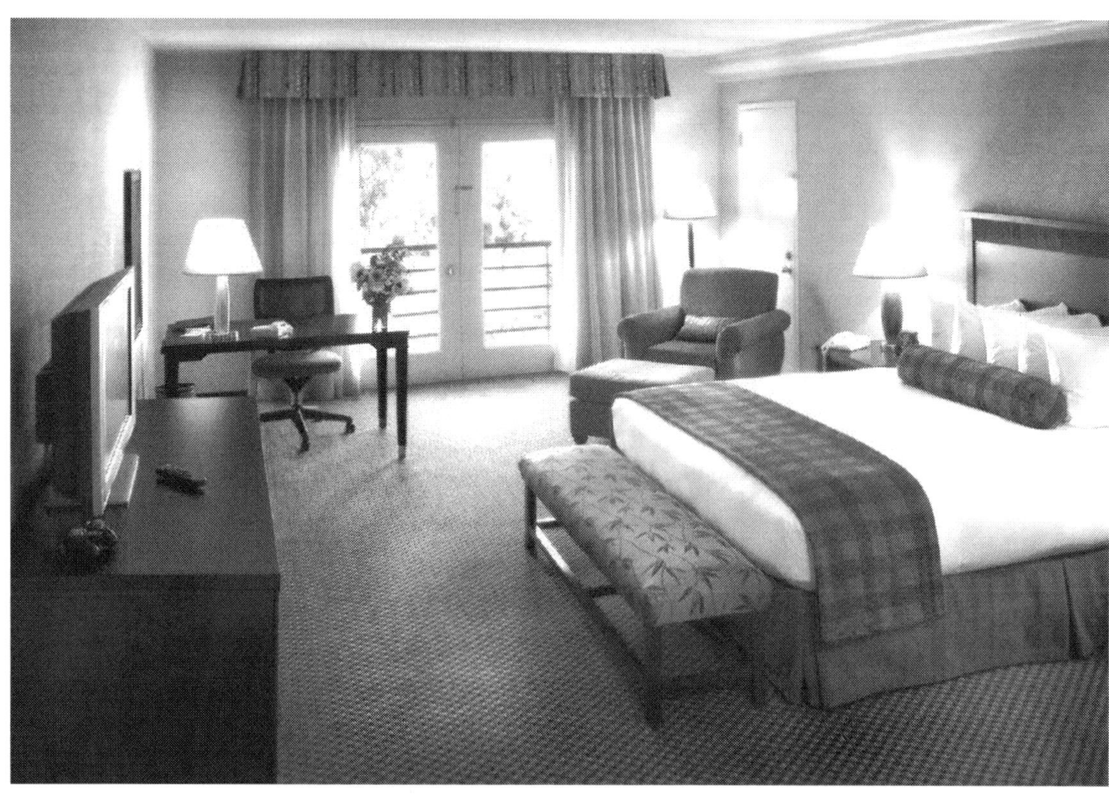

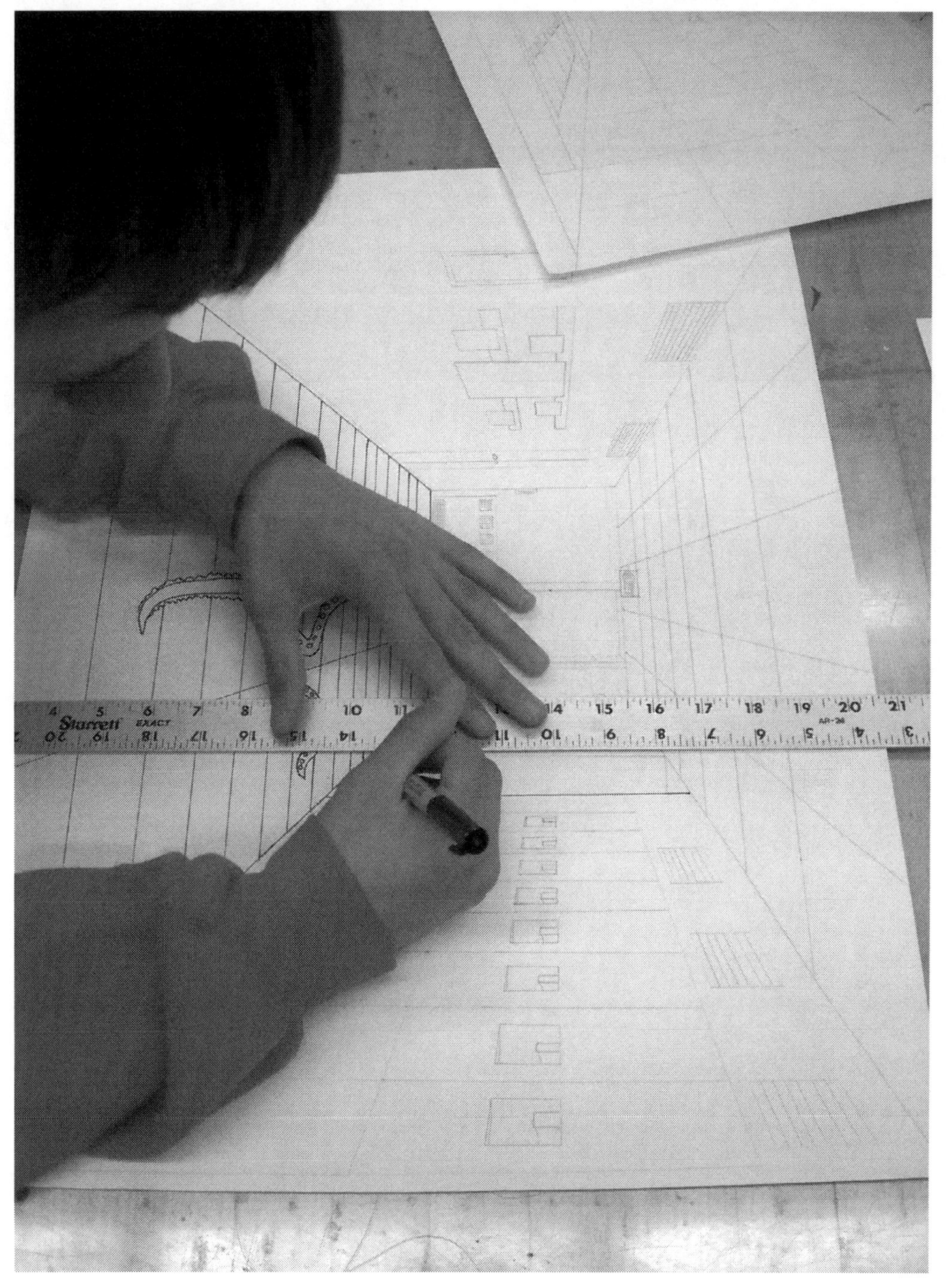

Students do a perspective drawing from observation in the school hallways, but finish by adding a surrealistic element. Here the student adds tentacles of some creature coming out of the floor.

This page is not in the student edition

Samples not in the student edition
Surreal school drawing samples in 1 Point Perspective.

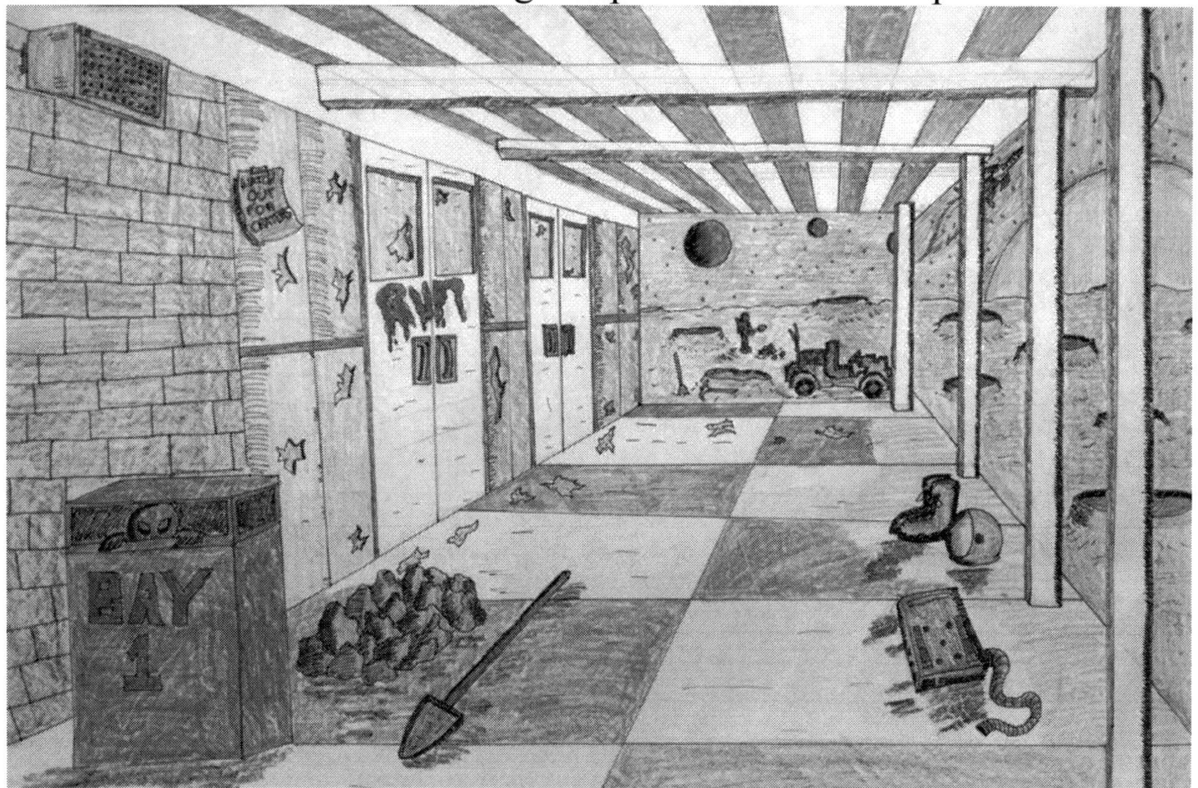

By Ryan Orlofsky

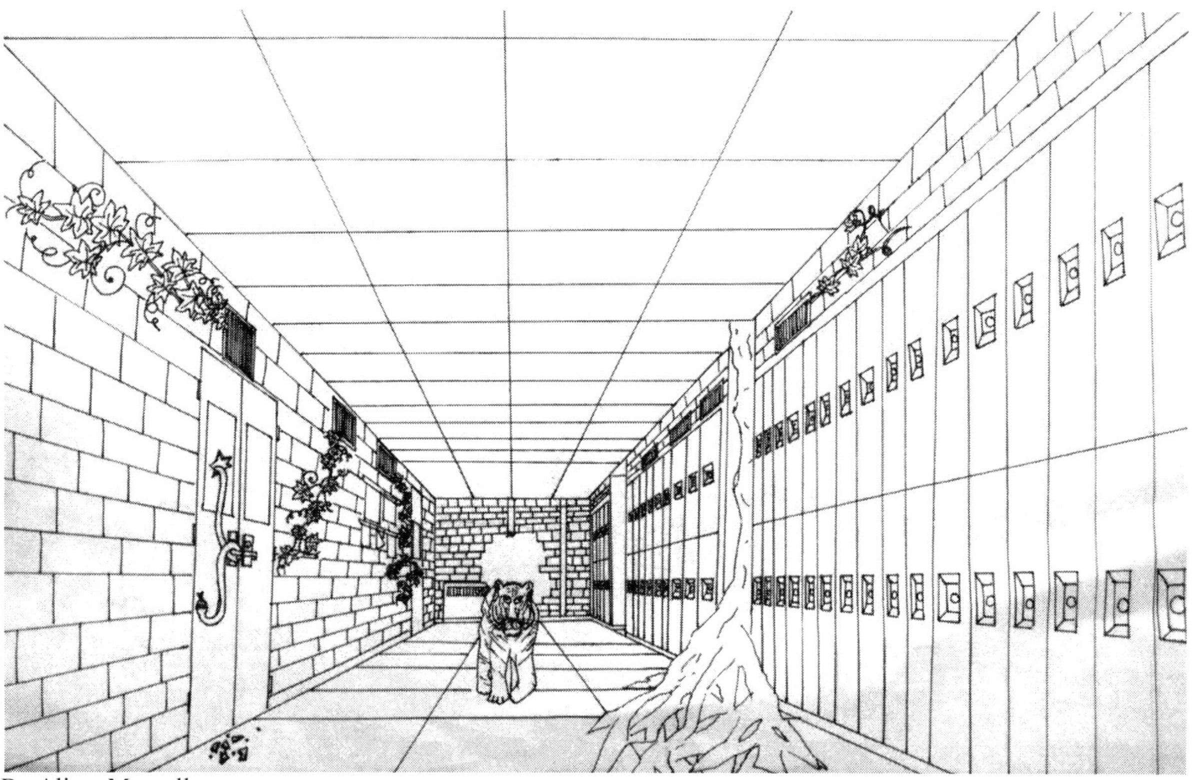

By Alissa Mazzella

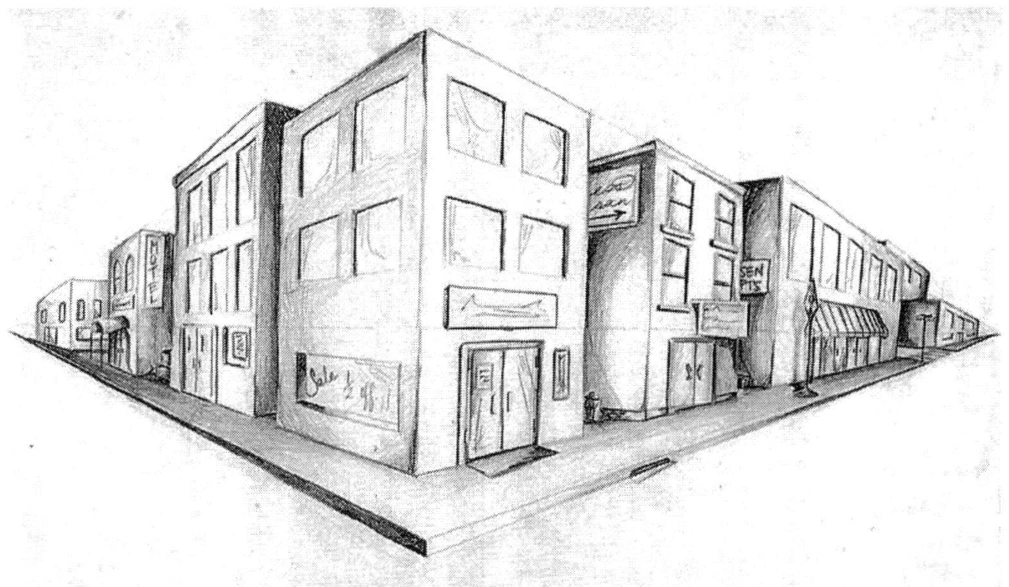

This is an example of 2 Point Perspective. See how both sides seem to converge to different points on the same horizon.

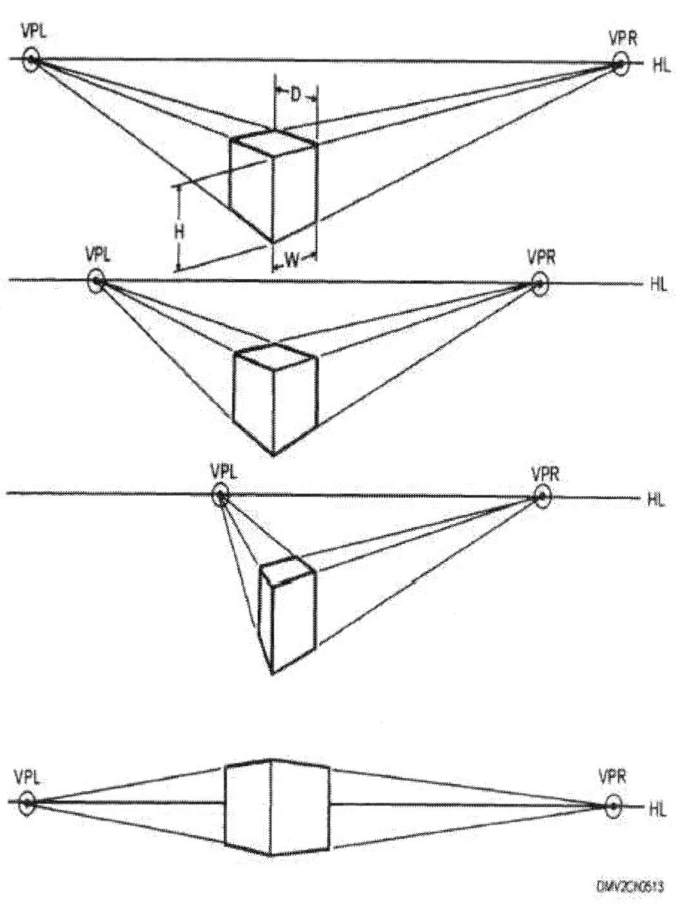

This is how 2 point perspective is used to draw boxes.

Drawing Boxes in 1 Point Perspective

1. Draw a horizontal line with a ruler, somewhere below. This is the *Horizon*.
2. Draw a **dot** somewhere on the line.
3. Make the corners of the squares connect to the **dot,** This is the *Vanishing Point*.
4. Erase any lines that cut through a square.

Crosshatching

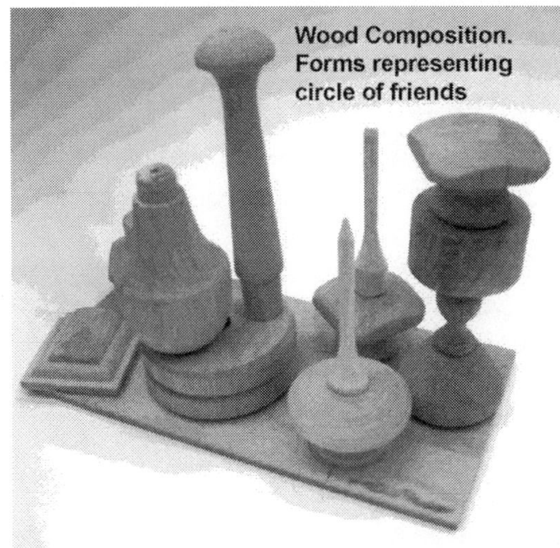

Repeated lines can create the look of shadow. The picture above was done step by step to the right. This is the same way you see shadow on a dollar bill.

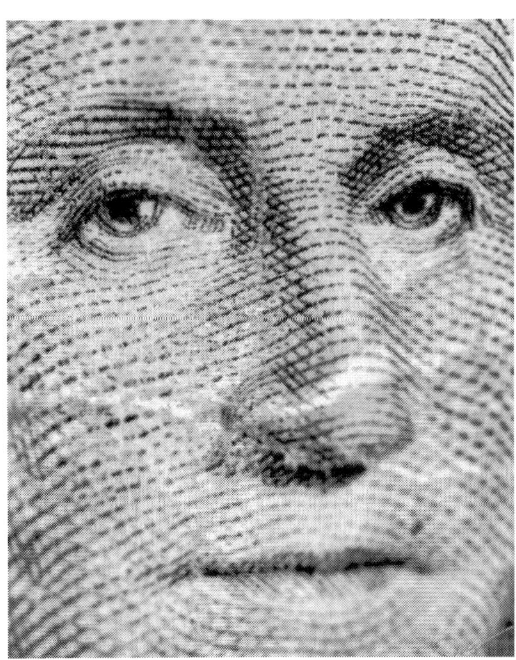

It can be done also with dots (Stippling) or any repeated line, even scribbles.

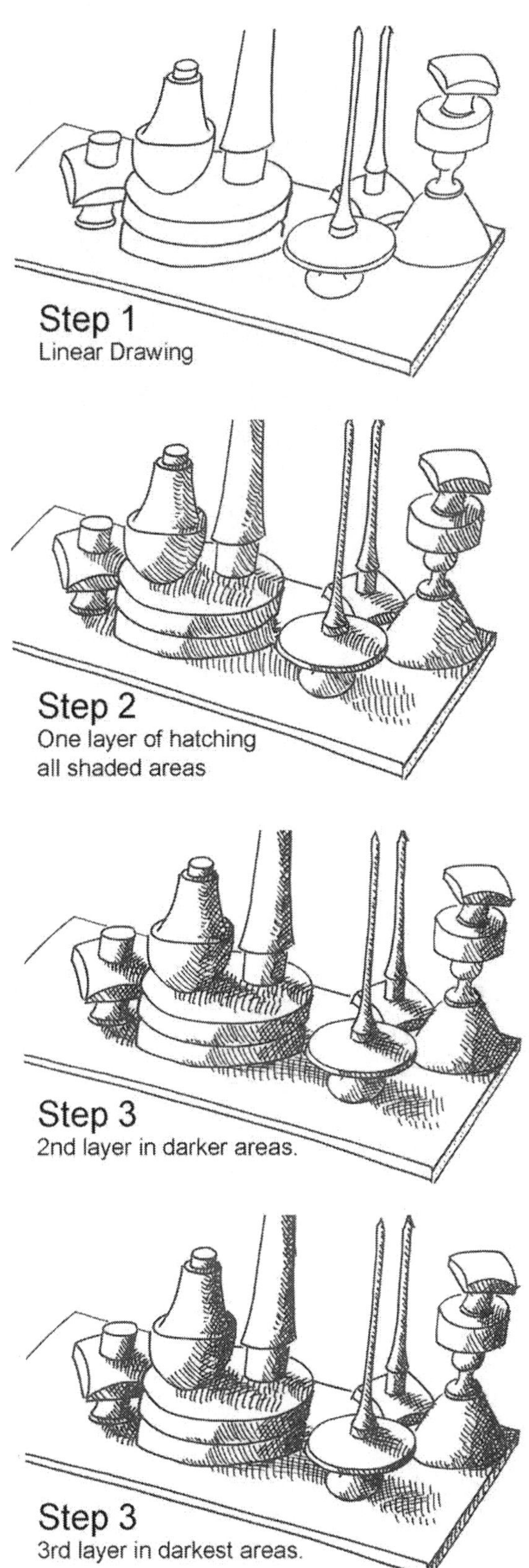

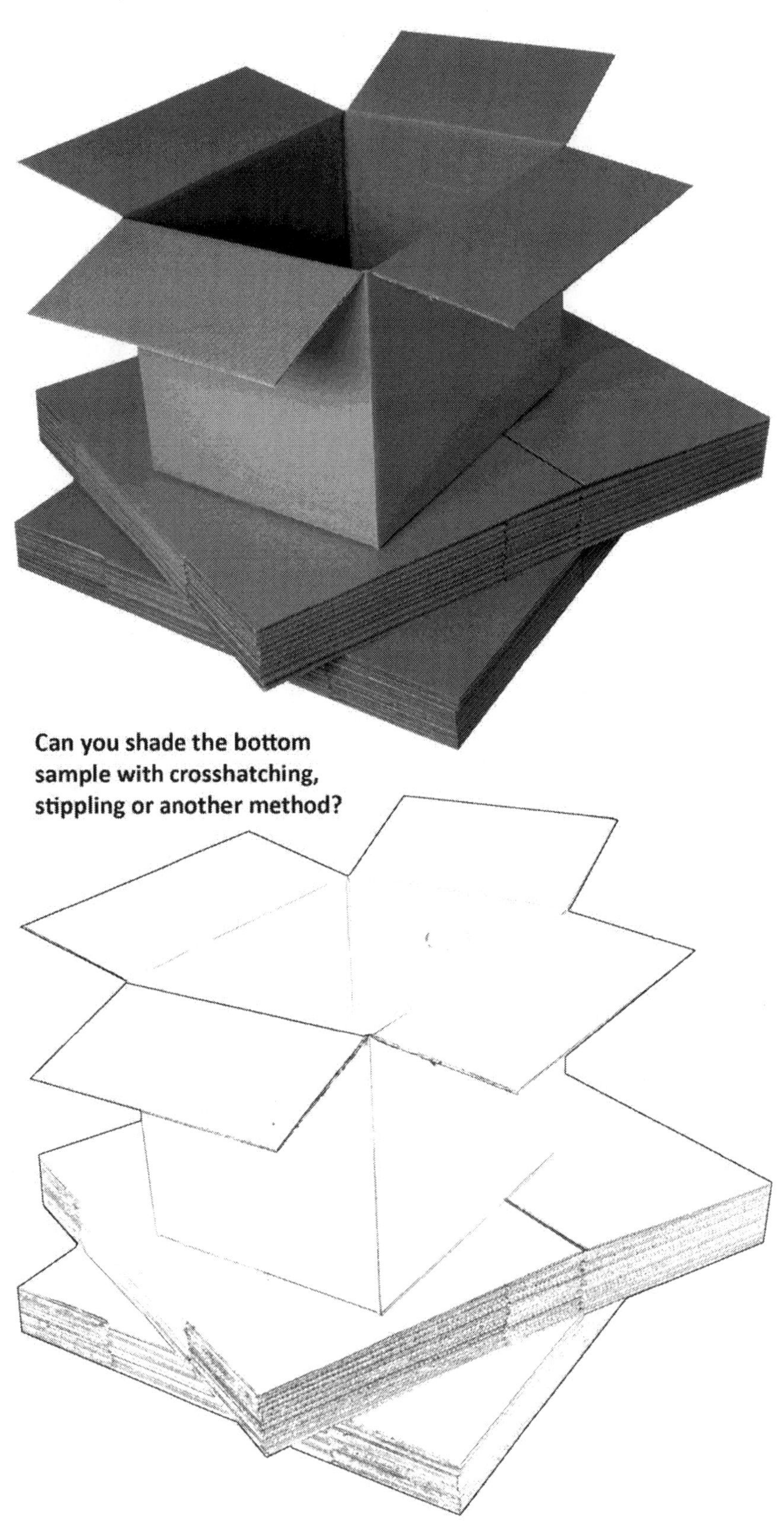

Can you shade the bottom
sample with crosshatching,
stippling or another method?

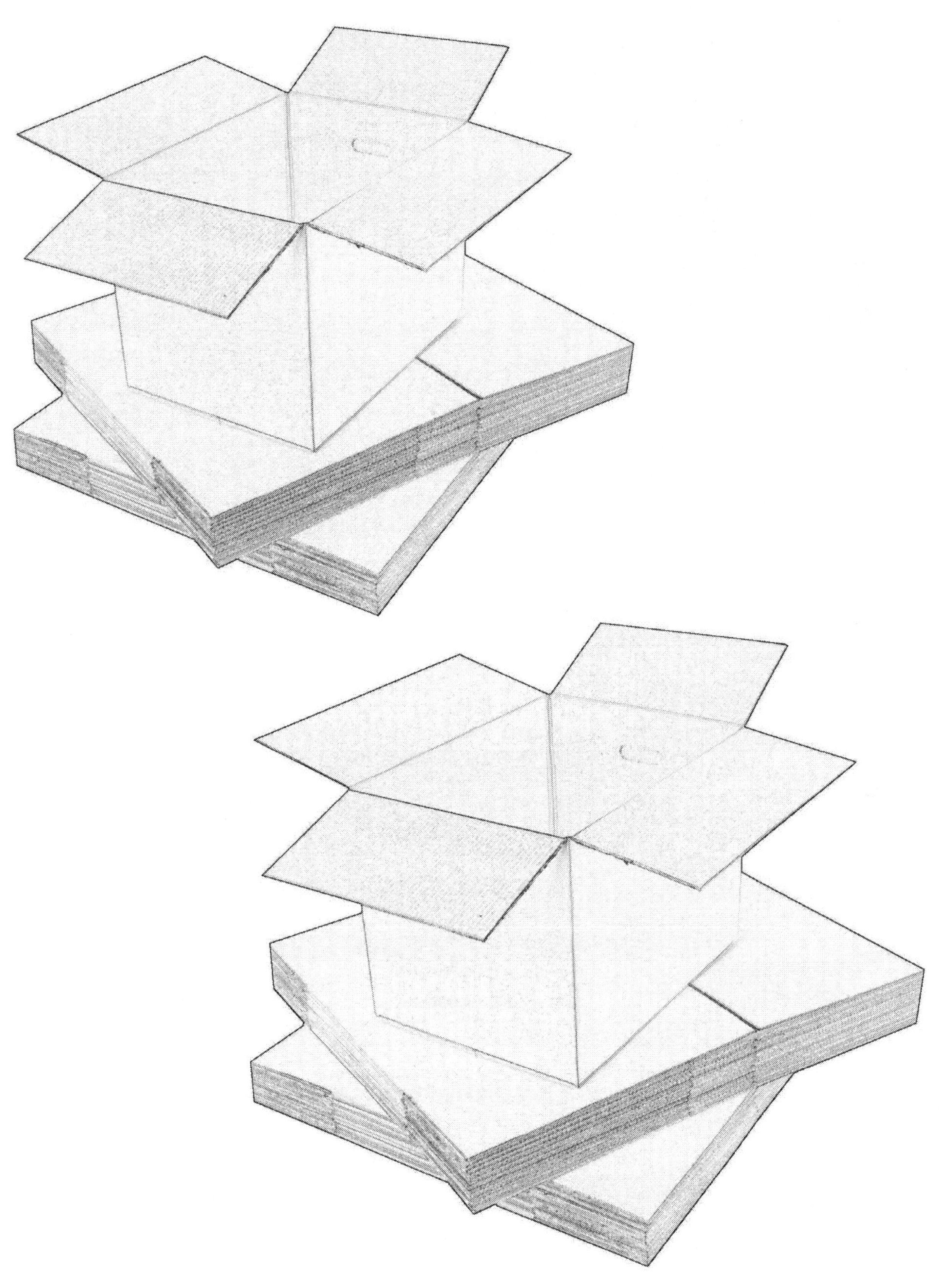

Coloring Spheres

Please color these spheres like in the example.

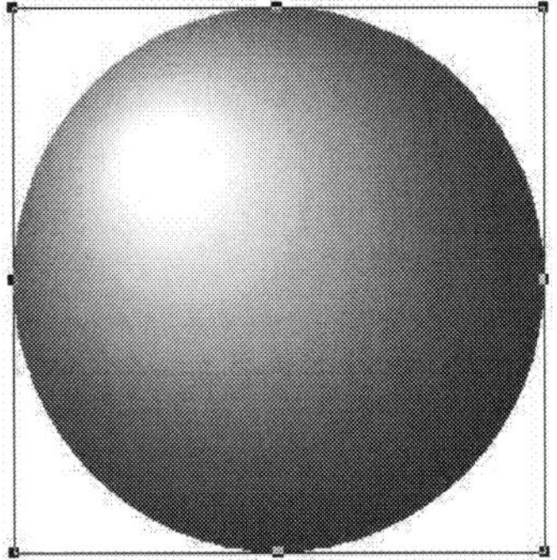

MONOCHROMATIC

Please color in the following 6 circles. See the sample so your circles look like shaded spheres too.

Primary colors
Secondary colors
Analogous colors
Complementary colors
Any color plus black and white
1 color, use pressure to show light and dark.

Primary Colors   Secondary Colors   Analogous Colors

Complimentary Colors   1 Color + Black + White   1 Color

4 Basic Forms

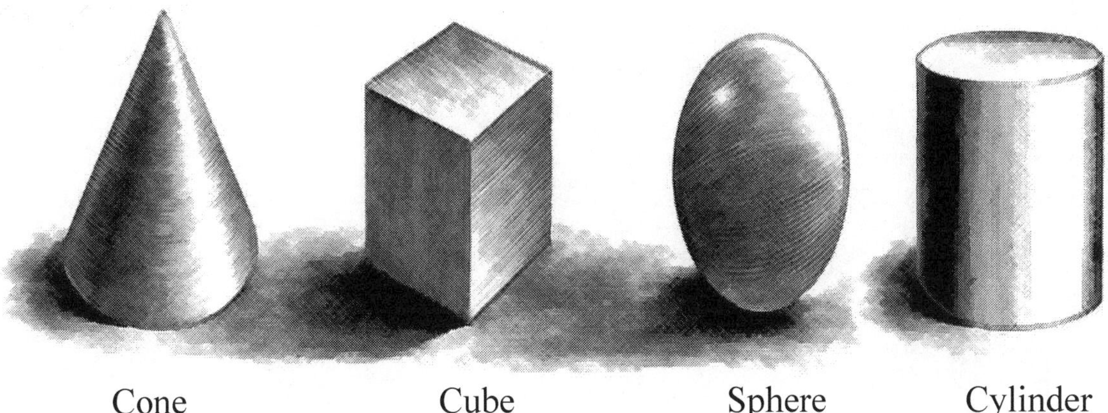

Cone   Cube   Sphere   Cylinder

Try drawing the 4 forms here. Color and shade them.

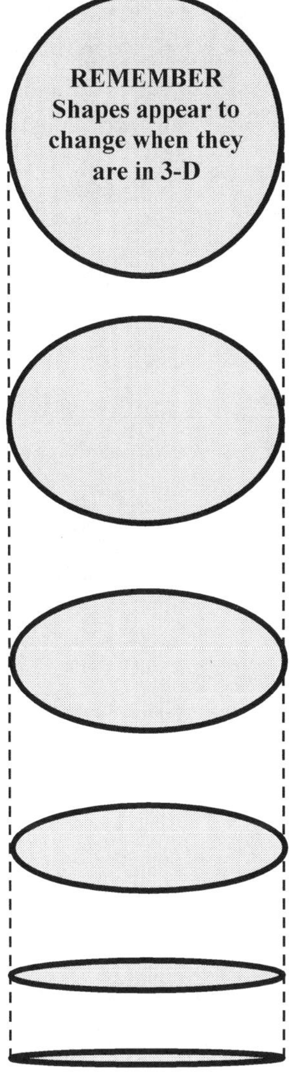

Face Proportions

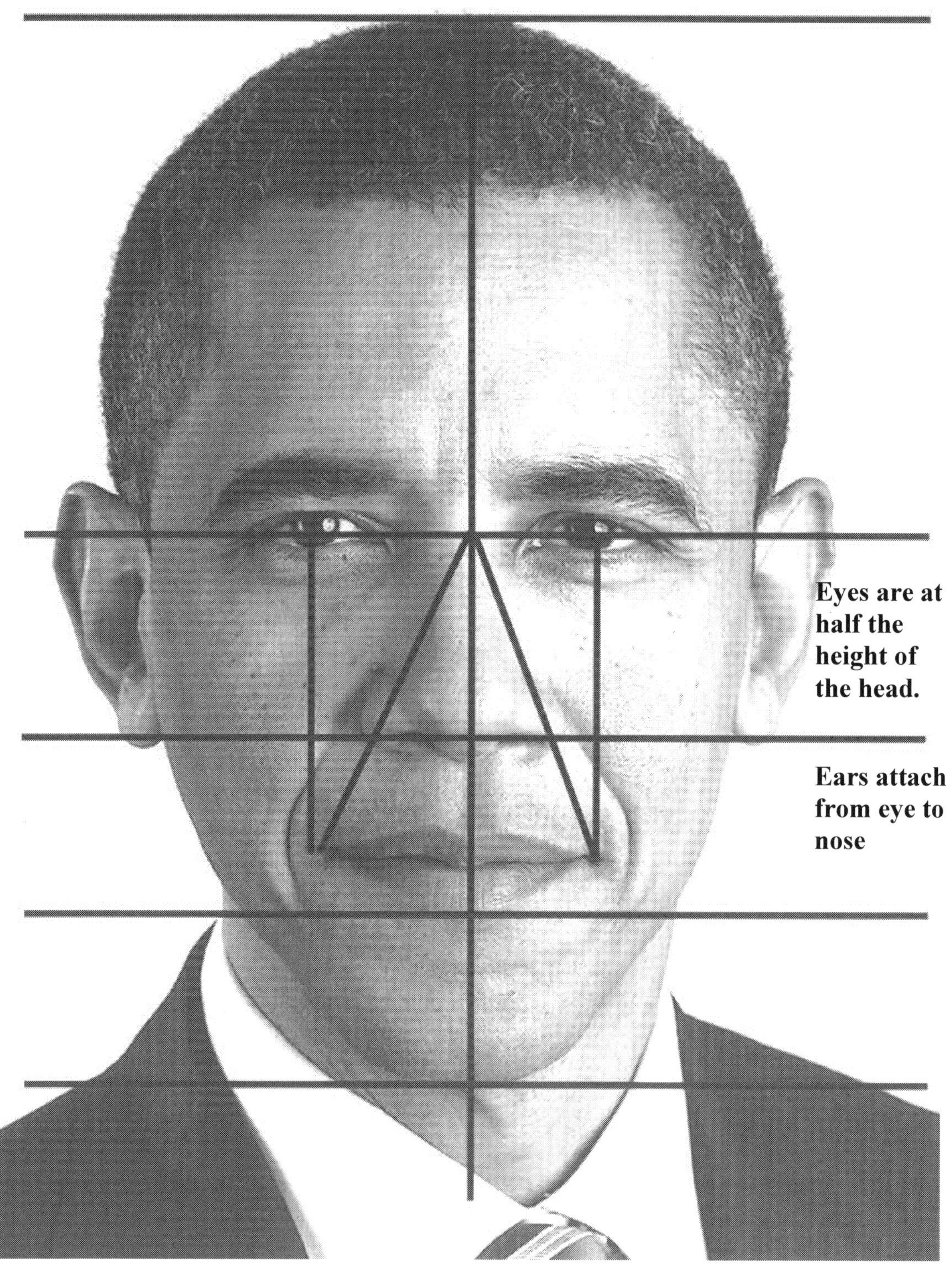

Face Map Proportions

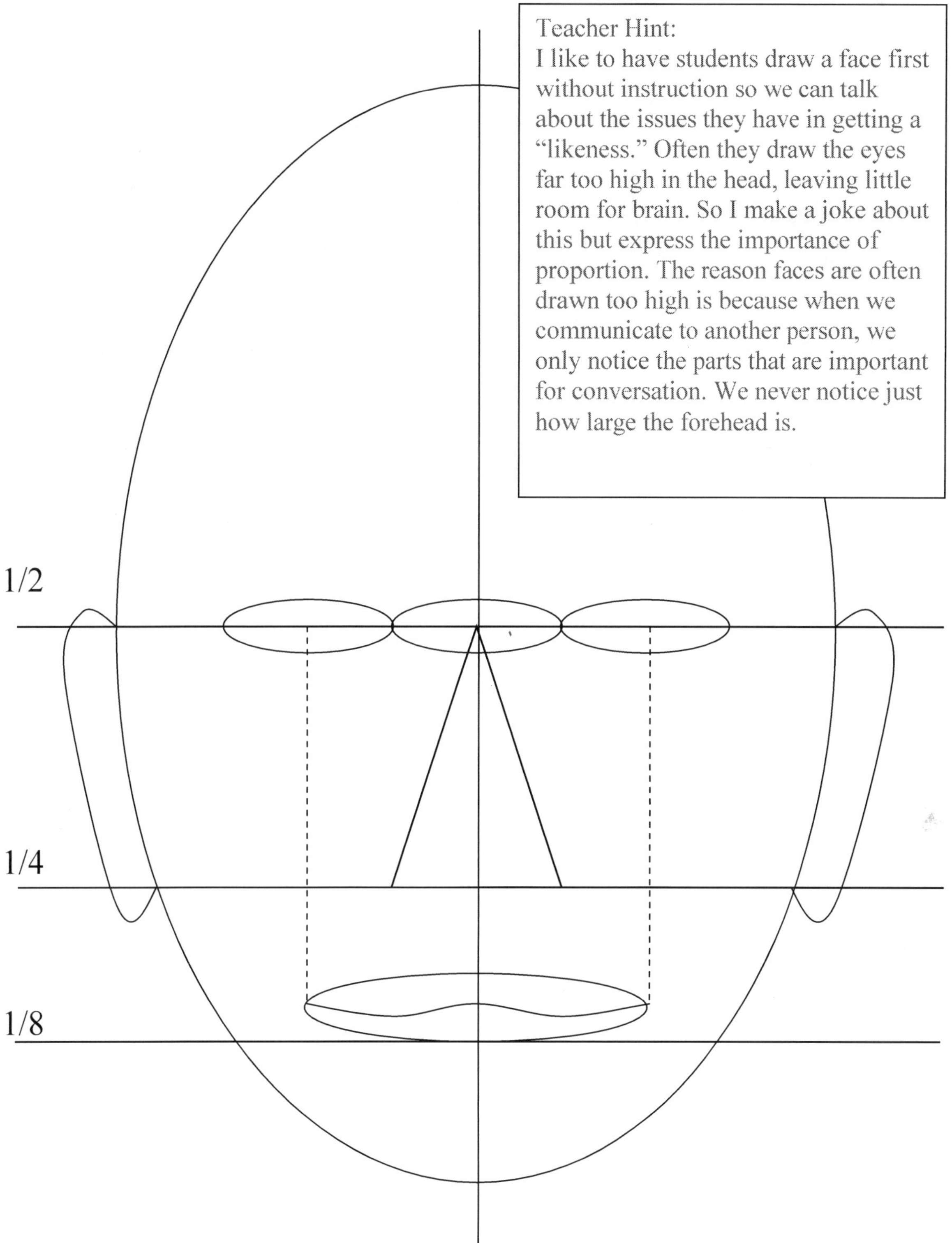

Teacher Hint:
I like to have students draw a face first without instruction so we can talk about the issues they have in getting a "likeness." Often they draw the eyes far too high in the head, leaving little room for brain. So I make a joke about this but express the importance of proportion. The reason faces are often drawn too high is because when we communicate to another person, we only notice the parts that are important for conversation. We never notice just how large the forehead is.

Plankton & Pollen

Find out about plankton, bacteria, viruses, and pollen. They often look really cool!
Can you make one from plaster, clay, or paper. Can you create a new one after
looking at many other ones? Maybe you can even make an Alien Pod?!?

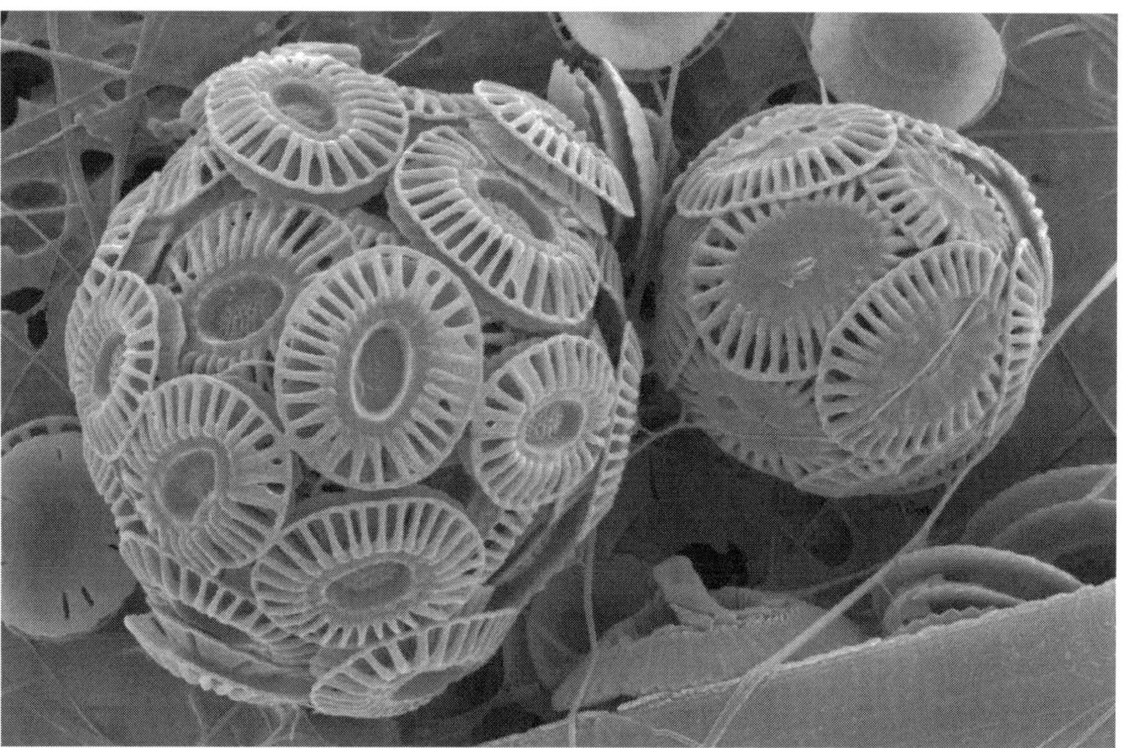

Plankton above

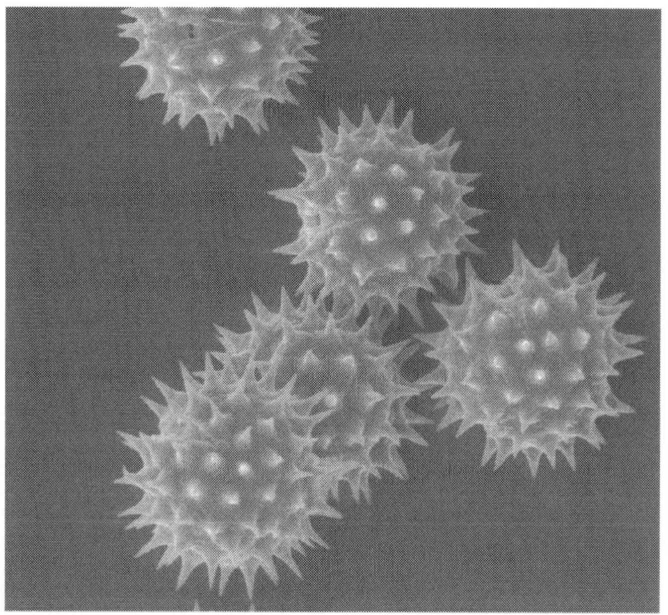

Pollen to the right

Sickness

Many sicknesses are caused by a virus, parasite, abnormal cells, or infection.
Name as many diseases or sicknesses that you can?

1.   3.

2.   4.

Pick one from above and use the internet or a book to see what it really looks like.

Draw it below and add color too.   **Your number** _________

What causes it? ____

Diseases and Other Creepy Crawlies

Find some time to go to the library or computer lab and look up viruses, bacteria and cancer cells. They can either print or sketch what they find. Below are Phages infecting a bacteria cell.

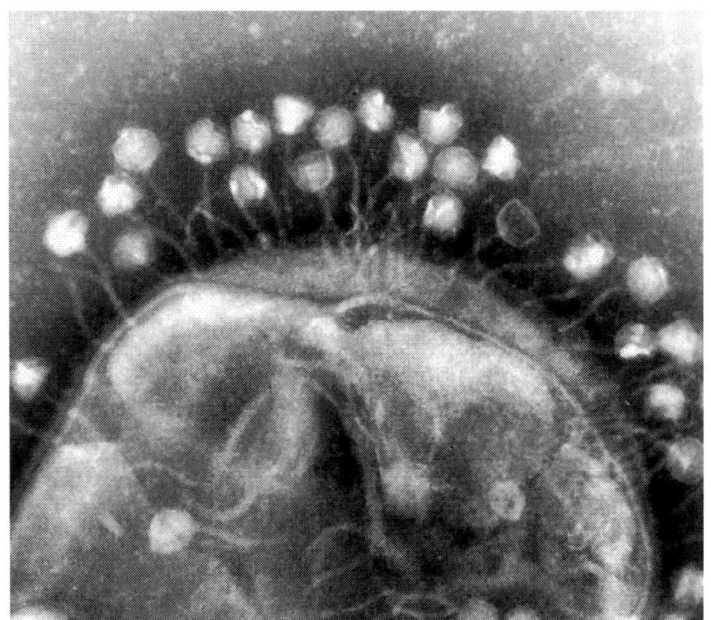

Above: *Mycobacteriophages*

TEACHER HINT:
I require my students to be able to find the proper scientific name for their cell, which later becomes the name of their project.

Students then re-create their cell with plaster over an aluminum foil base adding in straws, wire, dowels or pipe-cleaners to make it look as similar as possible.

When that is complete I ask them to finish their project with patterns, glitter, yarn, and artistic embellishments so that their work is not just clinical, but a work of sculptural art. You could have them use colors that express how the disease makes people feel.

Virus Project Samples

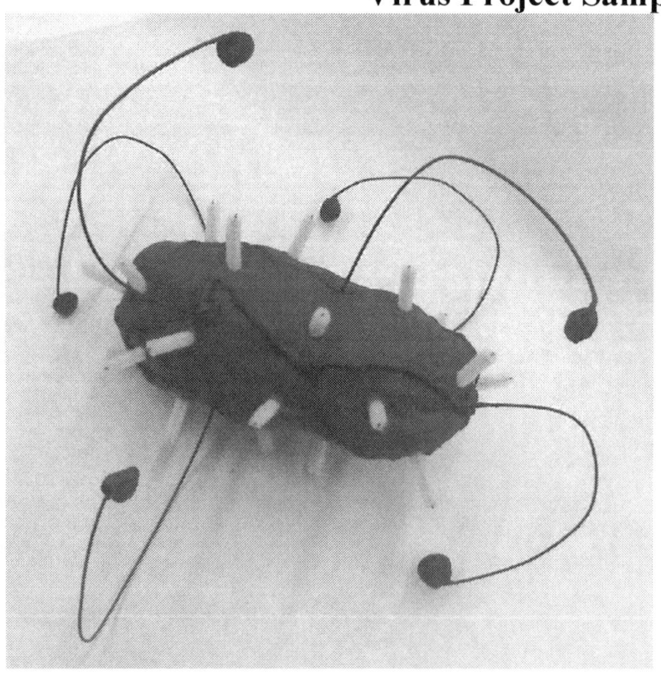

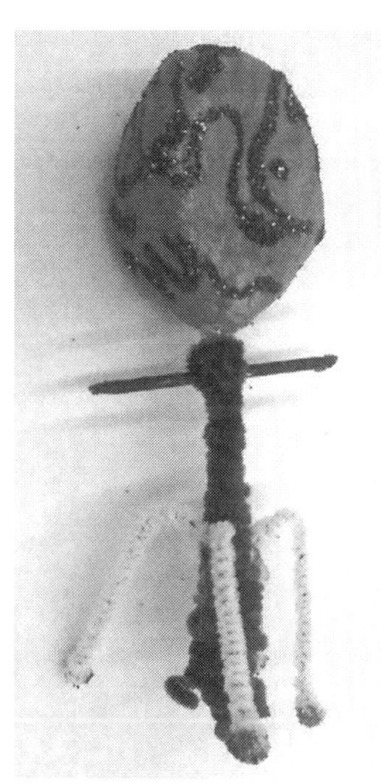

STUDENT WORKBOOKS HAVE A SKETCH PAGE HERE→

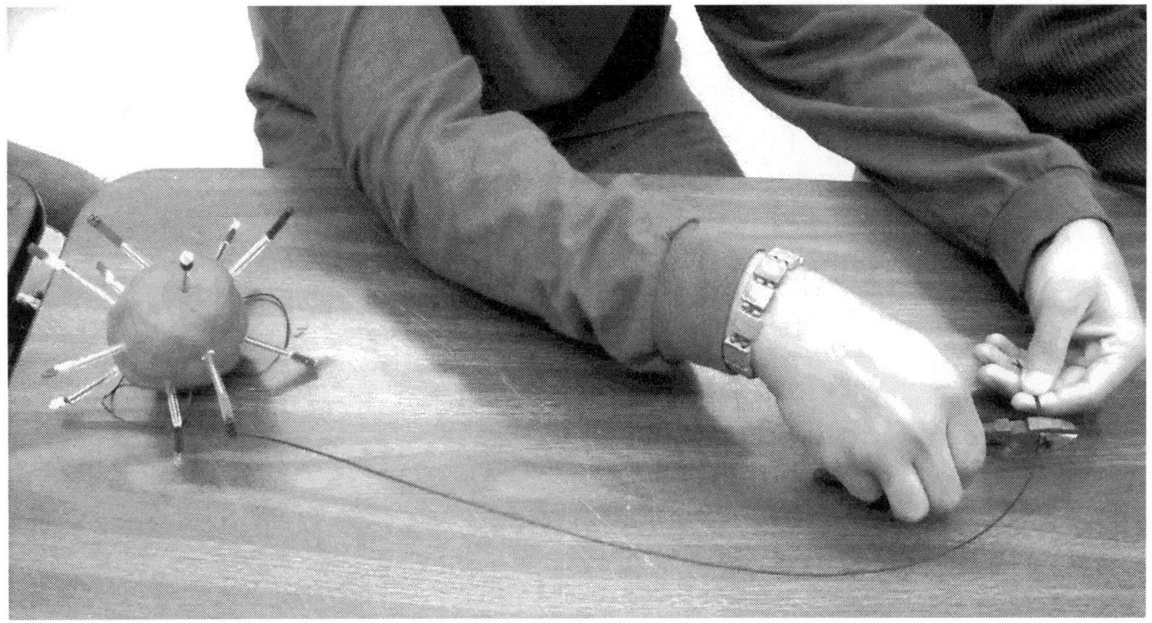

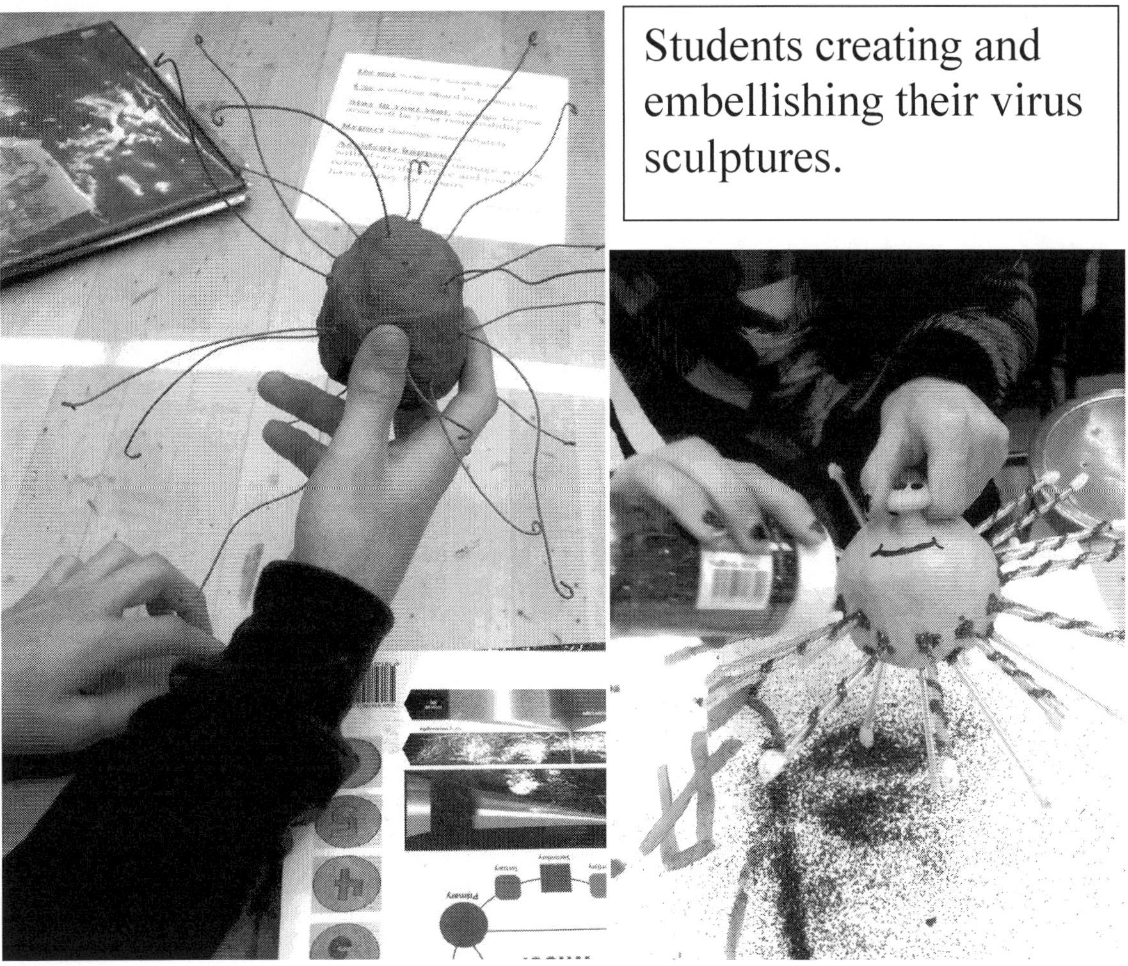

Students creating and embellishing their virus sculptures.

Wire Circus

The wire circus is the idea of Alexander Calder. He is an American artist famous for working with wire and metals to create different types of sculpture. He is most famous for his invention of the mobile.
(Provide internet examples, book images, or video)

Today, you will be joining the circus. You are going to choose one circus act/job and create a wire sculpture of it.   We can put them all together to make a circus.

Trapeze Artist
Lion/Tiger
Monkey
Elephant
Elephant Trainer
Ring Master
Unicycle Rider
Seesaw Acrobats
Contortionist
Clown
Strong Man
Bearded Lady
Lion Tamer
Peanut/Popcorn Vendor
Drink Vendor
Sea Lion Act
Acrobat
Tightrope Walker
Fire Breather/Dancer
Magician
Human Cannon Ball
Horses
Horse Rider/Tamer
Sword Swallower
Dog and Pony Show
Barker
Ticket Window
Trick Motor Cycle

Come up with your own act: ________________________________

Collage Projects with Meaning

Collage projects can be "loose and chunky" like the work of Robert Rauschenberg, or Pablo Picasso (provide samples) or they can be comical like the work of Romare Bearden (provide sample), or even cut and pasted in such a way that it look realistic or surrealistic, like the work of Salvador Dali or Rene Magritte.

Even if "loose and chunky," these projects should be done with good technique. Edges must be pasted well and have a flat, completed look.

Choose to go one of two ways to do this project.

#1. About Me: Choose pictures of the stuff you like to do, and the things you like in life. Cut out magazine pictures and even photo print-outs, images from the internet etc… to create a collection of pictures that tell us about you.

#2. Point-of-View: Choose images that have a message that shows how you feel about a situation. Some ideas might be: safety in school, stranger danger, save the earth, anti-bullying, protecting our pets, etc... Cut out magazine pictures and even photo print-outs, images from the internet and more to create a collection of pictures that tell us about how you feel about something.

What is your idea: ____

____

____

Add-On: Though the collage can be a finished project, here are some alternative uses of images:

— The collage can be scanned and printed on transparency plastic, then use an overhead projector to transfer the lines to a large canvas, OR use a grid to enlarge the original collage, OR scan in pictures and project them onto a canvas to be traced and painted.

— They can be photocopied and colored with expressive colors. If you photocopy four or six or nine, they can be placed in a grid like Andy Warhol would do, and color each one a bit differently.

My Cultural Background

Create a project based on things in your cultural background by creating a background pattern of repeated shapes of cultural objects and a foreground animal representing that your personality. Some people have many different cultural backgrounds.

Cultural Background #1 (Country of origin)	Cultural Background #2 (Country of origin)	Cultural Background #3 (Country of origin)
Cultural Objects *Flowers, crafts, trees, symbols*	Cultural Objects *Flowers, crafts, trees, symbols*	Cultural Objects *Flowers, crafts, trees, symbols*
Animals from that country	Animals from that country	Animals from that country

Pick an animal and symbol for your project to represent yourself:

Create a background pattern of objects based on information above found at the library or on the internet. Then cut and paste an animal symbol for yourself on top. Any media will work for this; try colored pencil, marker, or painted paper.

Pen Project

Shaman Dip Pen:

Pen nibs (Dip pen tips) are very inexpensive for a box or 12. They can be found at craft stores or through school vendors. Though a nib can be made, manufactured ones work better and can be attached to a stick with a little hot glue.

Start with a stick base. This can be a 1/4 inch hardwood dowel or a stick found outside with a similar diameter. Put a tip on it with a pencil sharpener. This is where you can add the nib later.

The concept or story is that the pen should look like it has some mystical quality about it beyond the simple fact it is a pen. What would the pen of a Medicine Man look like if it was used to write spells for victory in war, or to write a love spell, or one for revenge, healing, knowledge, peace…

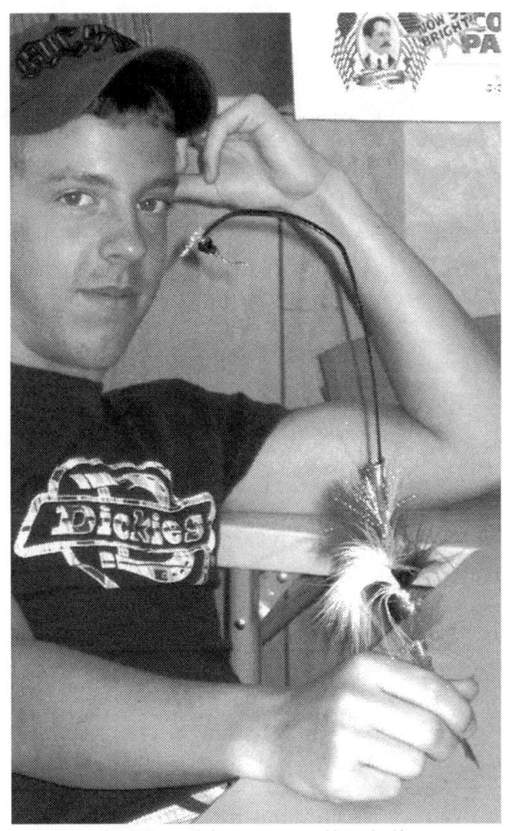

Student holding his personalized dip pen.

Older students (Grades 6+) may be able to cut a bit of their stick with an X-Acto blade, though the teacher will need to review proper use and safety. The bark may be completely or partially cut away so as to leave a desired texture.

Carve the stick to have a pattern that enhances your theme. Think of simple patterns you can carve in like rope, criss-cross, X's, waves, or whatever you think will work best.

The pen can be decorated with string, twine, raffia, beads, wire, feathers, felt strips, or whatever you can bring in. The pen nib can be glued on with hot glue and then tied on with whatever is available. The teacher can lead students through a demonstration of how to use traditional dip pens.

Not in student workbook - Sketchpage

My Name in Chinese

The Chinese written language is based on pictures that have been made simple over the years. In this project we try to turn the symbols back into pictures that tell a bit about you, the artist.

Students can rewrite the Chinese letters so that the personality of the person shows. If a student is an artist, the Chinese letters can be translated into art supplies laying in the same order, so we see both art supplies AND the writing that says their name in Chinese. To find Chinese translations of "English" names, use Google to search the words "Chinese name English."

As a cultural introduction, students can try to use bamboo brushes or round brushes to reproduce some Chinese characters easily found through a Google image search. To find names go here:

— chineseculture.about.com/library/name/blname.htm
— www.chinesenames.org
— www.chinese-tools.com/names
— chineseculture.about.com/library/name/family/blfn.htm

For example, the name "ERIC" can be written like this.

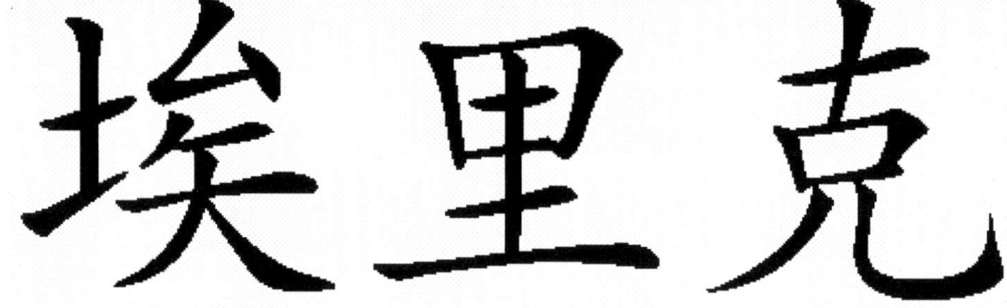

You can see the things that interest "Eric" by the drawing below.

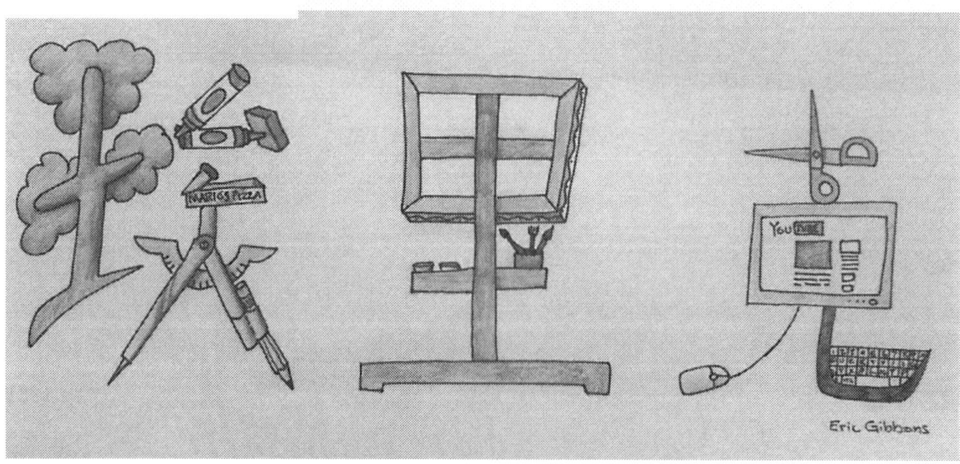

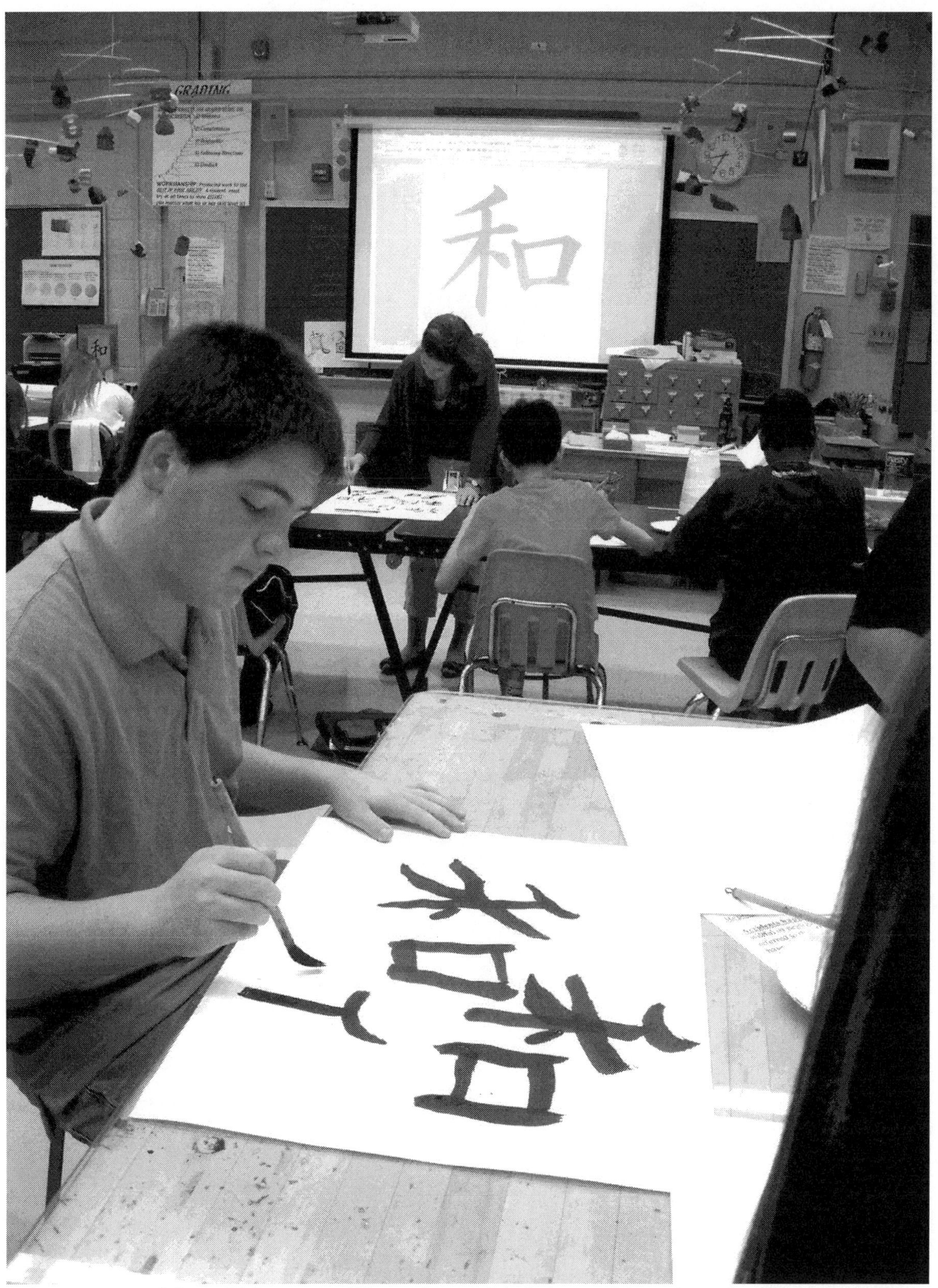

Students try writing Chinese calligraphy, with ink, and bamboo brushes before doing the name project. We looked up words like peace, love, hope, tree, person…

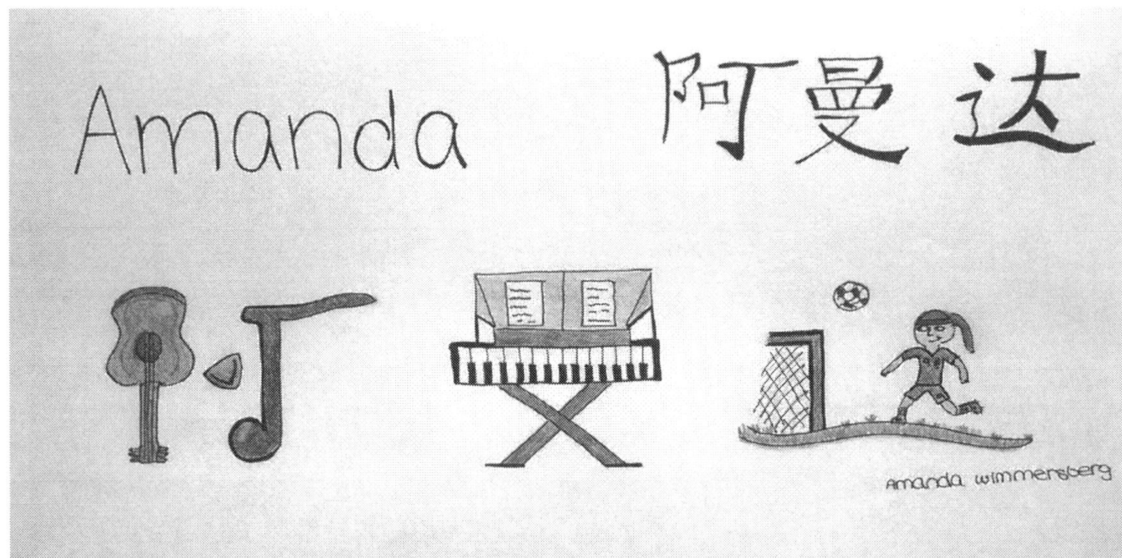

You can see that Amanda likes music and ports.

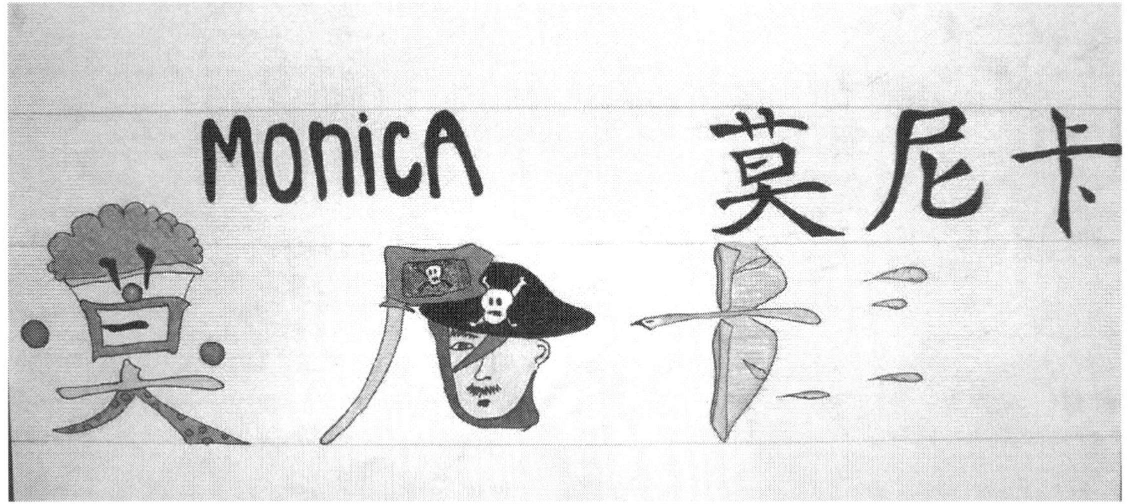

What does Monica like?

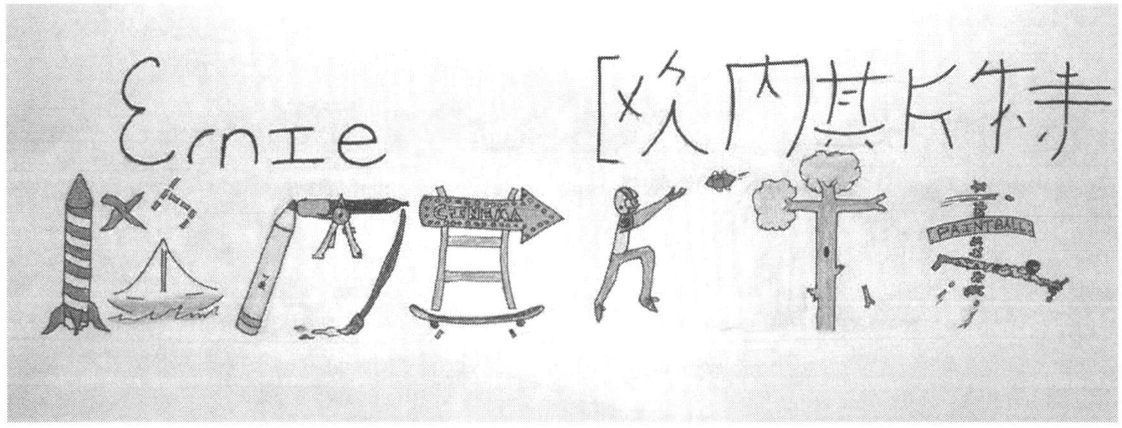

What does Ernie like to do?

Your name in Chinese looks like this:

Sketch how you would re-write your name to show what things you like, and the stuff you enjoy doing.

Sun Samples

Radial Design (Ray-di-el) (De-zyne) are shapes and lines that repeat in a circle. Some cultures make pictures called a Mandala (man-da-la).

Using the internet or library books, look up symbols of your own culture. Some students have many different cultures. Use the next page for your research.

What designs can you use from your culture to make a sun? What colors should you use? When you make your symbols repeat around a circle, you are making a radial design.

The suns below were made by drawing all our lines by pressing hard with white oil pastel on white paper. It is very hard to see, but when we used water colors, the white lines stay white and the colors look extra bright!

This same project can be done in markers, or cut-out construction paper, or nearly any material. Your teacher will tell you how they want you to do your project.

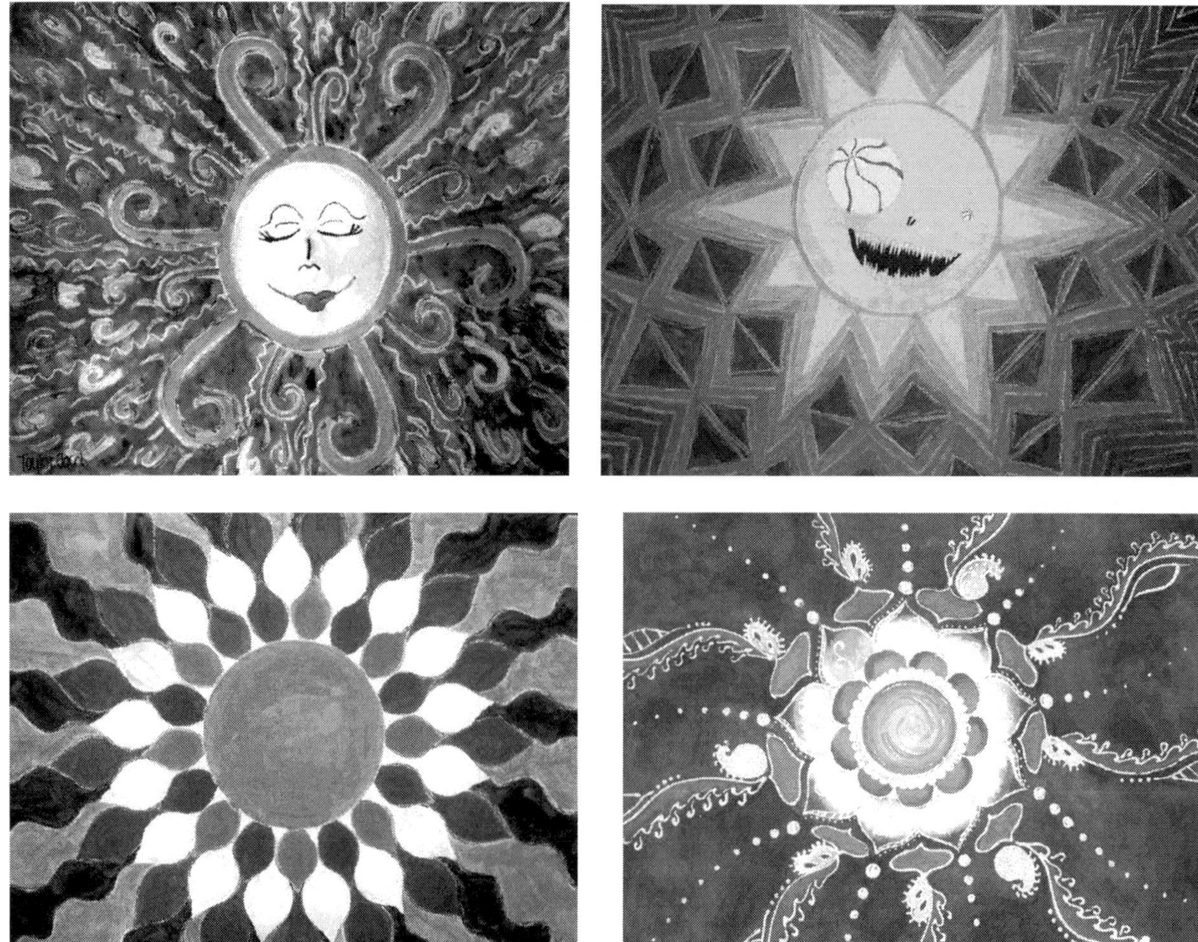

What is your cultural background(s)? ________________________________

____

Draw or write some symbols from your culture below:

NUMBERS as a Theme

Make a painting, illustration, or sculpture with a number theme. Work as a group or alone. Find out more these ideas, or discover a new one!

2
Good and evil
Yin and Yang
Noah's Ark, 2 of each animal

3
Holy Trinity
Ages of man
Branches of government
Jewels of Buddhism
Pure Ones of Taoism
Hear no evil, see no evil, speak no evil

4
Seasons
Beauties of China
Elements
Archangels in Islam
Four Horsemen of the Apocalypse
The four Gospels

5
Fingers
Basic pillars of Islam
Mayan Worlds
Mythological headless male warriors

6
Tastes
Foods placed on the Passover Plate
Articles of belief of Islam.
Degrees of Separation
Cardinal directions

7
Deadly sins **or** Virtues
Wonders of the world
Continents **or** Seas
Seven days of creation
Asian Lucky Gods

8
Days of Hanukkah
"The Immortals" China

9
Planets
Choirs of angels
Baseball Players

10
The Commandments
Plagues
Lost Tribes
Branches of the tree of life
Canadian provinces

11
Soccer, Cricket, or Football players
Guns in a military salute

12
Apostles or Tribes of Israel
Olympians
Days of Christmas
Months in a year

13
Attendees of the Last Supper
Witches in a coven
Colonies of the USA

My Number Theme is ____

What did you learn about your theme? _______________________________

____

____

Sketch out some of your ideas here:

SERVICE PROJECT - Survey

Art Students will create posters to help teach acceptance in our school. This could be about special needs students and other students using the word "*Retarded*" or some group you feel is bullied in your school.

What group should we focus on? _______________________________

Why?_______________________________

____

____

____

What do people not know about this group?

____

____

____

How does the bullying hurt this group and hurt our school?

____

____

____

What can be done to bring attention to this issue?

____

____

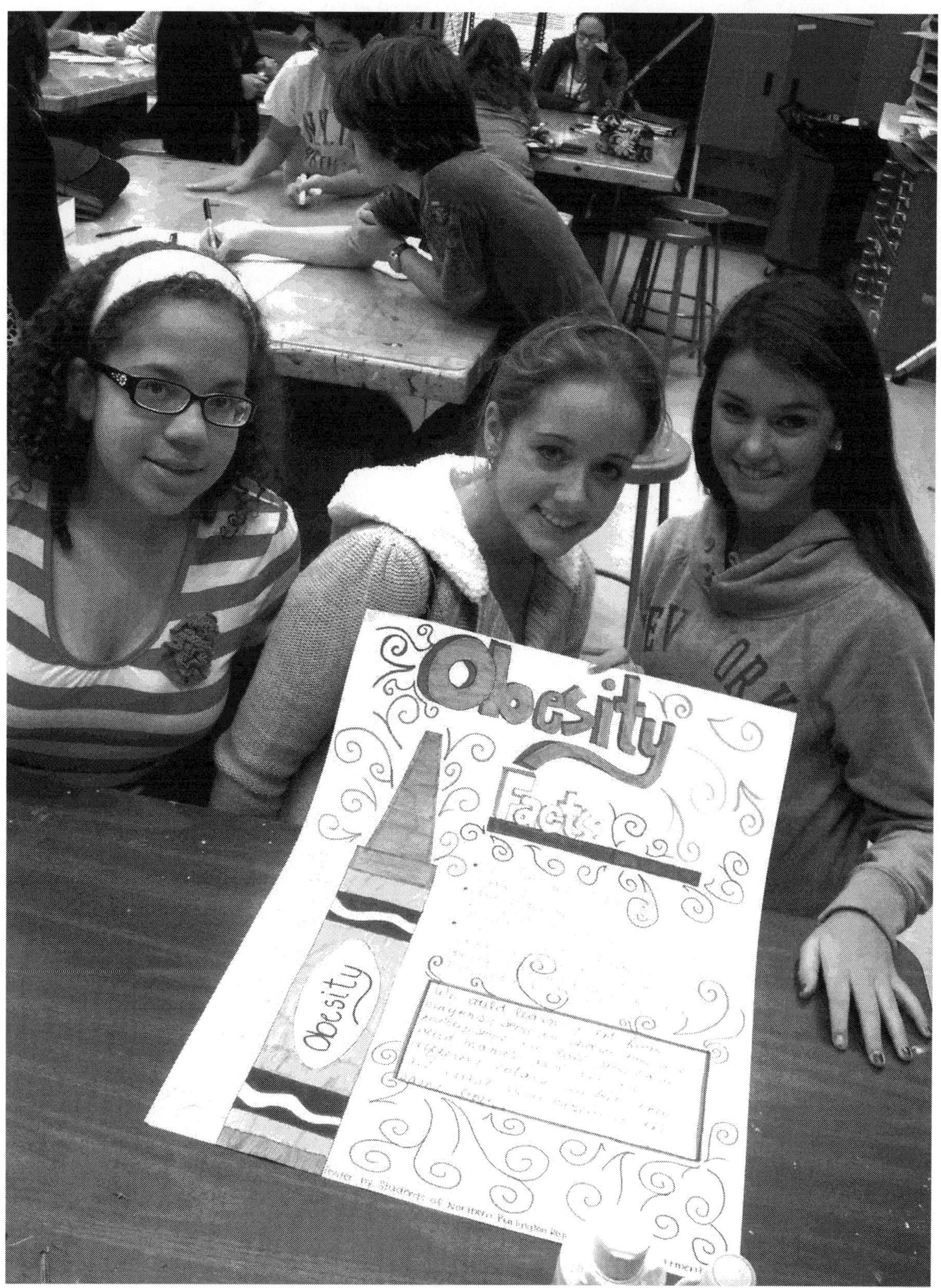

Student group with topic of obesity and bullying in school.

Design Agency

Team Name_____________________________ Topic _____________________________

Students ____ Period ______

Your job is to create a poster to make people understand the bullying in school and help teach our school through posters. Posters will need to have a neat and clean look and follow the example of the Autism poster on the next page. Your group will need to learn about the bullied students so that your facts are true. You can do this on the internet or the library. Finished posters will be shown to your teacher for a grade.

Posters that meet all of the requirements can be laminated and put around the school and later in your community. This will help teach everyone that bullying is something we need to try and stop, and it shows your neighborhood that your school cares!

Passes for research to the library can be given if necessary. When research and design is complete, your group will make a sketch before beginning a final poster.

Write your ideas below and show them to your teacher:

AUTISM

Students with Autism are in our school and community. Words like *"Retard"* are hurtful, mean and intolerant.

FACTS:

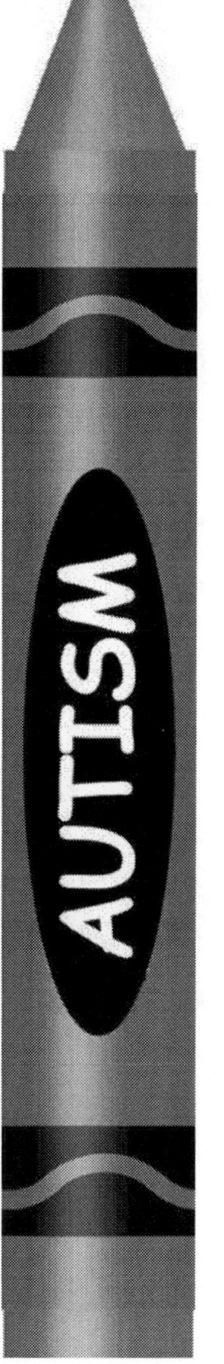

—Autism is a neurological disorder characterized by impaired social interaction and communication.

—1 in every 150 children is diagnosed with autism.

—The cause is currently unknown but does have a genetic link.

> *We could learn a lot from crayons; some are sharp, some are pretty, some are dull, some have weird names, and all are different colors....but they all exist very nicely in the same box.*

Poster by students: _______________________ **School Art Department**

SERVICE PROJECT PLAN

Team ____ Period ____________

Topic/Bullied group____

What do you already know about this topic? What are facts you think you know?

What are some wrong ideas people have about the bullied group you have chosen?

Who will be in charge of finding information about your bullied group?

Who will be in charge of planning out your poster?

Who will be in charge of writing on the poster?

Who will make sure coloring is neat and good-looking?

While your team member uses the pass below, please use the time to sketch your poster on the next page. This does not have to be neat, but should include all the required stuff from the example on the last page.

Pass to ___________ *to research the topic of* ________________________________

Student: ____ *Period:* ______ *From room* ______

DATE: ____/____/____ **Signature** ____

Service Project: *FOLLOW-UP*

Before putting posters in the hallway or neighborhood, share your poster with the class. As other groups share what they learned, write down about 5 of them below.

1. Poster theme: _______________________. I learned that… _______________

____

____

2. Poster theme: _______________________. I learned that… _______________

____

____

3. Poster theme: _______________________. I learned that… _______________

____

____

4. Poster theme: _______________________. I learned that… _______________

____

____

5. Poster theme: _______________________. I learned that… _______________

____

____

Where in the school was our poster placed? _________________________________

Where in the community was our poster placed? _____________________________

Social Issues Sculptures

Students decide for themselves an important social issue that affects themselves or their community and create a sculpture that symbolically illustrates the issue. Here we see "World Hunger" as food is within reach but still unreachable. Students also complete a statement about their topic to be placed with the sculpture to educate their audience.

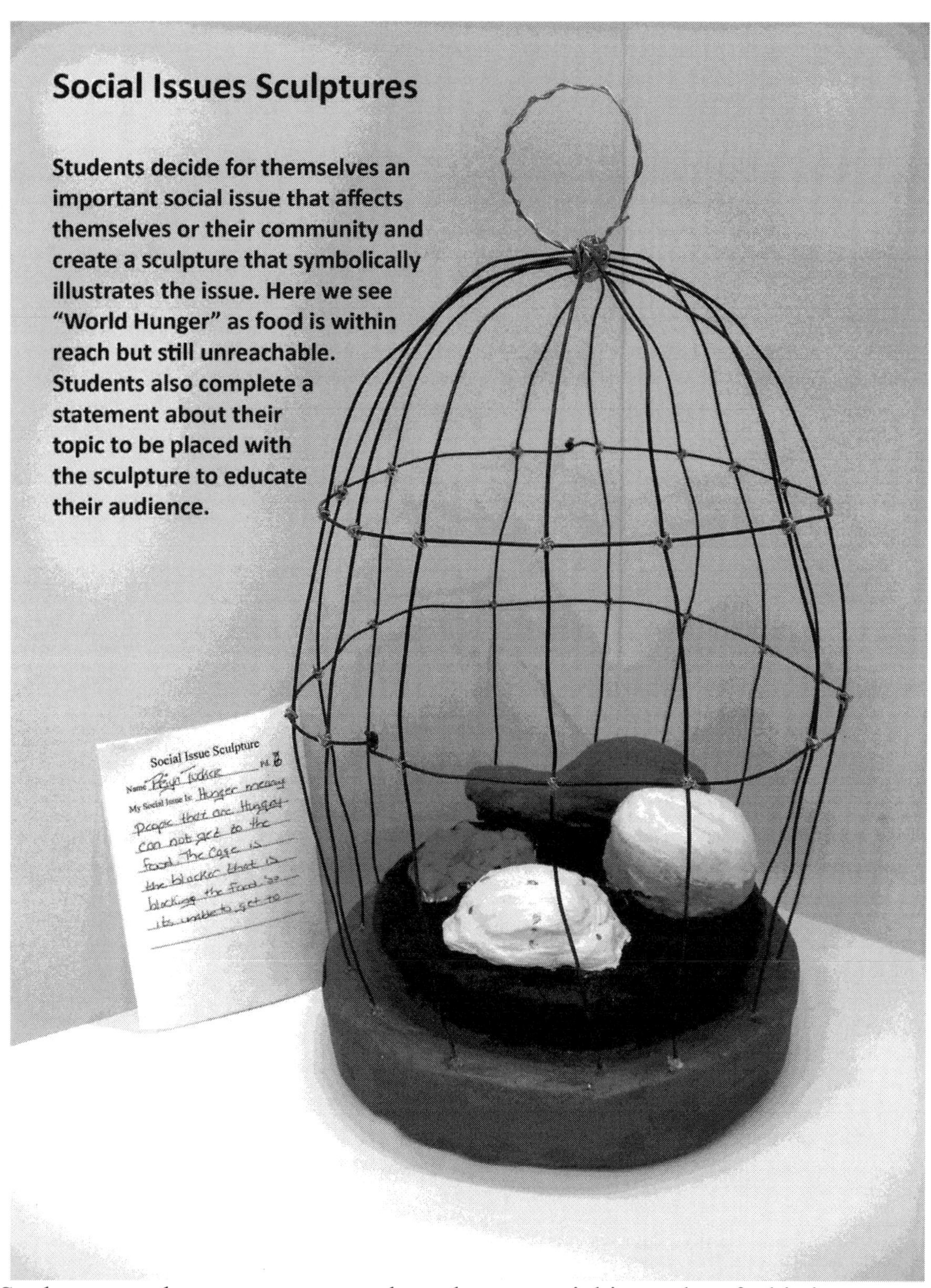

Sculpture students create art work to show a social issue they feel is important. Here we see "World Hunger." What social issue can you make a sculpture for?

THIS PAGE IS NOT IN THE STUDENT EDITION

Social Issues

What are some social issues that affect your family, community, or school?

____

____

____

Which one do you think you know the most about or would like to explore more?

____

What kinds of symbols can you use in an artwork? Sketch or write below.

Sunset Silhouette

(Sil-o-wet) The shadow your body makes
is a silhouette. It's like an outline that
has been colored in with one color.

Step 1: Start your colors from the bottom
with YELLOW, create stripes of color
that OVERLAP a little from one color
to the next. (About 1 inch of overlap.)
If you use paint you can just blend colors.

If you use pastels, fold a piece of paper
Towel about 6 times to blend the colors.
be sure the go from one color
to the next smoothly and blend well.

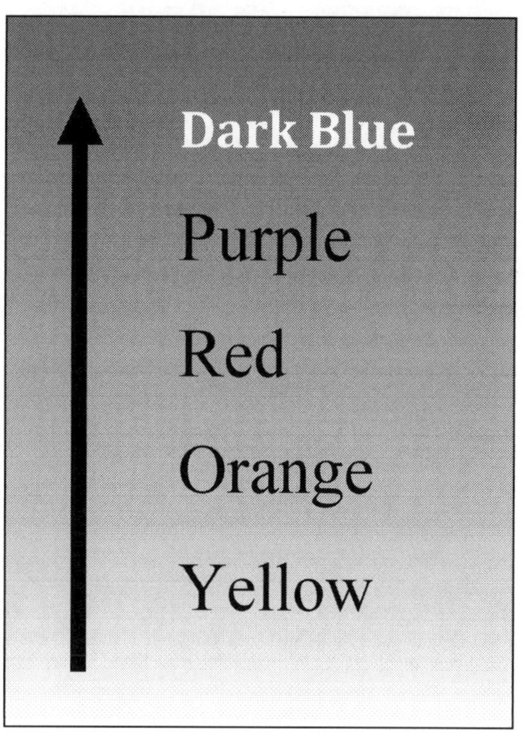

Step 3: Add a horizon with a dark cool color or black, and fill in below it.

Step 4: Add a tree and 2 objects in black to your picture. Avoid putting things ON
the horizon, they should be a bit below. Chose images that tell people something
about you. Do you play baseball? Maybe you should include a figure wearing a
baseball hat. Always include images that mean something to you.

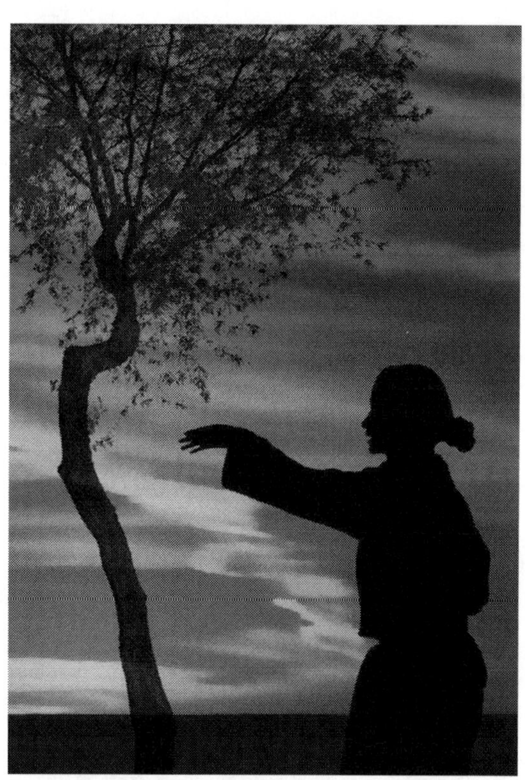

Comic Book Ideas

Parody: Making fun of something, twisting what you know for a funny effect.

Batman → Hatman
Wizard of Oz → Wizard of Odd
Sesame Street → Sesame Highway
The Hobbit → The Blob It

What are some movies or TV shows you could make fun of?

_________________________________ → _________________________________

_________________________________ → _________________________________

_________________________________ → _________________________________

Try changing the title of something for a funny idea…

■ Teenage Mutant Ninja _________________

■ Killer _________________ from Outer Space

■ Attack of the Mutant _________________

Your idea: _________________________________

Try a new situation…

Iron Man vs. Spongebob
T-Rex comes to Sesame Street
The President visits our school

Your idea: _________________________________

There are millions of possibilities!

Do you have an original cartoon you like to draw?
This is a great chance to make it look professional.

ORIGINALITY COUNTS: Don't COPY work.

All comic books need to include title, subtitle, dramatic action, logo, foreground, middle-ground, background, and overlap.

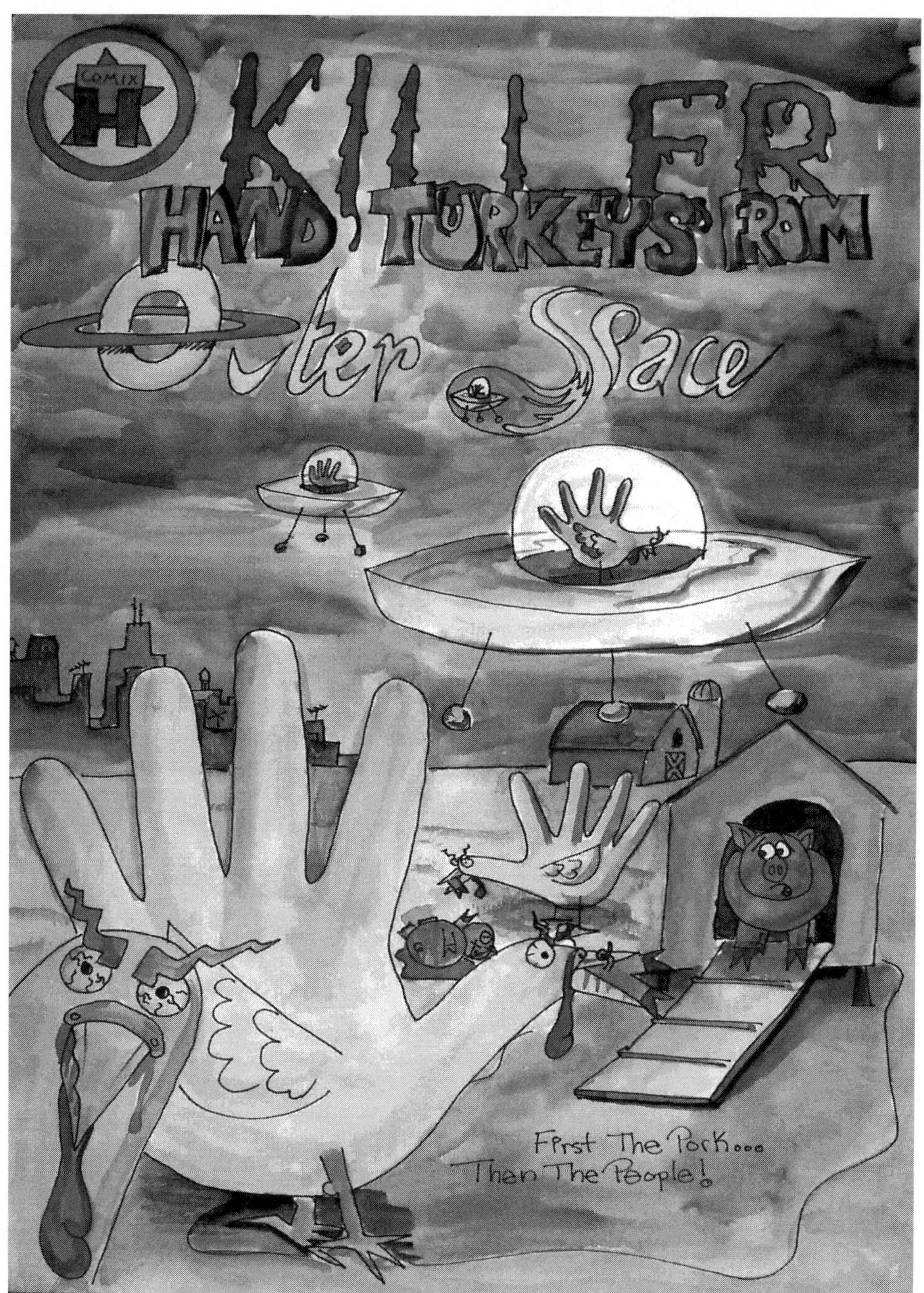

Try out your idea on the next page!

Sketch your comic book cover here. Remember to have a title, subtitle, dramatic action, logo, foreground, middle-ground, background, and overlap.

Compound Words: (Kom-pound) are two words put together that may have a different meaning than the words apart. A Butterfly is a bug with pretty wings, but butter is something you put on toast, and fly means to go up in the air.

In this project you should show the funny meaning of the compound word. For butterfly, you might show a stick of butter flying like an airplane, or house fly that is all yellow and looks like it is made out of butter. This is your chance to be silly.

Your artwork should include foreground, middle-ground, background, and overlap.

Horseshoe
House fly
Dragonfly
Football
Hotdog
Rainbow
Waterfall
Groundhog
Butterfly
Fireman
Firefighter
Dog food
Toenail
Jellyfish
Starfish
Family tree
Basketball
_______ball
Carpet
Honeybee
Hairnet
Hairspray
French fry
French toast
Hummingbird
Pancake
Shoehorn
Earring
Ponytail

Other? _________________

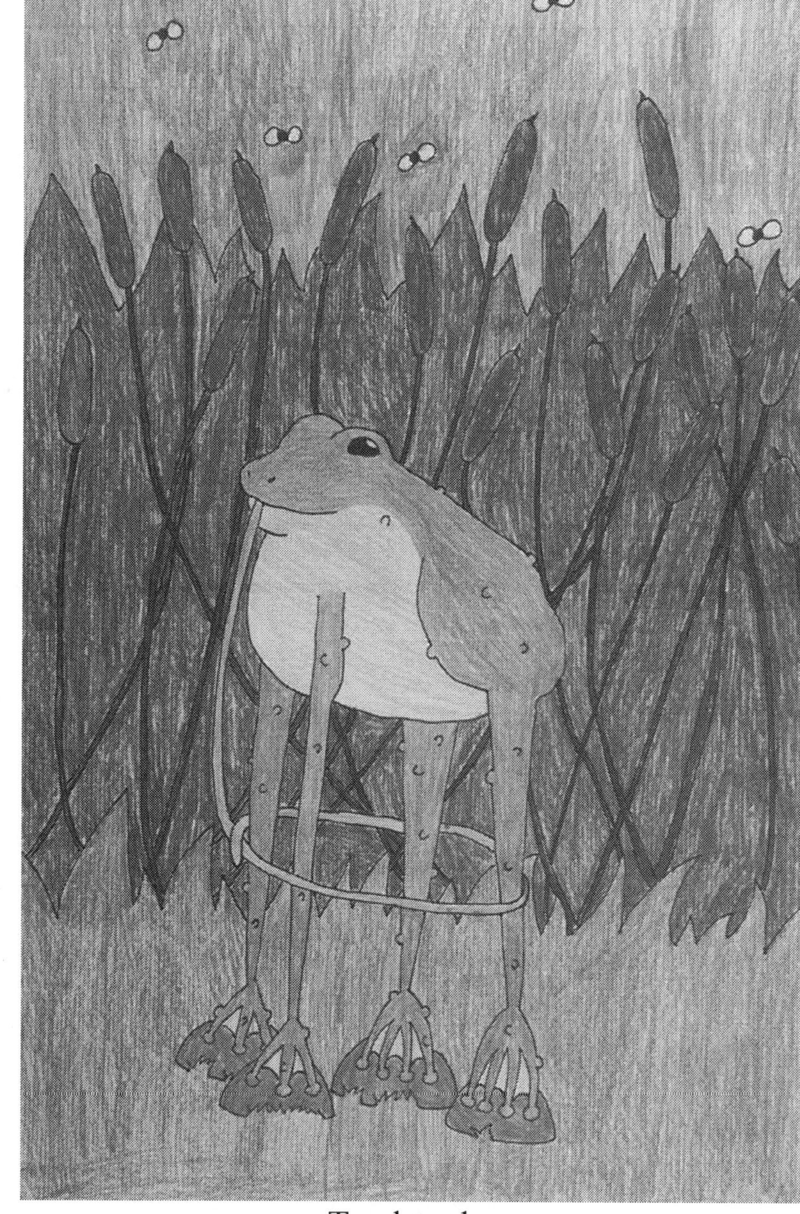

Toadstool

Compound Word Sketch: Include foreground, middle-ground, background, and overlap.

JABBERWOCKY
By Lewis Carroll
(*Through the Looking-Glass*, 1872)

`Twas brillig, and the slithy toves
  Did gyre and gimble in the wabe;
All mimsy were the borogoves,
  And the mome raths outgrabe.

"Beware the Jabberwock, my son!
  The jaws that bite, the claws that catch!
Beware the Jubjub bird, and shun
  The frumious Bandersnatch!"

He took his vorpal sword in hand:
  Long time the manxome foe he sought --
So rested he by the Tumtum tree,
  And stood awhile in thought.

And, as in uffish thought he stood,
  The Jabberwock, with eyes of flame,
Came whiffling through the tulgey wood,
  And burbled as it came!

One, two! One, two! & through & through
  The vorpal blade went snicker-snack!
He left it dead, and with its head
  He went galumphing back.

"And, has thou slain the Jabberwock?
  Come to my arms, my beamish boy!
O frabjous day! Callooh! Callay!"
  He chortled in his joy.

`Twas brillig, and the slithy toves
  Did gyre and gimble in the wabe;
All mimsy were the borogoves,
  And the mome raths outgrabe.

Try and do a understand each part of this poem. Often there is no correct answer, but try as best you can…

Repeated from first part of poem.

(Sample artwork on next page)

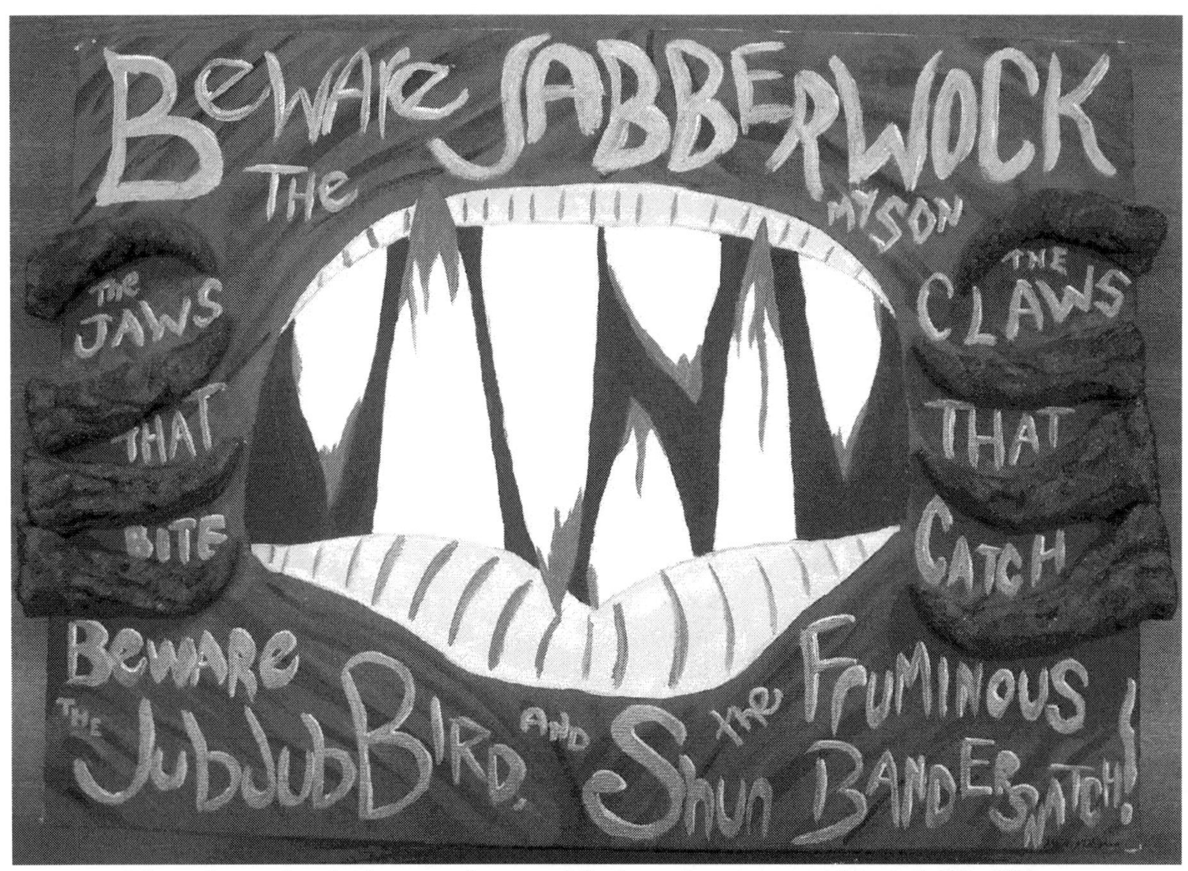

The above had plaster claws added to the canvas for a 3-D effect.
STUDENT EDTIONS DO NOT HAVE THIS PAGE

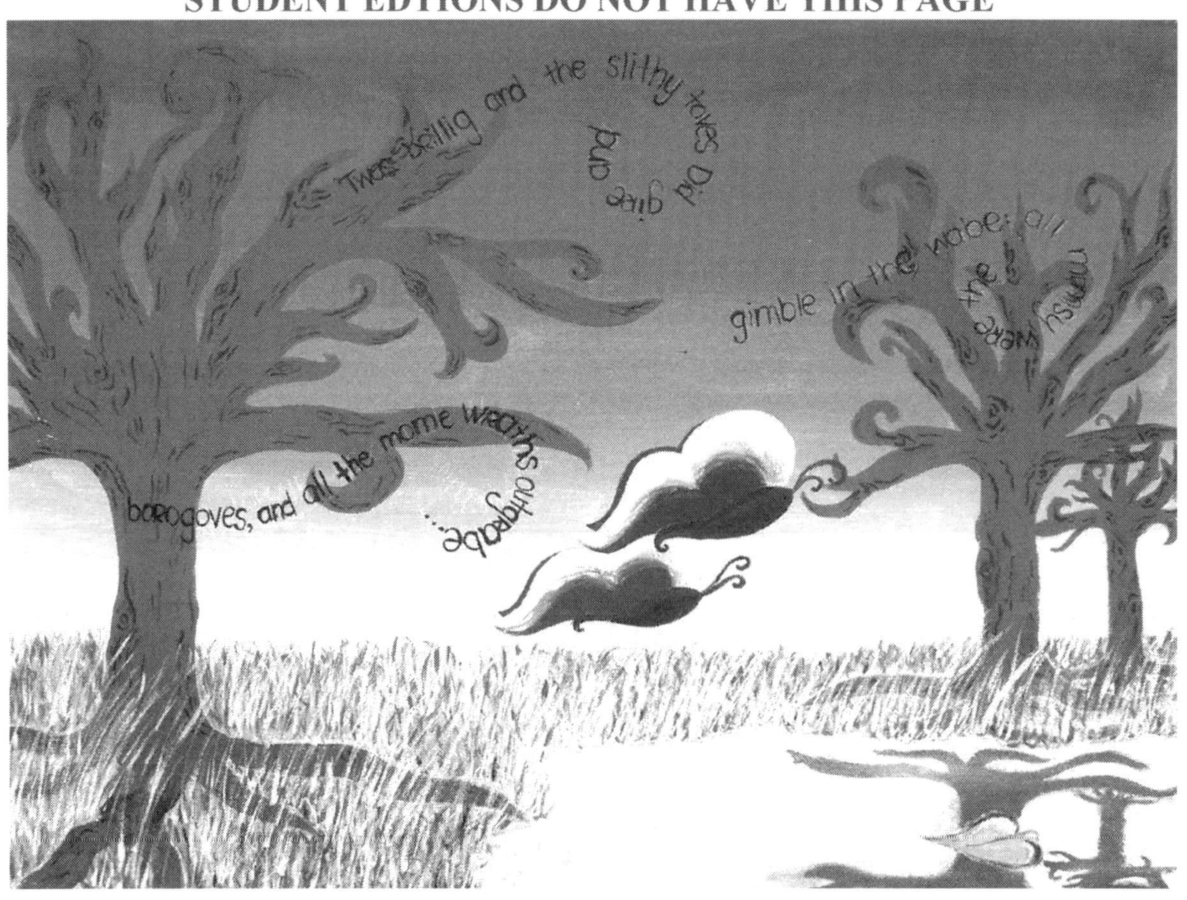

Jabberwocky sketch:

Teacher Note: This quotes section is a great way to include creative writing into your curriculum. I have my students start off every week with this; it takes just 3 minutes to write and 2 minutes to discuss. It is also an important way to prove to your district that your content is supportive of "core courses" as well.

I do not stress right or wrong answers, but offer my opinion at the end. These quotes can be interpreted in many different ways. The importance is in the thinking & writing.

A: Please take 2 or 3 minutes to write about the following quote.

What does this mean?

"Feet, what do I need you for when I have wings to fly?"
~Frida Kahlo

____

____

____

B Please take 2 or 3 minutes to write about the following quote.

What does this mean?

"Paintin's not important. The important thing is keepin' busy."
~Grandma Moses

____

____

____

C: Please take 2 or 3 minutes to write about the following quote.

What does this mean?

"Everything has its beauty but not everyone sees it."
~Confucius

____

____

____

D: Please take 2 or 3 minutes to write about the following quote.

What does this mean?

"Life is the art of drawing without an eraser."
~John W. Gardner

____

____

____

E: Please take 2 or 3 minutes to write about the following quote.

What does this mean?

"Colors are brighter when the mind is open."
~A. Alarcon

____

____

____

F: **Please take 2 or 3 minutes to write about the following quote.**

What does this mean?

"Lying in bed would be a perfect ... if only I had a colored pencil long enough to draw on the ceiling." ~Gilbert K. Chesterton

____

____

____

G: **Please take 2 or 3 minutes to write about the following quote.**

What does this mean?

"Art is a line around your thoughts."
~Gustav Klimt

____

____

____

H: **Please take 2 or 3 minutes to write about the following quote.**

What does this mean?

"Not everybody trusts paintings but people believe photographs."
~Ansel Adams

____

____

____

I: **Please take 2 or 3 minutes to write about the following quote.**

What does this mean?

"One should really use the camera as though tomorrow you'd be stricken blind."
~Dorothea Lange

____

____

____

J **Please take 2 or 3 minutes to write about the following quote.**

What does this mean?

"Painting is easy when you don't know how, but very difficult when you do."
~Edgar Degas

____

____

____

K: **Please take 2 or 3 minutes to write about the following quote.**

What does this mean?

"Every child is an artist. The problem is how to remain an artist once he grows up." ~Pablo Picasso

____

____

____

L: **Please take 2 or 3 minutes to write about the following quote.**

What does this mean?

"A day without art is like a garden without flowers."
~Lori McNee

____

____

____

M: **Please take 2 or 3 minutes to write about the following quote.**

What does this mean?

"Art washes away from the soul the dust of everyday life."
~Pablo Picasso

____

____

____

N: **Please take 2 or 3 minutes to write about the following quote.**

What does this mean?

"Art is like singing, some do it better than others,
but everyone can and should be doing it for their soul." ~Barbara Mason

____

____

____

O: **Please take 2 or 3 minutes to write about the following quote.**

What does this mean?

"A man paints with his brains and not with his hands."
~Michelangelo

____

____

____

P: **Please take 2 or 3 minutes to write about the following quote.**

What does this mean?

"Surely nothing has to listen to so many stupid remarks
as a painting in a museum." ~Edmond & Jules de Goncourt

____

____

____

Q: **Please take 2 or 3 minutes to write about the following quote.**

What does this mean?

"Art without heart is craft."
~Eric Gibbons

____

____

____

R: **Please take 2 or 3 minutes to write about the following quote.**

What does this mean?

"Imagination is more important than knowledge."
~Albert Einstein

____

____

____

S: **Please take 2 or 3 minutes to write about the following quote.**

What does this mean?

"Only the artists and children see life as it is."
~Hugo von Hofmannstahl

____

____

____

T: **Please take 2 or 3 minutes to write about the following quote.**

What does this mean?

"Create like a god, command like a king, work like a slave."
~Constantin Brancusi

____

____

____

U: **Please take 2 or 3 minutes to write about the following quote.**

What does this mean?

"As a painter, I will never amount to anything important.
I am absolutely sure of it." ~Vincent van Gogh

____

____

____

V: **Please take 2 or 3 minutes to write about the following quote.**

What does this mean?

"To be an artist you have to give up everything,
 including the desire to be a good artist." ~Jasper Johns

____

____

____

W: **Please take 2 or 3 minutes to write about the following quote.**

What does this mean?

"He who works with his hands and his head and his heart is an artist."
~St. Francis of Assisi

____

____

____

X: **Please take 2 or 3 minutes to write about the following quote.**

What does this mean?

"The EARTH without ART is just EH….."
~Unknown

Y: **Please take 2 or 3 minutes to write about the following quote.**

What does this mean?

"I want to paint with colors that rhyme."
~Dave Watland

Z: **Please take 2 or 3 minutes to write about the following quote.**

What does this mean?

"Painting is easy, getting it right is the hard bit."
~Danny Byrne

Review Pages: The 8 Art Elements

A line is the most simple thing in art. We call it an art element. You need lines to draw anything. What can you measure about a line? __length or how long it is__
What are some lines you see around you?

Table edges, edges of bricks, lines on paper, etc…

Draw 3 different kinds of lines here: *Any line is okay __if it is not a closed shape__*

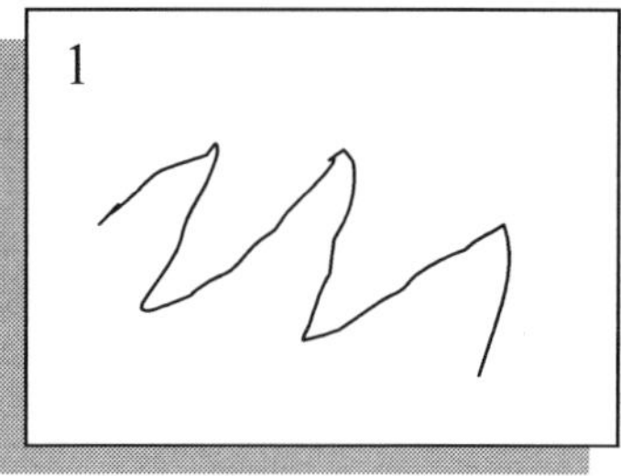 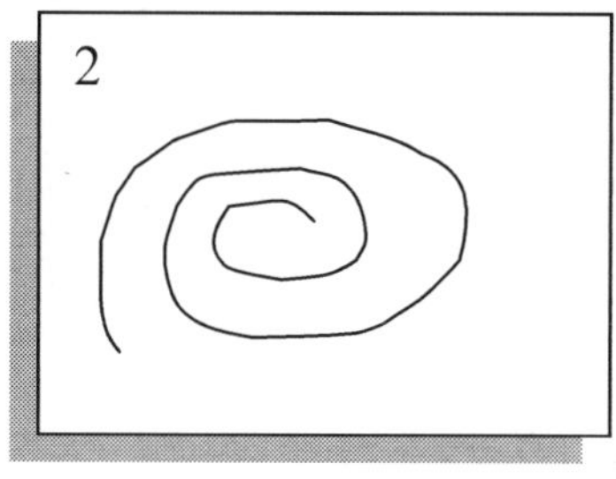 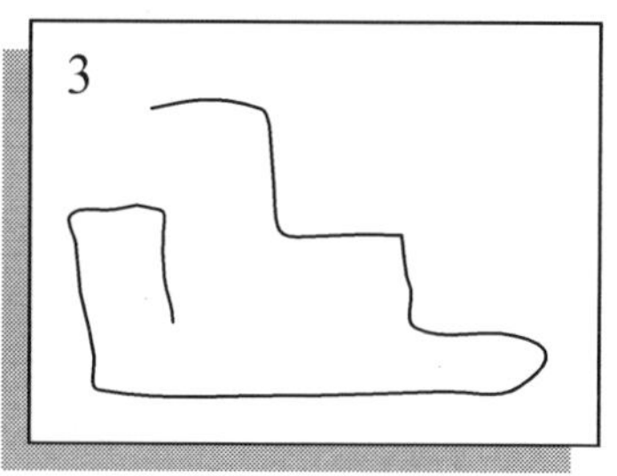

A line that touches itself makes a shape. A shape is __2__ -D because we can measure the __length__ and __width__ of it. "D" is short for Dimension. There are #__3__ basic shapes. Draw the basic shapes below:

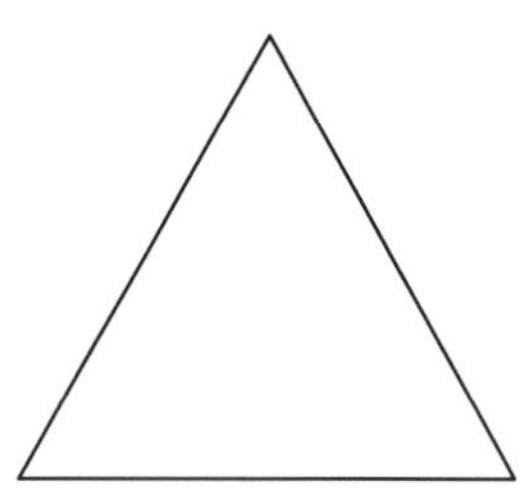 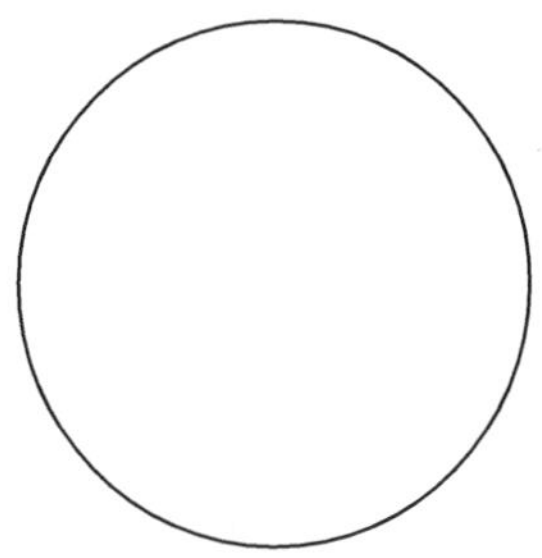 

__Shapes__ put together can create a form. A box is a form made from 6 square shapes. In art we call a box a special name. Think of the ice in your freezer at home. You don't call them *ice boxes*, you call them ice __cubes__. You eat ice cream in a __cone__, that's another basic form. What are the other two basic forms? __cylinder__ and __sphere__.

Can you draw all the forms below?

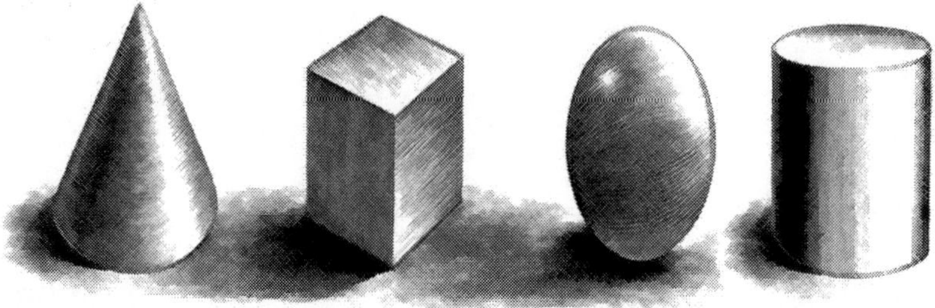

Color is sometimes the first thing we see. Most colors we see are mixed from just # **3** basic colors. These colors are **red** , **yellow** , **blue** . The other name for basic colors is **primary** colors. When basic colors mix, they make new colors. We call them **secondary** colors. Try mixing the basic colors below to see what colors they make. (Use marker, crayon, or color pencil)

Red and blue	Red and yellow	Yellow and blue
PURPLE	**ORANGE**	**GREEN**

All things, art and not-art, take up **space** . It comes in two kinds, **positive** where the thing is, and **negative** which is the empty area around it. When you swim in a pool, you are in the **positive** **space** of the water. When you are in school, you are in the **negative** **space** of the building.

Everything around us we can see has weight. Even air has weight! What is another word for weight? **mass** . Sometimes things look heavier or lighter than they really are. Metal and rocks are things we think of when we see dark colors. Cotton and clouds are things we think of when we see light colors. **dark** colors often look heavier than **light** colors.

Everything you touch has a feeling; smooth, rough, wet, dry, etc. This is the art element of **texture** .

Draw 3 examples below: *(Any 3 different textures would be fine)*

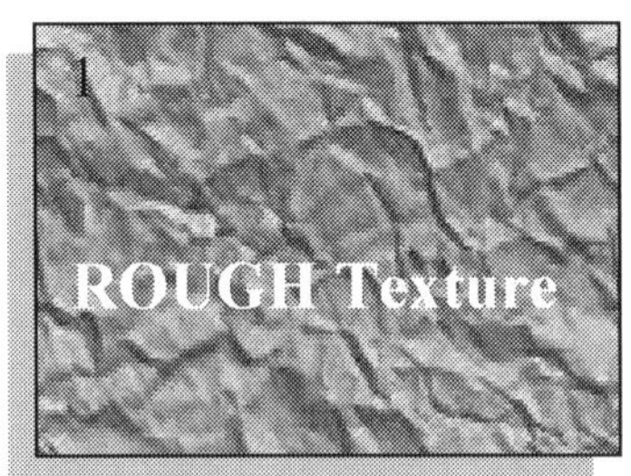

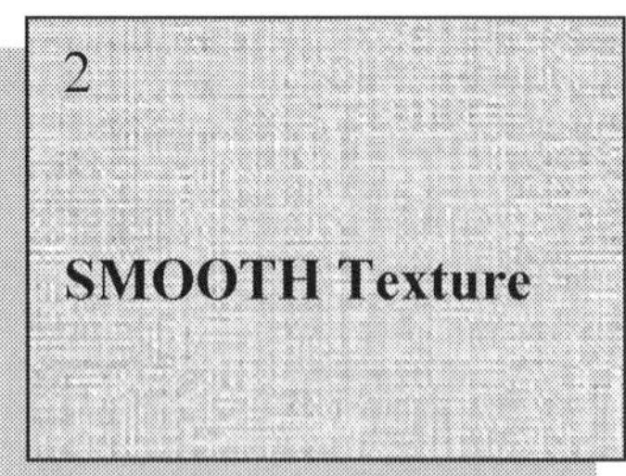

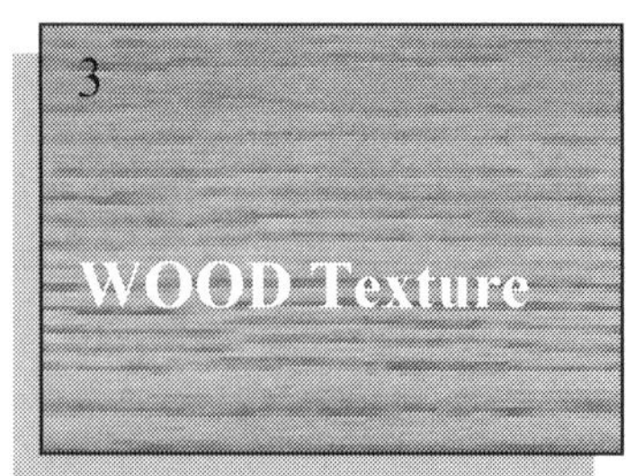

The last art element might be the most important. Without it we cannot even see any of the rest. What can it be? **light** . When we draw, we sometimes add shadows, which are the opposite of this art element.

Principles of Art & Design

1. What does **balance** mean?

   Two things of equal visual weight

2. Draw two things balanced below:

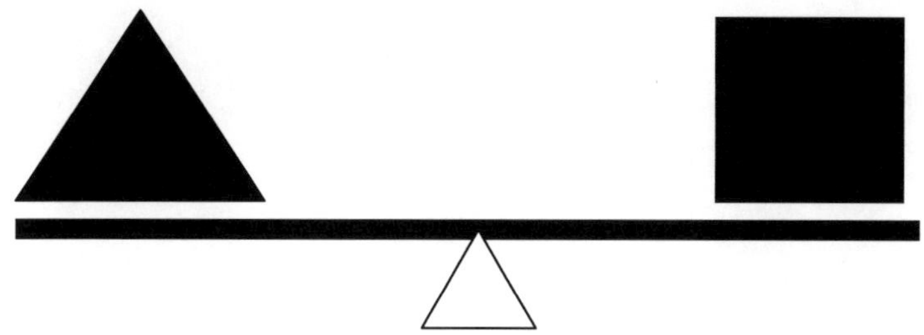

3. Can you draw one thing balanced by many smaller ones below?

   Something like this is fine

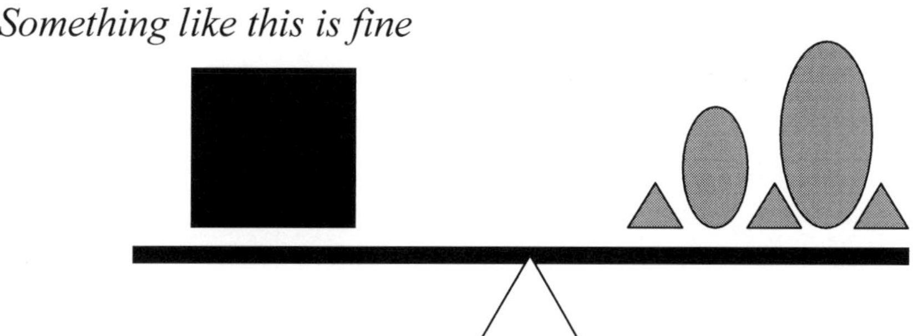

4. Try drawing something that is moving. How do you make it look like its moving? **Movement** is an art principal.

   Swish lines are okay, or something in the act of moving.

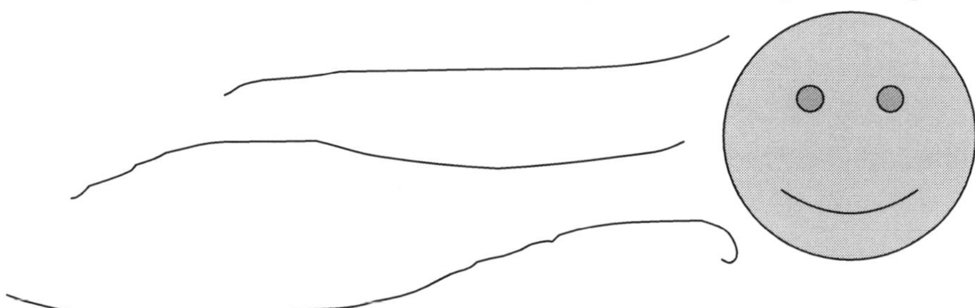

5. What is **contrast**? <u>**opposites like light and dark, or big and small…**</u>
Can you draw two opposite objects below?

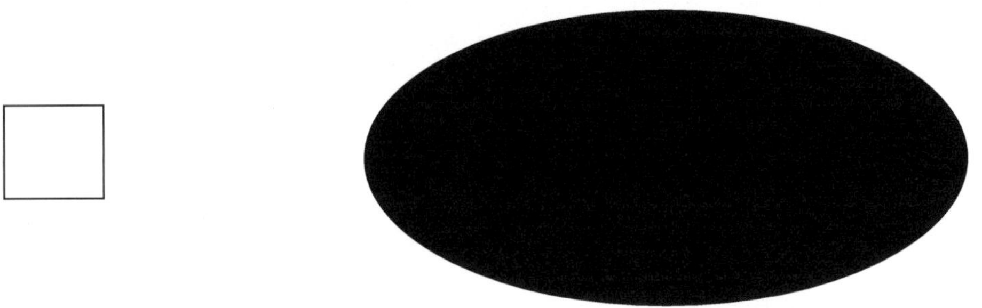

6. What is **unity**? <u>**having something the same, like most trees are green**</u>
Can you draw some things in unity below?

All circle shapes:

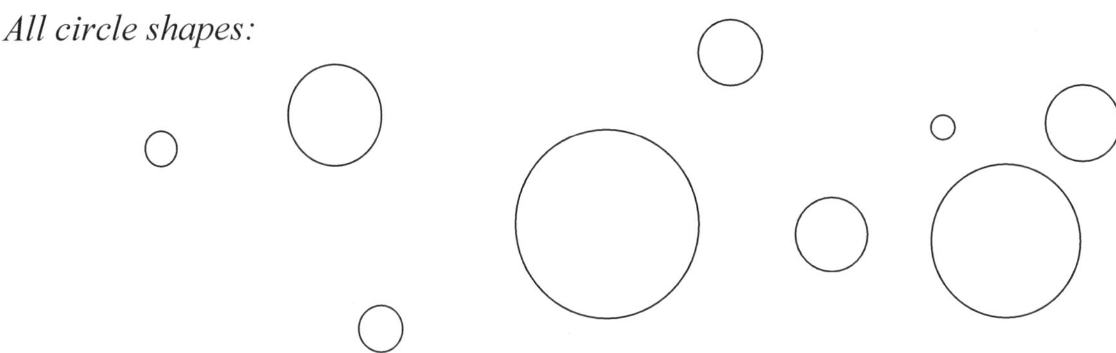

7. What is **emphasis**? (*em-fa-sis*) <u>**something that stands out because its different**</u>

8. Draw sometime below and make one thing stand out with emphasis.

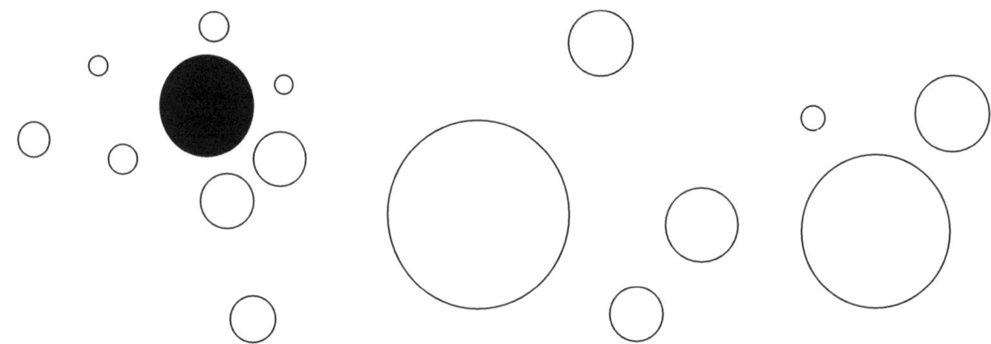

9. What is **pattern**? <u>**A repeated shape or line, it can be planned or natural**</u>
Please draw 3 patterns below.

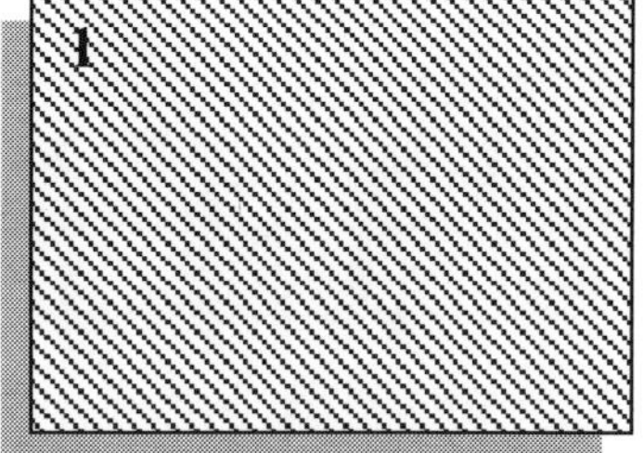 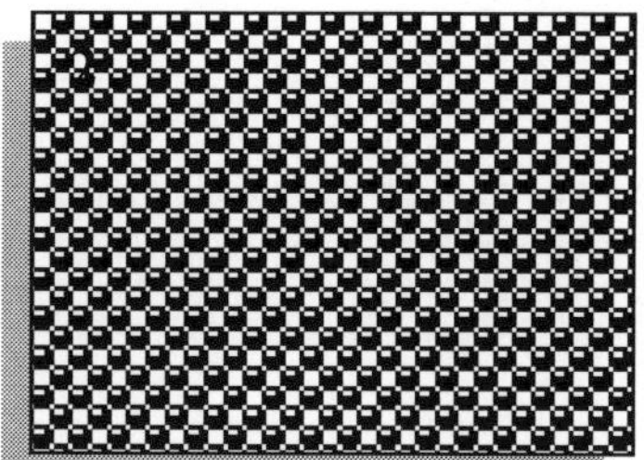 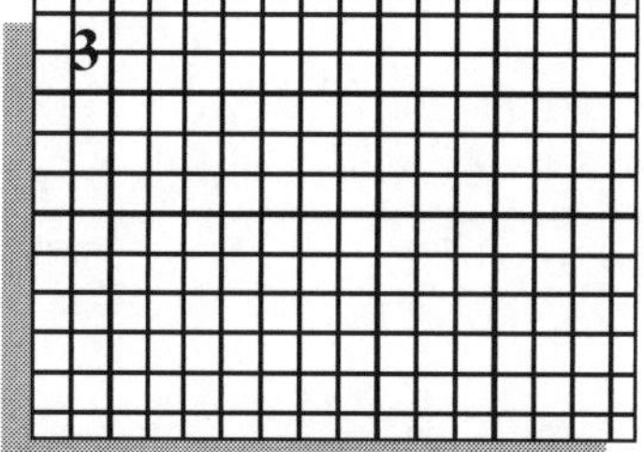

10. Draw two kinds of patterns below: a planned pattern and an organic pattern.

Planned/Mechanical   Organic/Natural

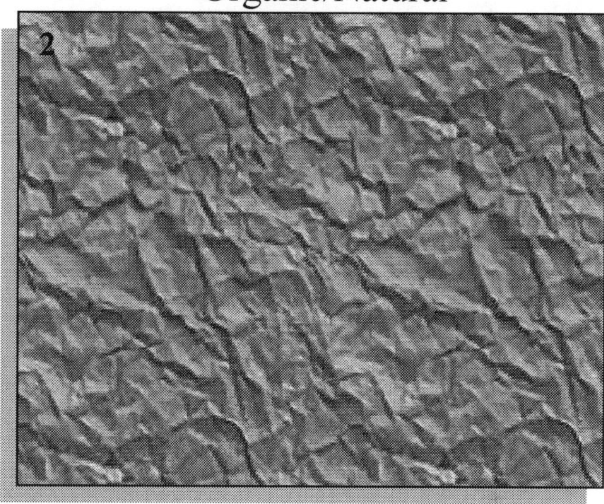

11. What is **variety**?

    Having many different things in a picture; people, trees, houses, cars...

12. How is variety different from **contrast**?

    Contrast is just 2 things being opposite, variety is many different things.

Let's Learn About Color - ANSWERS

Shade is the opposite of <u>**light**</u>. Without shadow we would all look flat like a magazine picture. In art we draw shadows to show that things take up space. They usually have one side in light, and another that is shaded. Sometimes people draw shadows with black or gray, but you can also use cool colors like green, purple, or blue. I drew a ball below with a shadow.

Primary Colors are sometimes called the basic colors. Primary means first or the beginning. Just like Primary school is for grades one through about six. There are <u>**# 3**</u> primary colors. These colors are <u>**Red**</u>, <u>**Yellow**</u>, and <u>**Blue**</u>.

Secondary Colors

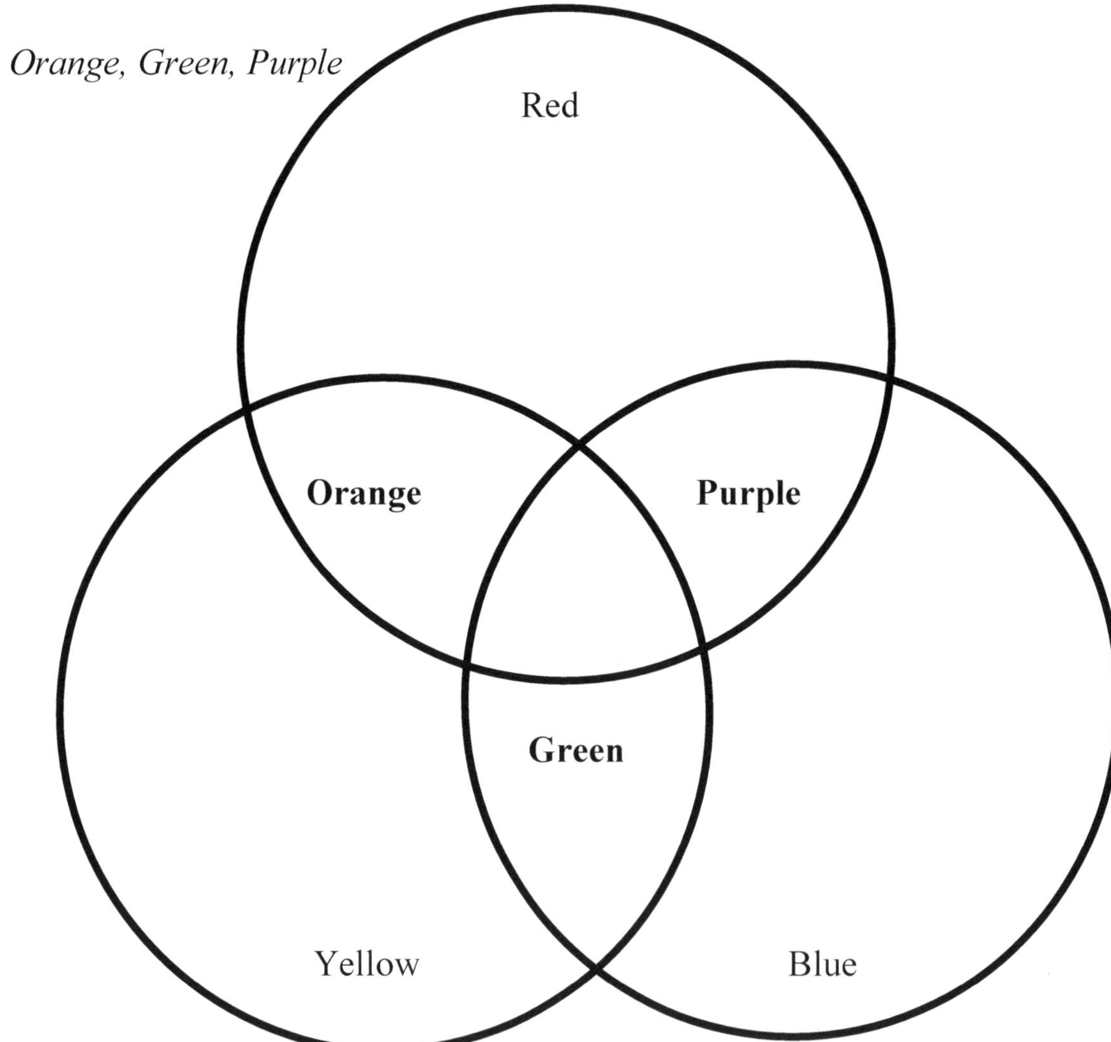

Want to know more? The color in the middle has a long and special name.

<u>**Chromatic**</u> <u>**Gray**</u>.

138

Warm Colors: Warm colors should remind you of warm things. Think of fire, the sun, a hot stove; what colors are these things?

 __Red__ , __Orange__ , __Yellow__

Cool Colors: cool colors should remind you of cool or cold things. Think water, the ocean, a river, grass, or the sky when it's getting dark; what colors are these?

 __Blue__ , __Purple__ , __Green__ .

Perspective

Vocabulary:

— Perspective: The illusion of three dimensional space on a flat surface.
    (It is how flat pictures look 3-D)

— Horizon: Where the sky meets the land.

— Vanishing Point: The place where all lines going away from you look
    like they will meet each other. (They converge)

— Parallel: Lines that are side by side and never touch or meet.
    (Like rail road tracks.)

— Converging: To come together. Lines that meet each other.

— Vertical: Up and down lines.

— Eye Level: The level of your eyes. The horizon is always at your eye level.

Colors and Shapes have feelings too! - Answers

Red is the color of blood, stop signs, and lava. How do these things make you feel?

Scared, troubled, danger, fear...

Orange is the color of a hot stove burner, warning signs, and some spicy sauces. How do these things make people feel?

Worried, anxious, nervous, excited, full of energy...

Yellow is the color of the sun, smiley faces, and many flowers. How do these things make people feel?

Cheerful, joyful, energy, warm...

Green is the color of grass, healthy vegetables, and many things that grow. What feelings does this give people?

Growing, happy, pleasant, smart, healthy...

Blue is the color of the ocean and the sky. When you are relaxing at the beach or laying down looking up at the sky on a beautiful day, how do you feel?

Nice, calm, quiet, restful...

Purple is the color of royalty, deep oceans, and starry nights. What kinds of feelings does this give people?

Sleep, silence, cold, alone...

Triangles are sharp like broken glass, knives, and arrows. How would you feel if you were surrounded by these things?

Scared, troubled, danger, fear...

Circles are soft like balloons, balls, bubbles, and hoopla-hoops. How do these things make people feel?

Cheerful, joyful, energy, playful, child-like...

Squares are used to make bricks, boxes, buildings, and tables. We do not use circles to make bricks, boxes, and buildings because squares are more... What?

Sturdy, strong, dependable, boring, useful...

Schools of Art - History

A "School Of Art" is another way to say a group of art or a style of art. We put things in groups all the time. We can put people in groups too like girls and boys. Religions are kinds of groups like Christians, Muslims, Jews, and Buddhists… Even your pets are put in groups like poodles, bull dogs, spaniels, and beagles…

We group these things by the way they look. Poodles all have curly hair, Dalmatians have black spots, Beagles are smaller and have brown spots.

Art is the same way. If you see a painting, with people wearing rich clothes like from a Cinderella Movie, and the trees look very fluffy, and the people look like they are rich and playing around, then it might be from the Rococo (Row-co-co) school of art.

If you see a painting of something you might see in a TV commercial, and it has very bright colors, it might be from the Pop Art school of art.

Rococo and Pop Art are schools of art. We will learn about 13 important ones. You should know there are hundreds of schools of art, but you will learn about just a few important ones. They are:

Renaissance (Re-na-sance)
Baroque (Ba-roke)
Rococo (Row-co-co)
Neo-Classical (Neo-Clas-si-kul)
Romanticism (Ro-man-ti-si-zum)
Realism (real-is-um)
Impressionism (Imm-pre-shon-is-um)
Cubism (Qb-is-um) or (Cube-is-um)
Dada (Da-da)
Surrealism (Sur-real-is-um)
Expressionism (X-pre-shun-is-um)
Abstract Expressionism (Ab-stract, X-pre-shun-is-um)
Pop Art

Research:

Pick one school of art from the previous page. Maybe your teacher will have you pick from a hat, so not everyone does the same thing. Write it here:

____

Use the internet or the library to answer these questions:

1. What is the year that your school of art began? _________________*
(* this may not be exact, but get as close as you can)

2. Name three artists of your school of art and their birth year

____ born in _____________

____ born in _____________

____ born in _____________

3. Many artists start after they are 20 years old. If you add 20 to their birth year, is your answer to number 1 still correct? Do you need to change it?

4. Name three famous artworks (painting, drawing, or sculpture) and the artist.

_________________________________ made by _________________

_________________________________ made by _________________

_________________________________ made by _________________

5. What must art from your school of art need to look like to be from that style?

____

____

____

POSTERS:

Working with a small group of two to four people, you are to create a poster that will teach others about that school of art.

Who is in your group? (Put your name in too)

________________________________,

________________________________,

________________________________,

________________________________,

RULES: You must include:
- Title (That's the school of art)
- General dates of the school of art
- ART from that period IN COLOR (You may photocopy and color in)
- Label all artwork

Written information should include:
- Written history of that school of art
- 4 or more artists working in that period
- Each artist must be shown with an artwork on the poster
- CLUES: If you saw a painting, how would you know it was from your "School Of Art?" List some clues to know how to know the art's school

BONUS: Extra Credit
- Include an interesting fact like –Van Gogh went crazy because he held his brushes in his mouth and was slowly poisoned by his paint!
- QUOTE: Include a famous quote from artist in your school of art.

There is a sample poster on the next page and a sketch page after that.

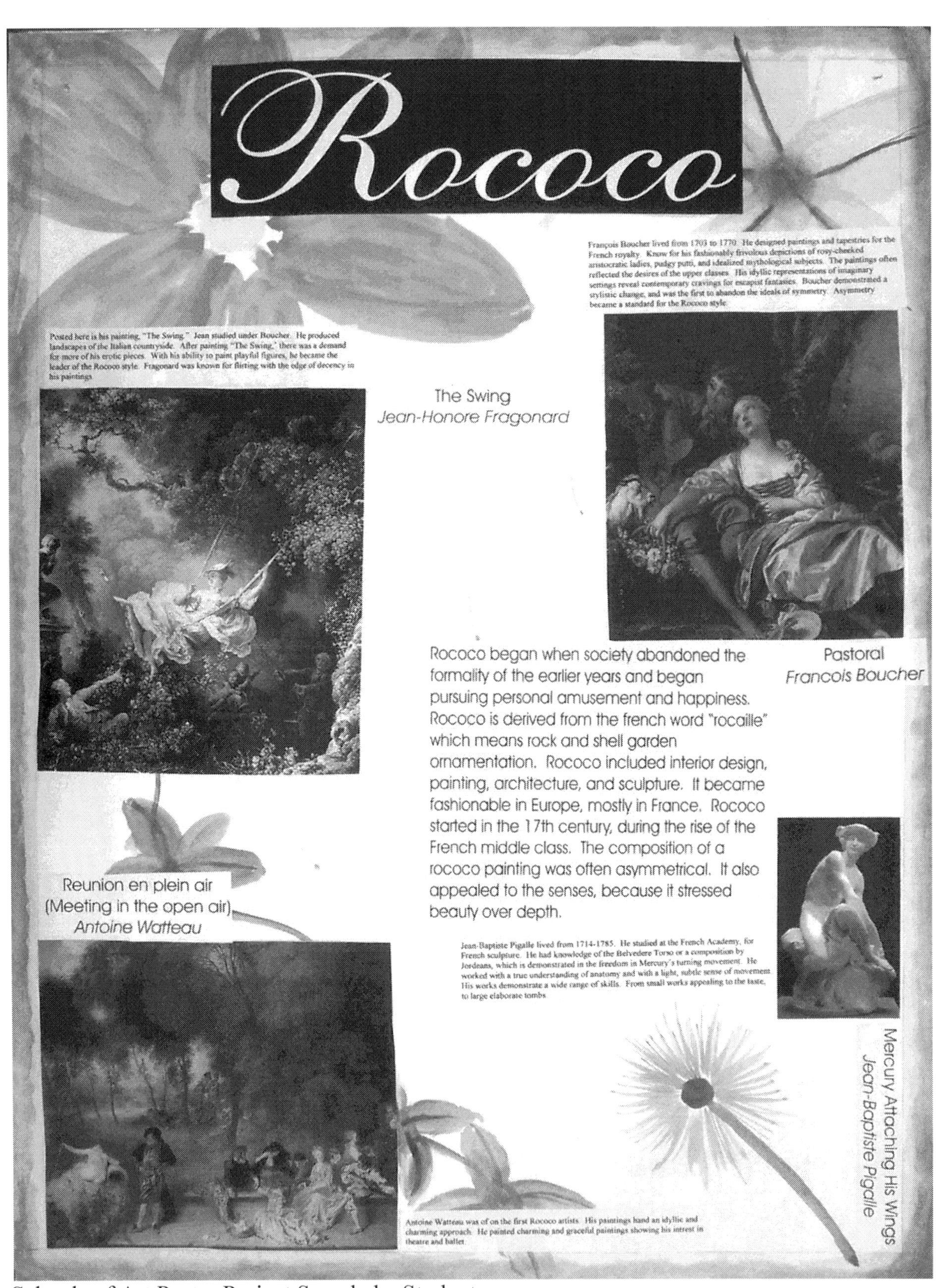

François Boucher lived from 1703 to 1770. He designed paintings and tapestries for the French royalty. Know for his fashionably frivolous depictions of rosy-cheeked aristocratic ladies, pudgy putti, and idealized mythological subjects. The paintings often reflected the desires of the upper classes. His idyllic representations of imaginary settings reveal contemporary cravings for escapist fantasies. Boucher demonstrated a stylistic change, and was the first to abandon the ideals of symmetry. Asymmetry became a standard for the Rococo style.

Posted here is his painting, "The Swing." Jean studied under Boucher. He produced landscapes of the Italian countryside. After painting "The Swing," there was a demand for more of his erotic pieces. With his ability to paint playful figures, he became the leader of the Rococo style. Fragonard was known for flirting with the edge of decency in his paintings.

The Swing
Jean-Honore Fragonard

Pastoral
Francois Boucher

Rococo began when society abandoned the formality of the earlier years and began pursuing personal amusement and happiness. Rococo is derived from the french word "rocaille" which means rock and shell garden ornamentation. Rococo included interior design, painting, architecture, and sculpture. It became fashionable in Europe, mostly in France. Rococo started in the 17th century, during the rise of the French middle class. The composition of a rococo painting was often asymmetrical. It also appealed to the senses, because it stressed beauty over depth.

Reunion en plein air
(Meeting in the open air)
Antoine Watteau

Jean-Baptiste Pigalle lived from 1714-1785. He studied at the French Academy, for French sculpture. He had knowledge of the Belvedere Torso or a composition by Jordeans, which is demonstrated in the freedom in Mercury's turning movement. He worked with a true understanding of anatomy and with a light, subtle sense of movement. His works demonstrate a wide range of skills. From small works appealing to the taste, to large elaborate tombs.

Antoine Watteau was of on the first Rococo artists. His paintings hand an idyllic and charming approach. He painted charming and graceful paintings showing his intrest in theatre and ballet.

Mercury Attaching His Wings
Jean-Baptiste Pigalle

Schools of Art Poster Project Sample by Students

Famous Artists for Research

If your teacher assigns a research paper, this is a list of artists that may be helpful. There are many thousands of artists, but this is a short list of some famous ones.

Pablo Picasso

Marcel Duchamp

Henri Matisse

Vincent Van Gogh

Claude Monet

Édouard Manet

Georgia O'Keeffe

Piet Mondrian

Paul Klee

Roy Lichtenstein

Claes Oldenburg

Christo and Jeanne-Claude

Michelangelo

Salvador Dali

Jackson Pollack

Mark Rothko

Paul Cezanne

Jasper Johns

Andy Warhol

Ansel Adams

Wayne Thiebaud

Georges Seurat

Rauschenberg

Albers Joseph

Grant Wood

Andrew Wyeth

Pierre Renoir

Chuck Close

M. C. Escher

Mary Cassatt

Alexander Calder

Rembrandt Van Rijn

Dorothea Lang

Edvard Munch

Duane Hanson

Louise Nevelson

Raphael

Frank Stella

Romare Bearden

Frida Kahlo

Katsushika Hokusai

Edward Hopper

Jacob Lawrence

Henri Rousseau

Marc Chagall

Augustus Rodin

Norman Rockwell

George Segal

Artist Research Paper

Work copied from the Internet or plagiarized will be a zero and referred to the office for disciplinary action. Use the Internet or library to find information, just… PUT IT IN YOUR OWN WORDS. Read, understand and then write.

Pick an artist from the list or find another one in an art book.

You must write a one page paper about an artist and their work plus include a photo and cover page.

Your paper must have:
— The name of the artist
— Birth and death dates of the artist and what country they are from
— "School of art" (This is the name of the style of their art, like Surrealism, Impressionism etc.)
— Basic history (a simple life story)
— Talk about his/her work and what is it that makes it special
— Write about one work of their art, answer why it is important or special.
— Include a copy, photocopy, print-out of the painting you are writing about on a separate page. Label it with name of the artists, and name of the art!
— On cover page, write where you found your information. (**Bibliography**)

Paper Rules:
— 1 full page.
— 1 inch borders/margins all the way around
— 14 pt font (Simple font like this one "Times New Roman" is good)
— SINGLE SPACED with NO spaces between paragraphs. (See the sample)
— Cover page with your name and additional information. (See the sample)

ALL WORK IS CHECKED FOR COPYING! Don't copy work!

DUE DATE ________________, _______ points off for every day late.

A SAMPLE PAPER IS ON THE NEXT 3 PAGES

Your Name
Period

Artist's Name
Birth/Death Dates
School of Art

Bibliography

Book Title, Author, ISBN number
Or full web address
http://www.artcyclopedia.com/artists/hassenflaffa.html

Arthur Framanmatt was born in 1892 in New York City and died in 2001 in his beloved Antarctica. He was a surrealistic painter who was fascinated by painting fruit pits and animal hair, which he included in every painting.

Although born in New York he was raised on the top of Mount Fuji by his adopted Egyptian family; famous fur traders from Mexico. His mother specialized in selling seas shells by the sea shore, while his father was well known for his "Peter Piper" brand pickled peppers. Arthur loved drawing rubber baby buggy bumpers at a nearby factory. He was often seen by the factory custodian while drawing and became his student, soon covering the walls of the factory with murals of all kinds. This is when he began to paint peach pits with a few apple seeds into his paintings of giant wooly mammoths covered in French braids.

Framanmatt attended Burlington County Community College in his 80's, getting an advanced degree in fine art. He was commissioned by the college to create more murals, these became, what are known today as, the Fuzz Murals. Though fully recognized for their genius today, at the time of their installation, they were hated.

Later the artist completed a series in the same style, though miniature, for the Bordentown Street Fair. The works were a great hit and one sold to a major New York gallery owner. This gallery brought Mr. Framanmatt to Manhattan, holding several successful exhibitions where his "Fur and Seed" paintings would sell for several thousand dollars each.

Arthur experimented with many other subjects including Gum Wads, Pastry Crumbs, Kitty Dandruff, and the modestly successful series based on his photographs of belly-button fuzz. His works can be found in most major collections of art including the Museum of Modern Art of New York, Los Angeles, Paris, Baghdad, Fiji and the Bikini Islands.

Arthur is one of a small group of artists in the Dada School of art who created an offshoot called "Da-Dee" art. It is known for use of natural elements and the addition of odor to their works of art. Other Famous artists of this group were Pablo Dyapar, Samual Steekey, Michael Farfrumfartin, and Jennifer Deodorante', famous for her actual lack of smell, and her paintings of toenail clippings and dandruff.

The attached work is called *White Polar Bear in a Snowstorm* where the artist uses his lesser-known technique of white on white on white. All the elements of the painting are shown through the subtle use of texture, but the show was not popular, and nobody liked his work.

His great disappointment led to a deep depression and he moved to Antarctica and eventual died there in 2001. Recent video images do conclude that he was viciously attacked and killed by a pack of wild rabid penguins.

Though Arthur Framanmat is dead, his legacy lives on in museums around the world, though much of his work remains hidden in vaults in museums.

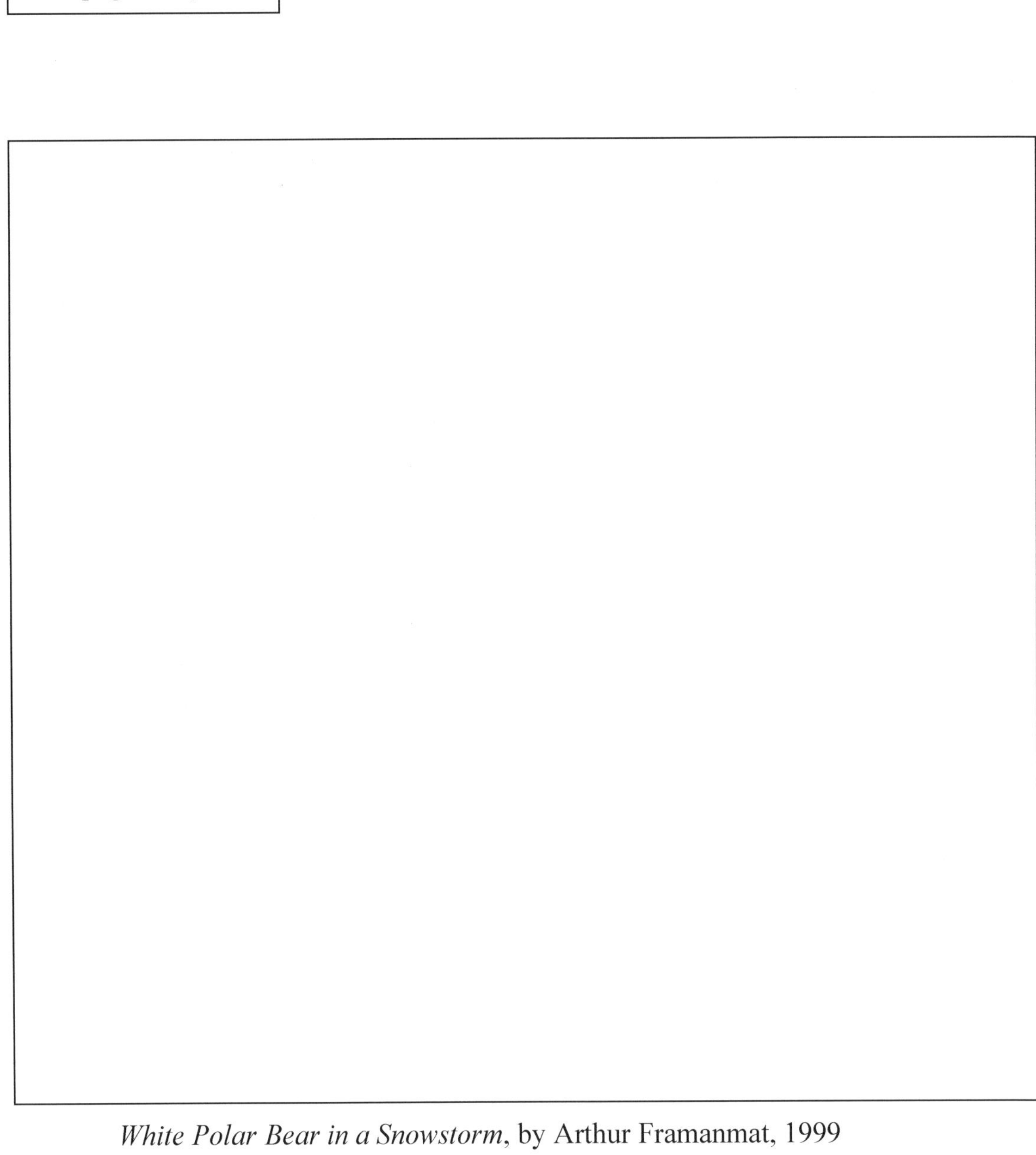

White Polar Bear in a Snowstorm, by Arthur Framanmat, 1999

<u>The student edition has a page where students can check off what they included in their report before they hand it in. See page 199 for a copy here.</u>

Schools Of Art - Introduction

Let's find out more about the schools of art. Using textbooks, the Internet, or library, try to complete as much of this information as you can.

1. Renaissance: Dates:_____________

Definition:

What is special or unique about this school of art?

Two Artists: _____________________ & _____________________

2. Baroque: Dates: _____________

Definition:

What is special or unique about this school of art?

Two Artists: _____________________ & _____________________

3. Rococo: Dates: _____________

Definition:

What is special or unique about this school of art?

Two Artists: _____________________ & _____________________

4. Neo-Classical: Dates: _____________________

Definition:

What is special or unique about this school of art?

Two Artists: _____________________________ & _______________________________

5. Romanticism: Dates: _____________________

Definition:

What is special or unique about this school of art?

Two Artists: _____________________________ & _______________________________

6. Realism : Dates _____________________

Definition:

What is special or unique about this school of art?

Two Artists: _____________________________ & _______________________________

7. Impressionism : Dates ____________________

Definition:

What is special or unique about this school of art?

Two Artists: ______________________________ & ________________________________

8. Expressionism: Dates ____________________

Definition:

What is special or unique about this school of art?

Two Artists: ______________________________ & ________________________________

9. Cubism: Date ____________________ (*This one is an exact year*)

Definition:

What is special or unique about this school of art?

Two Artists: ______________________________ & ________________________________

10. Dada: Dates _______________________

Definition:

What is special or unique about this school of art?

Two Artists: _______________________________ & _______________________________

11. Surrealism: Dates _______________________

Definition:

What is special or unique about this school of art?

Two Artists: _______________________________ & _______________________________

12. Abstract Expressionism: Dates _______________________

Definition:

What is special or unique about this school of art?

Two Artists: _______________________________ & _______________________________

13. Pop art: Dates _____________________

Definition:

What is special or unique about this school of art?

Two Artists: _____________________________ & _______________________________

14. What style seems the most interesting and why?

____

____

____

15. What painting did you see that you liked the most and why?

____

____

____

Schools of Art Overview
Write 3 facts about each.

Renaissance

1. _______________________
2. _______________________
3. _______________________

Baroque

1. _______________________
2. _______________________
3. _______________________

Rococo

1. _______________________
2. _______________________
3. _______________________

Neo-Classical

1. _______________________
2. _______________________
3. _______________________

Romanticism

1. _______________________
2. _______________________
3. _______________________

Impressionism

1. _______________________
2. _______________________
3. _______________________

Realism

1. _______________________
2. _______________________
3. _______________________

Cubism

1. _______________________
2. _______________________
3. _______________________

Dada

1. _______________________
2. _______________________
3. _______________________

Surrealism

1. _______________________
2. _______________________
3. _______________________

Expressionism

1. _______________________
2. _______________________
3. _______________________

Abstract Expressionism

1. _______________________
2. _______________________
3. _______________________

Pop Art

1. _______________________
2. _______________________
3. _______________________

Schools of Art List

Renaissance – French word for "rebirth," This work showed Greek, Roman or Bible stories, they tried to make the work look 3-D with perspective. It is the oldest style we need to know, and looks old. Some artists would include Leonardo da Vinci, Michelangelo, (and the other Ninja Turtles ;-)

Baroque – Looks like it might be on stage and have a spotlight. Look for drama in the action or the lighting. Often has very dark and very light areas, but not always. You might see Musketeer's style clothes of the 1600's.

Rococo – Sickeningly Sweet, everything is rosy and RICH, it shows people playing. Cute and fluffy were their main ideas. Rococo is like Baroque but topped off with a tub of sugar. Look for Cinderella style dresses.

Neo-Classical – The opposite of Rococo. The Neo-Classical artists were trying to kick out the King and queen. The paintings are VERY organized, serious, often with big shapes hidden in the paintings. These paintings often included Greek and Roman images so be careful to not confuse it with Renaissance. Most buildings in Washington DC are examples of this style.

Romanticism – In the early 1800's, it usually showed man and nature but not always peaceful. Sometimes man is using nature—like hills or mountains to fight a war, or hunt to feed his family, but man is never hurting nature in this work, the opposite may be true.

Realism –Is what it sounds like. Realism showed the good and the bad. It began before there were cameras, so the artists tried to paint as much detail as they could. Today, some of these paintings look like photographs. Before, people were usually painted prettier than they were.

Impressionism – Started in France in the 1860's, the artists tried to paint to show how important light is. Monet, Cassatt, Van Gogh, Cézanne, and Pissarro are Impressionist painters. These paintings are usually THICK with paint. Paintings are made while looking at what you are painting. Many of these paintings have a "Z" pattern hiding inside them.

Cubism – Started by Pablo Picasso with his painting in 1907 of Demoiselles d'Avignon. Usually the art looks shattered, and broken into shapes like broken glass, but you can still see what's going on.
NOT ALL work with shapes is CUBISM!

Expressionism – These paintings must have images you can understand but it is a little weird, or very strange to express emotions. All art should show emotion, the artists of this school of art use color or shape to help make the emotions stand out. Edvard Munch is an artist of this style.

Abstract Expressionism – NO pictures can be seen. The work looks like splashes, or layers of color, or child-like. *If you can't tell at all what's going on in the painting it is probably this style.*

Dada – A strange art movement that started in Germany in the early 1920's. The artists tried to make fun of art and the people who liked museum art. They would make things that most people thought was junk, or not "real" art, like a toilet up-side-down. Marcel DuChamp is a famous artist of this style.

Surrealism – Started in the 1920's and was often about dreams or the secrets in your brain. Art in the Surrealist style often looked dreamlike or impossible. Some artists were De Chirico, Salvador Dali, Rene Magritte, and Joan Míro.

Pop Art – Started in New York in the 1960's, a style of art that comes from popular culture including stuff you buy in a store (like soup or soda), commercials, simple every-day stuff, and cartoons. Some famous artists Keith Haring, Claes Oldenburg, and Andy Warhol.

Important art to remember

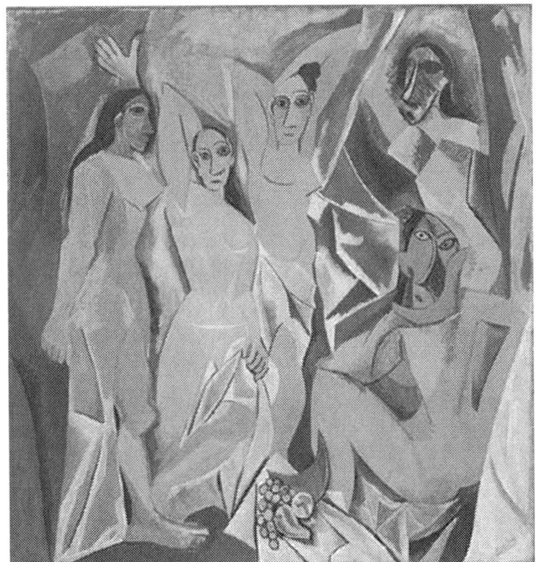

Pablo Picasso, **1907** of *Demoiselles d'Avignon.*

The painting above is the first painting in human history that a person was painted in a way that was different on purpose. They style is called Cubism, it was the first one! **Below** is the *Mona Lisa*, by Leonardo Da Vinci, a Renaissance Artist from the late 1400s. It is the most famous painting in the world!

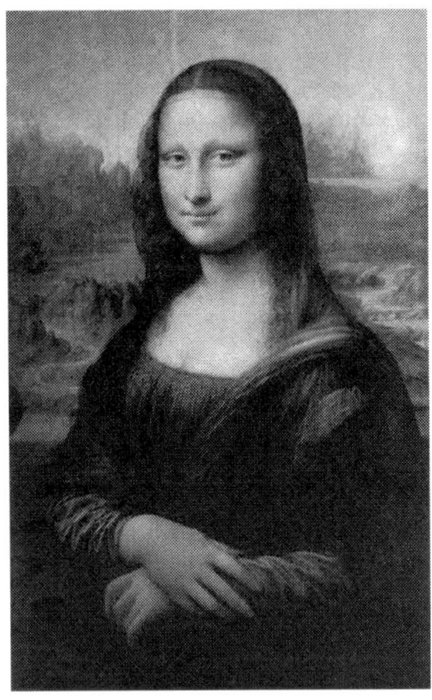

The painting to the right →
…is a painting of a dream. The stuff in the painting is not real, but it is painted to look very real. This is called surrealism.

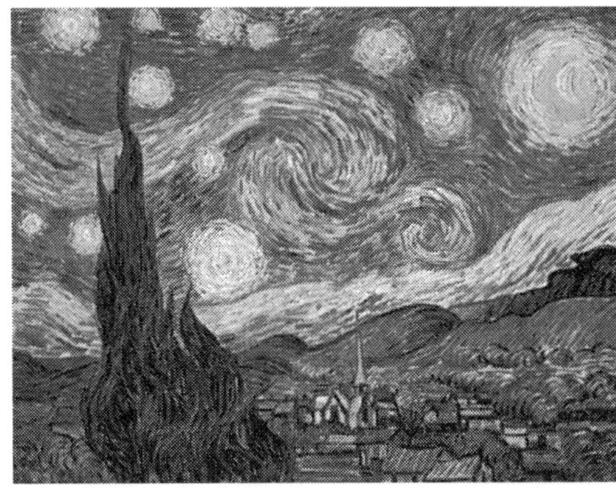

Starry Night, by Vincent VanGogh,

The painting above is special too, because the artist starts to use color to express his feelings. It is an Impressionist painting but some people call it post-impressionism.

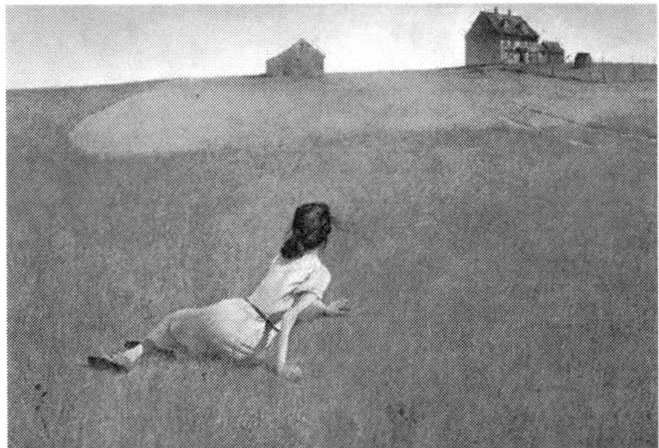

Christina's World (above) by Andrew Wyeth is an example of Realism. It shows a lot of detail, and had both good things and bad things in the painting. People think it is a young girl, but it is really older lady named… Christina.

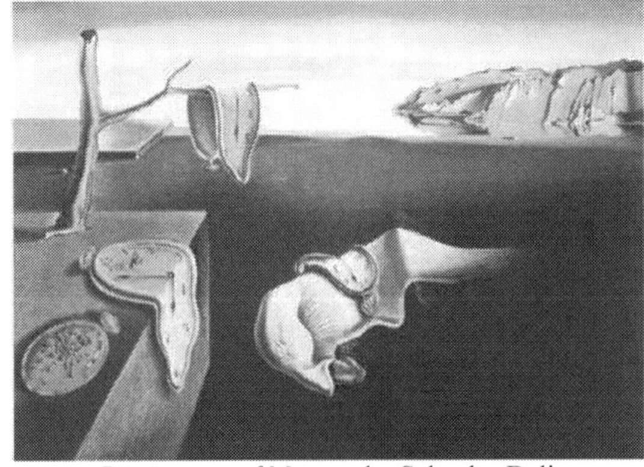

Persistence of Memory by Salvador Dali

Schools of Art: Matching

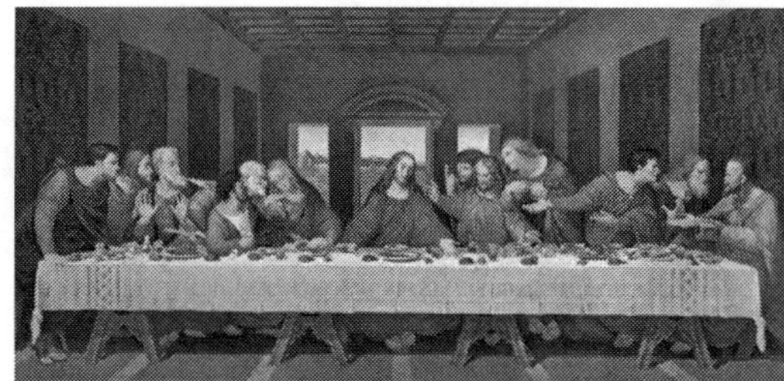

Draw a line connect the art and the correct school of art.

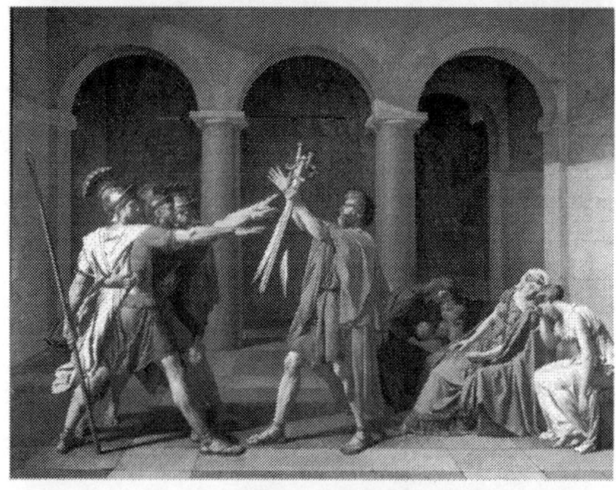

Baroque: Looks like it might be on stage and have a spotlight. Look for drama in the action or the lighting. Often has very dark and very light areas, but not always. Musketeer's style clothes of the 1600's.

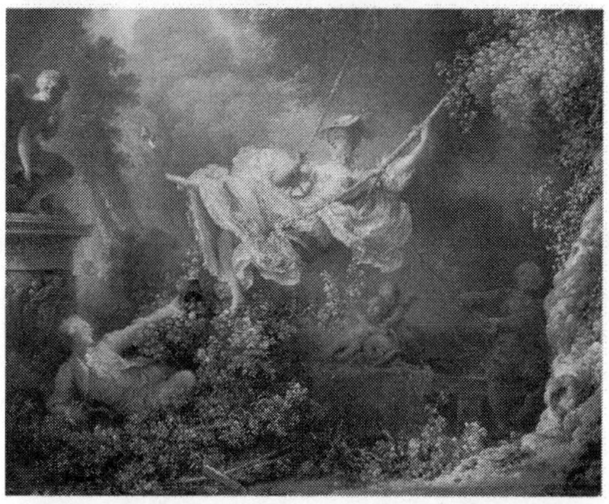

Neoclassical: The paintings are VERY organized, often with big shapes hidden in the paintings. These paintings often included Greek and Roman images so be careful to not confuse it with Renaissance.

Renaissance: This work showed Greek, Roman or Bible stories, they tried to make the work look 3-D with perspective. It is the oldest and looks old fashioned.

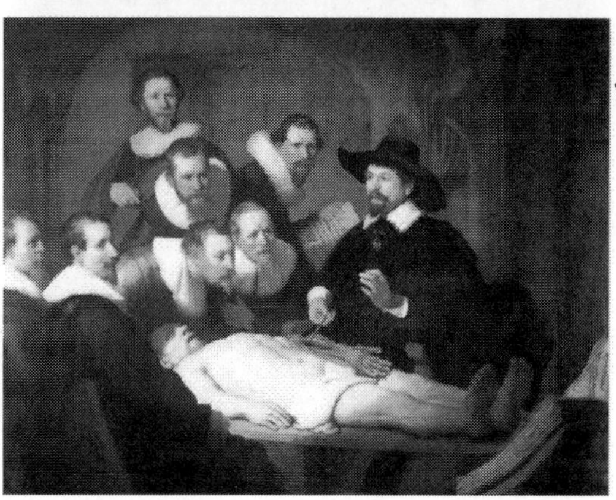

Rococo: Sickeningly Sweet, everything is rosy and RICH, it shows people playing. Cute and fluffy were their main ideas. Rococo is like Baroque but topped off with a tub of Sugar. Look for Cinderella style dresses.

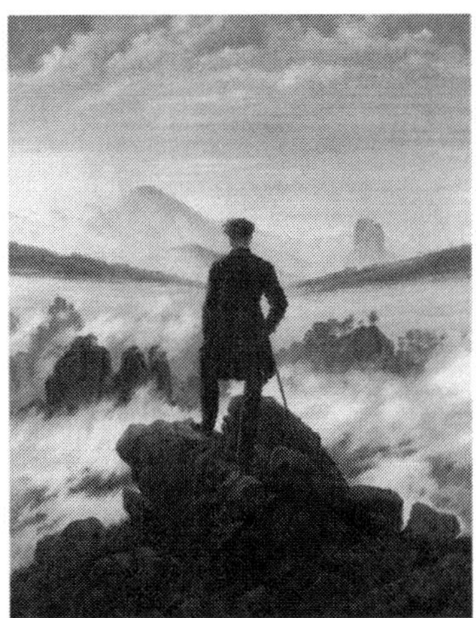

Schools of Art: Matching

Draw a line connect the art and the correct school of art.

Dada: The artists tried to make fun of art and the people who liked museum art. They would make things that most people thought was junk, or not "real" art, like a toilet up-side-down.

Romanticism: Usually showed man and nature but not always peaceful. Sometimes man is using nature (like hills or mountains to fight a war, or hunt to feed his family, but man is never hurting nature in this work, but the opposite may be true.

Realism: Realism showed the good and the bad. It began before there were cameras, so the artists tried to paint as much detail as they could. Some of these paintings look like photographs.

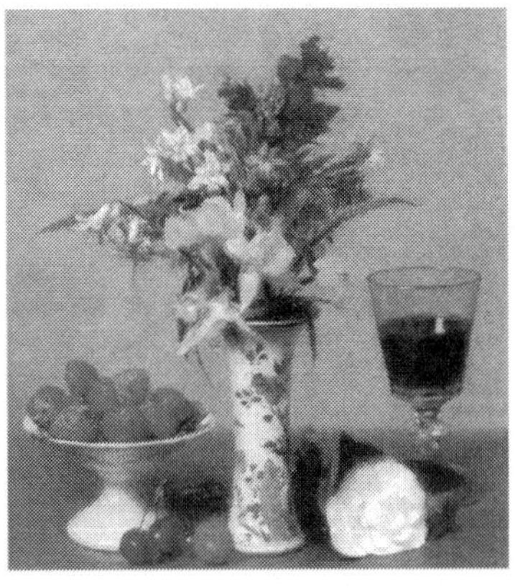

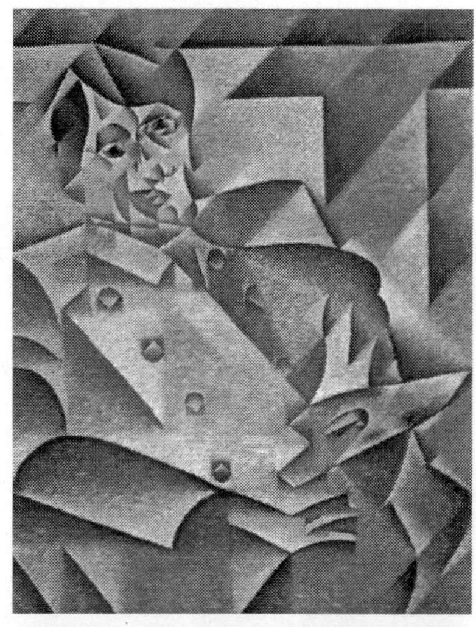

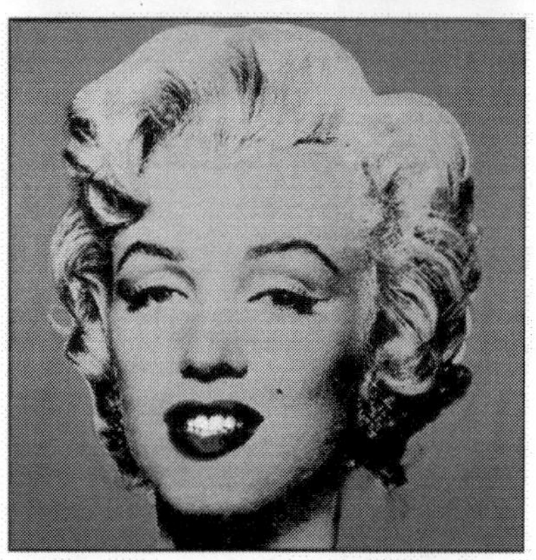

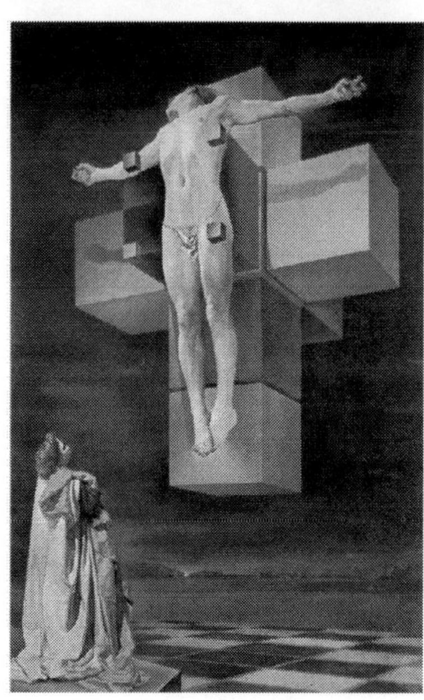

Schools of Art: Matching

Draw a line connect the art and the correct school of art.

Surrealism: Sometimes very real looking but somehow impossible or dream-like. Sometimes about the secrets in your brain.

Pop Art: A style of art that comes from popular culture including stuff you buy in a store, like soup or soda, commercials, simple every-day things, and cartoons.

Cubism: Usually the art looks shattered, and broken into shapes like broken glass, but you can still tell what's going on. **NOT ALL art with shapes is CUBISM!**

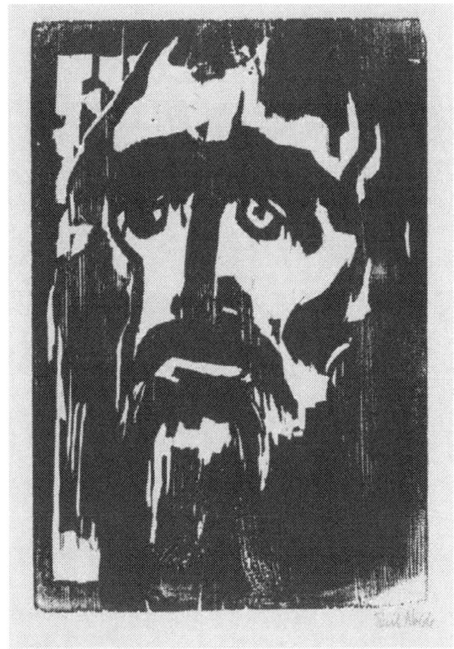

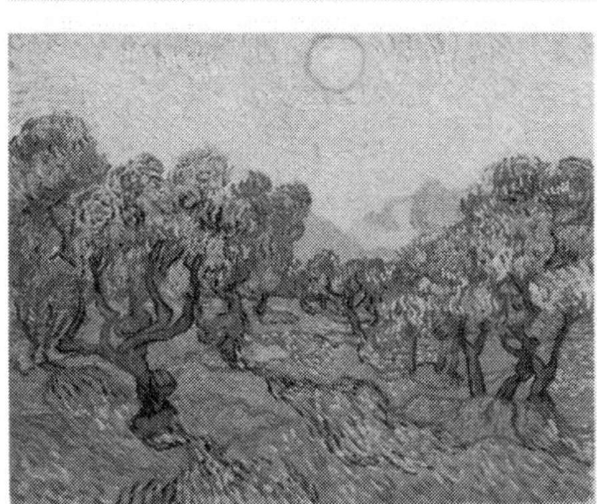

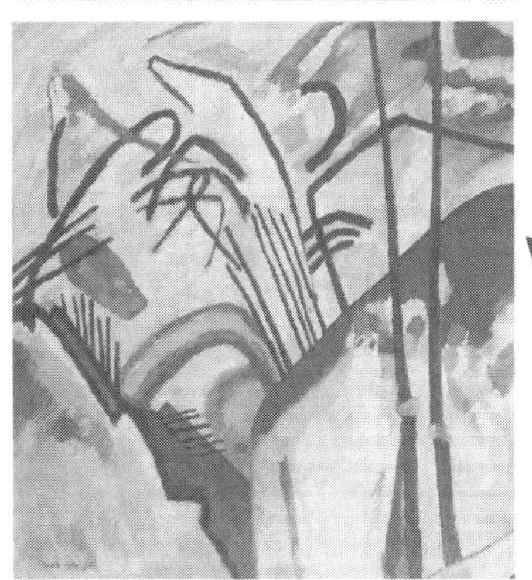

Schools of Art: Matching

Draw a line connect the art and the correct school of art.

Abstract Expressionism: NO pictures can be seen. The work looks like splashes, or layers of color, or child-like. If you can't tell at all what is going on in the painting, it is probably this style.

Expressionism: These paintings must have images you can understand but it is a little weird to express emotions. Though all art generally shows emotion, the artists of this school of art use color or shape to help make the emotions stand out.

Impressionism: The artists tried to show the way light changes the way things look. These paintings are usually THICK with paint. Paintings are made while looking at what you are painting. Many of these paintings have a "Z" pattern hiding inside them.

Teacher: Though strictly speaking Van Gogh was a Post Impressionist, I feel that on a pre-college level it is helpful to express him as an Impressionist as he displays the key qualities of Impressionism in an exaggerated way.

What is abstract? (Ab-stract) means changed from what it really looks like. Some art is very abstract, some is just a little. Here are some pictures of President Obama that are abstracted.

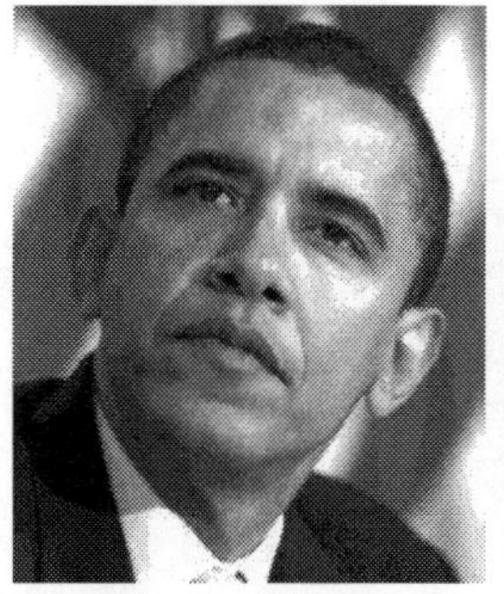 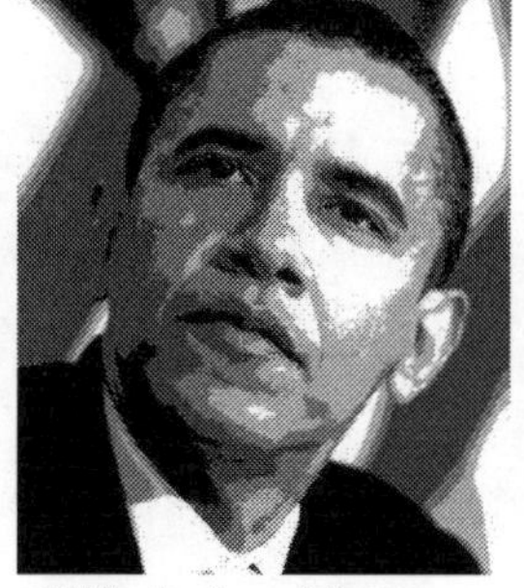 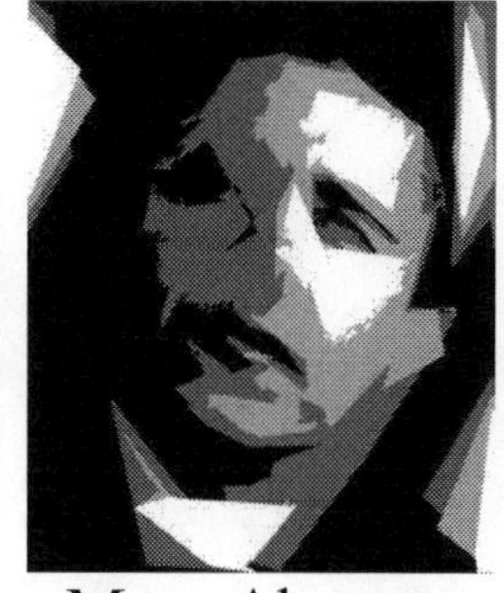 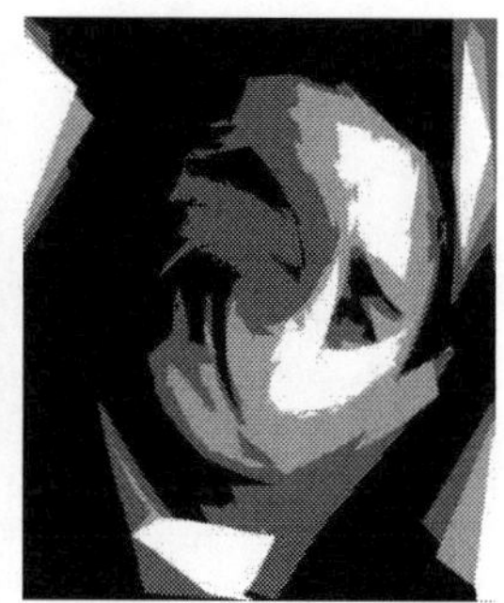

Realistic Photo   Slightly Abstract   More Abstract   VERY Abstract

REMEMBER, if there is a subject, and the art is from a real thing, then it cannot be abstract expressionism. How about below? Is there a subject?

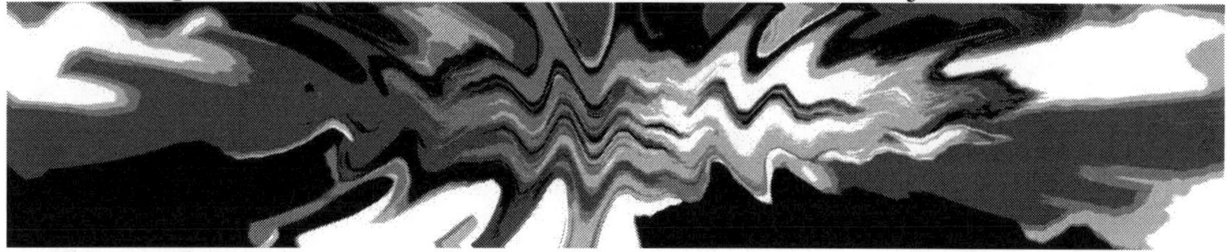

Your teacher will be able to show you many famous painting samples. Decide what school of art they belong to based on clues you see within the artwork.

Sketch Below: What school of art do you believe it to be from?

____

What 3 pieces of evidence can you see?

1. _______________________________

2. _______________________________

3. _______________________________

What was the real answer?

____

If you were wrong, what did you miss?

____

What school of art do you believe it to be from?

Sketch Below:

____

What 3 pieces of evidence can you see?

1. _________________________

2. _________________________

3. _________________________

What was the real answer?

____

If you were wrong, what did you miss?

Sketch Below:

What school of art do you believe it to be from?

____

What 3 pieces of evidence can you see?

1. _________________________

2. _________________________

3. _________________________

What was the real answer?

____

If you were wrong, what did you miss?

NOTE Taking

Project:_______________________ Date __/__/__

Sketch Page for: Project:_____________________ Date __/__/__

Video Notes

Throughout the year, art videos will be played by the teacher or substitute. These will help with your art history information, or teach you how to do some art, or teach you something special about art. You will have to take some notes about what you see. This work is graded. You get a 100% if you participate and a zero if you do not. This will be very easy to do, but you must do some writing.

Writing one or two words is NOT enough. You must write a short sentence that tells us what you saw or what you heard. If the artist in the movie is painting a bird, you can write down, "The artist painted a bird." If the artist says, he was born in Mexico, you can write down, "The artist was born in Mexico." It is not hard but you need to pay attention.

We will try below. Your teacher will call out the first few facts to write down, then you need to try on your own. Spelling does not count, just try your best.

VIDEO NOTES – Sample

TITLE______________________________________

Period___ Date __/__/__

Directions: Write 10 facts below based on the video WHILE YOU WATCH.
Two word facts, silliness, will not be acceptable. *This is GRADED.*

1. ____
2. ____
3. ____
4. ____
5. ____
6. ____
7. ____
8. ____
9. ____
10. _______________________________________

Double check that all facts have MORE than 2 words.

GRADED BY TEACHER: FULL CREDIT 100%   OR _______________% Credit

Some Art Videos on Youtube.com
This was a working list in the Spring of 2010.

http://www.youtube.com/watch?v=ub6GTjY031Y	Food Art
http://www.youtube.com/watch?v=1qdYJmiLV2Q	Hand Turkey
http://www.youtube.com/watch?v=s7GYGmEcQJA	Hand Art
http://www.youtube.com/watch?v=JjUMvnsE4zo	More Hand Art
http://www.youtube.com/watch?v=2itCiI-ykYg	Hand Shadows
http://www.youtube.com/watch?v=hibyAJOSW8U	Fake Face
http://www.youtube.com/watch?v=orjALWsyaR4	Burger Painting
http://www.youtube.com/watch?v=HVhVClFMg6Y	Kinetic Sculpture, BMW Spheres
http://www.youtube.com/watch?v=WcR7U2tuNoY	Theo Jansen
http://www.youtube.com/watch?v=b694exl_oZo	Theo Jansen
http://www.youtube.com/watch?v=PH6xCT2aTSo	Inflatable Bag Monsters
http://www.youtube.com/watch?v=fZvoqNiOnG4	Coffee Art
http://youtube.com/watch?v=rV5NLOL7Fjk	"Sand Dancer"
http://youtube.com/watch?v=Gw933kKz7w8	23 Scraps of Paper
http://youtube.com/watch?v=EkUbYBo5xgs	Banksy in the Museum
http://youtube.com/watch?v=SIf3dfqIVg8	Lobo Skank Onesong
http://youtube.com/watch?v=JwsBBIIXT0E	Reverse Graffiti
http://www.youtube.com/watch?v=zl6hNj1uOkY	Doll Face
http://www.youtube.com/watch?v=i1wfWPtjxMA	Dirt Painting
http://www.youtube.com/watch?v=ONqgaVU_XPk	Cube Animation
http://www.youtube.com/watch?v=vPIpvFtZ4-k	Makeup Artists
http://www.youtube.com/user/notblu?blend=1	Blu Art, Animated Drawings
http://www.youtube.com/watch?v=awKJQ-HfEHc	Shepard Fairey (Obama Hope Poster)
http://www.youtube.com/watch?v=iXT2E9Ccc8A	Salvador Dali
http://www.youtube.com/watch?v=lRai9x8aD3A	Bansky London Show
http://www.youtube.com/watch?v=3SNYtd0Ayt0	Street Mural
http://www.youtube.com/watch?v=f4zoQSNX1Ys	Electronic Garden
http://www.youtube.com/watch?v=NZsqd-OgKhE	Vogal Art Collection
http://www.youtube.com/watch?v=BDlLh0jcJVY	60 minutes: Is this art?
http://www.youtube.com/watch?v=0CFPg1m_Umg	Spraypaint Art
http://www.youtube.com/watch?v=ghqoqz3yvts	Spraypaint Art
http://www.youtube.com/watch?v=eftdfXNICbY	Paper Towers
http://www.youtube.com/watch?v=3Un20p1NGuw	Black Hole - Office
http://www.youtube.com/watch?v=NmxX2r-uD8I	Thief?
http://www.youtube.com/watch?v=OjTOs1L3SBg	InSide, Short Film
http://www.youtube.com/watch?v=ZxmvRDTELy8	Sliding House
http://www.youtube.com/watch?v=4HMm9jrgDzM	Artistic 1-10 in Japanese Theme
http://www.youtube.com/watch?v=d2Y5mUJiaZI	Duchamp's Fountain
http://www.youtube.com/watch?v=QrtCcXXNcGA	Coin Making
http://www.youtube.com/watch?v=BM-JpePRWB8	Coin Manufacture
http://www.youtube.com/watch?v=10gStfTPBfg	Relief Sculpture
http://www.youtube.com/watch?v=HdXNWH06mPc	Tourist Trap Animation
http://www.youtube.com/watch?v=pLAma-lrJRM	Twitch Art

YOUTUBE Video Notes   DATE________________

Just write the title of the video and a short sentence about what you saw. 1 per video. As always, 1 and 2 word statements do not count.

1. _________ | ____
2. _________ | ____
3. _________ | ____
4. _________ | ____
5. _________ | ____
6. _________ | ____
7. _________ | ____
8. _________ | ____
9. _________ | ____
10. ________ | ____

YOUTUBE Video Notes   DATE________________

Just write the title of the video and a short sentence about what you saw. 1 per video. As always, 1 and 2 word statements do not count.

1. _________ | ____
2. _________ | ____
3. _________ | ____
4. _________ | ____
5. _________ | ____
6. _________ | ____
7. _________ | ____
8. _________ | ____
9. _________ | ____
10. ________ | ____

VIDEO NOTES – GRADED

TITLE_______________________________

Period____ Date ___/___/___

Directions: Write 10 facts below based on the video WHILE YOU WATCH. **Two word facts, silliness, will not be acceptable.** *This is GRADED.*

1. _______________________________________
2. _______________________________________
3. _______________________________________
4. _______________________________________
5. _______________________________________
6. _______________________________________
7. _______________________________________
8. _______________________________________
9. _______________________________________
10. ______________________________________
11. ______________________________________
12. ______________________________________
13. ______________________________________
14. ______________________________________
15. ______________________________________
16. ______________________________________
17. ______________________________________
18. ______________________________________
19. ______________________________________
20. ______________________________________

Double check that all facts have MORE than 2 words.

GRADED BY TEACHER: FULL CREDIT 100%   OR ________________% Credit

Lesson Ideas – Not in student editions

Drawing and Painting Project Ideas:

Some lessons can be augmented to work in different media.

Alphabets: [Problem Solving and illustration] Students pick a broad theme of their own interest and create a word, their name, or an entire alphabet based on that theme. Objects should be in the shape of the letters. See supporting pages in this book. See examples in book.

Portraits: [Problem Solving and Biology] First without any instruction, then with exposure to proper proportions, detailed in this book. They can also do portraits as blind drawings for working more abstractly or with a grid for realism in grades 4 and up. Students should be assigned to bring in a photo of a family member or figure they admire. Magazines, internet print-outs, or photos work well. I have also done this project with a surrealistic component, where students mix a symbol of their personality and merge it with their portrait.

Pop Art Pop: [Problem Solving, and history] Students find a common object like a soda can, re-draw and paint it in as many different modes as possible, blind drawing, contour, blind contour, stipple, crosshatch, color field. All work should be on the same size paper or canvas and when complete, images should be placed side by side to create a Warhol-inspired image. To make this easier, each student can be given a similar object and as a class create a larger mural-like project.

Tessellations: [Geometry] M.C. Escher. Plenty of support info on the internet to do this. I like Crystal Productions' posters for this lesson with simple techniques illustrating how to make tessellations from square pieces of paper. A Tessellation is a pattern that repeats infinitely. Grades 4 and up can do this well.

Abstract Representation of Family with Shapes and Colors: [Problem solving, Interpretation Skills] Students list 8 members of their family and write 5 descriptive words about each. Using the *Color and Shape Have Feelings Too* worksheet in this book, they create symbolic shapes and colors for each and create a composition to represent their family. Klee and Kandinsky are good samples for work like this.

Jabberwocky: [Literature] Poem in this book. Without showing students any illustrations, they interpret the poem and illustrate one stanza. Work is collected and put on display. Include foreground, middle-ground, background, and overlap. See examples in this book.

Cubism Simplified: [Geometry and problem solving] Using a ruler, criss-cross a page in every possible direction with a pencil or pen. Choose an image from a magazine you like and "force" the image into these geometric shapes. Seeing Picasso samples is helpful. Lines can also be used less abstractly to divide areas of color.

Comic Book / Movie Poster Parody: [Career Awareness, literature, advertising design, and problem solving] Taking a favorite movie, change the name a bit and create a new image for the parody. Include foreground, middle-ground, background, overlap, title, subtitle, logo, and dramatic action. (see sample in this workbook) See Warhol and Lichtenstein for Pop Art Samples of comic art.

Aboriginal Family Story: [World Cultures, multi-media research] Using samples of aboriginal paintings, and internet samples of aboriginal symbols, create a work that describes an important event from your own family history, recent or old, good or bad. Use the page of expressive shapes and colors to help. Fill all areas with pattern.

Drawings from Observation: [Biology] When weather permits, go outside and draw a scene from nature. Make it fun by adding a surrealistic element, changing colors, or exaggerating elements within the scene. In spring-time it is helpful to tag a branch when budding with loosely tied yarn, and redrawing that branch as a bloom grows, showing the biological process. Andrew Wyeth is a good example artist here.

Sun Mandela: [World cultures, library and research skills] See samples of Asian mandelas and create your own based on the sun as a theme. It can be done in watercolor with oil pastel resist. Consider the use of a cultural tie-in by asking students to use themes found in their own cultural background. Mandelas can also be made by using information from the *Color and Shape Have Feelings Too* worksheet. By repeating shapes based on personality traits of themselves or family members they can cut these shapes from oak-tag and repeat them in a radial design. Corners of rectangular paper can be filled in too with the 4 seasons of ourselves either abstractly or with imagery. (FYI: Rubber cement is a good resist media too for bright whites, in well-ventilated area.)

Sunset Silhouette: [Problem Solving, color theory, physics] Teach students to color blend with sunset colors, overlay black on the bottom quarter to create a land silhouette in black. Add in a tree, a man-made element and person in profile to complete it. See example in book. It is helpful to tie in the imagery with student's experiences. Figures and elements should be related to what the individual student values or feels is important.

Compound Word Illustration: [English and literature] Create a list of compound words and illustrate them in a way that shows their incorrect meaning. Include foreground, middle-ground, background, and overlap. (Butterfly, a stick of butter flying) See list in book.

Wild World Collage: [History, illustration, political history] Collecting images from magazines, kids create crazy combinations of images (Jets with butterfly wings, people with animal legs etc…) All of this is glued down to one large background image. Wavy Gravy is a collage artist of the 60's. Themes can be chosen, like current events or an event in history to create a historical tie-in. Students can also choose a social theme (Environment, cancer, hunger, etc…) they wish to illustrate as political activism was a key component in the 60's.

Perspective: [Geometry and history] One-point perspective of a school hallway. Use rulers and worksheets in this book to prepare for the project. At the end have students add in 1 surrealistic element to make the scene subtly spooky or funny. (Ninja dropping in from ceiling tile, T-Rex tail coming out a door…) See artists of the Renaissance for good examples of perspective, and surrealists for the dreamlike portion.

Cut-Out Still Life: [Tool skills, geometry, history, problem solving] Students do a large contour drawing of a simple still life. Behind this layer newspaper, magazines, construction paper, to create 4 or 5 layers. Staple this packet and cut out contours. Reconstruct the still life on a new paper mixing layered cut-outs. Add drawing lines on top for shading and define contours as needed. Picasso and Braque had good examples of work like this. If you create multiple still life compositions, then a Warhol pop art connection may be helpful.

Environmental Drawing: [Earth Science and biology] Teacher will need to have MANY examples set aside. Students create their own environment (Desert, forest, jungle, coral reef…) and use examples from teacher showing how things should look. No one should draw from imagination but mix and match images from several sources to create one complete image. All elements come from observation of available images. (I get books at Barnes and Noble on discount, cut them up, and laminate the pages) Students are to include foreground, middle-ground, background, and overlap.

5 Step Transition: [Geometry, problem solving] Using a long strip of paper, students draw 2 objects, unrelated to each other, on opposite ends. In 5 steps (including the 2 images) students show a transition or "morph" of one image into the other. (Scissor turning into a coke can in 5 steps.) The middle image should be half of one object merged with the other.

Treasure Maps: [Geometry, Geography, Cartography] Students create a treasure map of an imaginary island. The island can take on the contour of an object, but break it into small pieces so it is not too obvious. Include the following: Detailed border, rose compass, longitude/latitude, 5 land feature symbols, key for symbols, 2 landmarks, 2 water symbols in the water, 1 sea monster and 1 ship. Maps can be aged by wrinkling and soaking in watered-down acrylic paint or strong tea/coffee. See example in this book.

Wrinkle World or Cave Painting: [Problem Solving and history] Take a large piece of paper, wrinkle it into a ball, open and stare at it, and trace shapes you see that make images. This is very similar to watching clouds and trying to see shapes and creatures in them. Color in and make as detailed as possible. If you use brown paper, and wrinkle it, it can look rather stone-like. Have students imagine they are cave-people drawing what is important for them to survive. Scenes may include themselves and their family and their lives at home – their own "cave."

Flower Dissection: [Biology, library research] Drawing and labeling with research. Students can gather flowers or bring some in, maybe a donation of old flowers from a flower shop. Students dissect flowers with an X-Acto knife and draw from observation. (For younger students I would recommend the teacher cut samples open in half. Later, within the library or computer lab, students label the parts that they have observed. Enlarge sketches and use as references for larger paintings like Georgia O'Keeffe.

Drawings of Decay: [Biology] Students can gather soft tissue plants, even lettuce can work and do one sketch a day of the decaying process. This could even be done in the form of a flipbook. Sketches can also follow the various color changes observed in the plant. I would suggest this as a five-minute sketch at the beginning of each class while doing another project. Sketches can later be more fully completed.

Flipbooks: [Biology] of science based observations. Similar to drawings of decay, students could also make flip books based on observations of processes like cell division, plant growth, weather movements.

Pi Painting: [Math] Students create a visual code and key of colors and shapes to represent numbers, then illustrate Pi through these colors, shapes, and composition. This can result in some very abstract works of art but reinforce the math concepts the students have chosen to base their work on. Images should be examined afterward to see if any larger patterns emerge. Other math functions can be explored in this same way, though additional visual codes would need to be made for functions and letter place-holders.

Board Game: [History] Students work in groups to create a board game based on an historical event, time period, or school of art. Research will help them create playing pieces and images for their board games. Game board can be made with a canvas board or covered cardboard. A game can also be based on something the student is excellent at and knows a lot about, like skateboarding…

Political Cartoon: [Current Events/History] Students could create a political cartoon for a contemporary event or historical one, choosing a side to support for a clear point of view.

Mash-Up: [History] Students could make a satirical recreation of a famous work of art or combine two very different famous works to create a new one. There should be accompanying information about the images created that indicate student understanding of context.

Museum Tour: [History] Students can create a diorama of a museum hall setting up an exhibition of images from that particular time. Images should have a companion paper labeled with historical details of the works of art. This can be done for specific schools of art, artists, themes, or based on interests of the students. (ie: finding images of game playing from 8 different centuries). Larger exhibitions can be created as a group project, each group setting up an exhibition in the room for a day or week each.

Art History: [History] Students could take a famous event in human history and create a work of art based on that event. They can even be required to choose a school of art that was from the time of the event from which to create their artwork. (ie: WWI scene in expressionism style.)

Holiday Projects with Substance:

Note: I am of the opinion that art classes need not be slaves to the season at hand. I understand though that many schools practically require the art department to decorate their schools. I also know that the holidays are great motivators to younger children. However, it is no excuse to create vapid, pieces of decoration with no redeeming educational value like hand turkeys, or paper plate Santa heads with cotton ball beards. Doing so only reconfirms the stereotype to others that art is not a subject of substance.

Halloween: [Anatomy and World Cultures] An easy go-to for Halloween is a study of Mexico's Day of the Dead holiday. It is festive, colorful, and teaches art from a multi-cultural point of view. Students can create a painting or sculpture of themselves as a skeleton doing what it is they like most.

Halloween: [History] Pop art candy paintings or sculpture. Using either Andy Warhol or Claes Oldenburg students create either paintings or sculpture of food after seeing samples of the artist's work. Please include some discussion of the 60's political climate, and how Pop Art was in direct opposition to the accepted norms of art at the time. This project can also be done by making paper staple pillows, stuffed with scraps. (Two sheets of paper, stapled 80%, stuff with scraps, and staple closed. Similar to sewing but with staples and paper.)

Thanksgiving: [History, Social Studies, Service Learning] Students can learn about world hunger during this season of bounty and create a work of art that illustrates and educates others about world hunger. This can be in the form of drawings or paintings of food still lives, or sculptures of food. Clay projects can also be made of place settings with food, or individual pot-luck plates. This project can also be done by making paper staple pillows, stuffed with scraps. (See above)

Thanksgiving: [Parody, History] The Anti-hand Turkey. Students trace their hands but turn it into something that is not a turkey. Aliens, animals, bugs, and creatures emerge. Trace hands in different positions. Encourage students to explore four possibilities through quick sketches, and choose one to explore in depth. Tie this lesson into an exploration of the surreal work of Salvador Dali or Rene Magritte.

Winter: [Problem Solving, World Cultures] Negative Space Drawings. Students cover their paper with graphite and do all their drawing work with an eraser. Create a winter scene that includes foreground, middle-ground and background using only an eraser. This does NOT have to be a snowy landscape, it can be a scene of what individual students do on their holiday. They should focus on things specific to their family or culture.

Valentine's Day: [History] Historically, Valentine's Day is in honor of St. Valentine who was killed for marrying soldiers so they could avoid going to war. At that time, only single men were able to serve. The Emperor had him killed for doing this. Students can use this time to study the origins of holidays we celebrate and illustrate their history. Often the facts surrounding the holiday are very different that what it is we celebrate.

Valentine's Day: [Illustration] Students illustrate WHY they value the friendship or individual important in shaping their lives with a drawing. Students should show a shared activity, and include foreground, background, and middle-ground.

Spring Holidays: [Biology] See flower dissection illustration project in 2-D art lesson suggestions.

Spring Holidays: [World Cultures, History, and research skills] Students focus on their cultural background and research holiday traditions for Easter or spring for their country of origin. They create an illustration of the holiday, celebratory objects, or sculpture of these objects. At the end they should do a short show-and-tell explaining what they learned about their own cultural traditions from their countries of origin.

Sculptural Projects

Some projects may be augmented to create 2-D projects as drawings or paintings.

Family Mobile: [Geometry/Physics] Students use information from this book , *colors and shapes have feelings too*, to create mobiles of their family unit by creating symbolic shapes and colors for each family member and create a composition to represent their family. (8 – 10 shapes recommended) Alexander Calder is a wonderful artist for examples. See example in book.

Dinosaur Eggs: [Science, History] Students create dinosaur eggs from plaster and balloons, then crack them open and create a baby dinosaur to fit inside as if in the process of hatching. Students research what their chosen dinosaur would look like as a baby. Eggs and creatures should be related by color to reinforce form and function concepts. To put plaster into a balloon, create a funnel with a 12 oz. or 1 liter soda bottle by cutting off the bottom. Attach a balloon to the cap-end, fill with about 1 cup of plaster, then holding the funnel to your face, blow in both plaster and air into the balloon. Carefully tie off, and roll the balloon in your hands until the plaster hardens. Rolling will even coat the inside of the balloon leaving a hollow center to the "egg" form. Work outside as this can potentially be very messy, but very fun!

Wire Tree: [World Cultures] Using stovepipe wire, copper or any other "soft" wire, students take 50 to 100 thin strands at about 1 ft in length and twist the wires to make a tree, splitting bunches and twisting roots and branches. Foil, craft jewels, or other leaf-like objects can be added as leaves. See the internet for many examples. Couple this project with research about Bonsai trees and their expressive forms emulating wind blowing through their branches.

Wire People/Portraits: [Problem Solving, History] Using thin wire, students create a self portrait. Include elements unique to themselves. This project can be extended by creating a body as well, doing an activity the student does often, or what they wish to be able to do. Students could also create a character from a circus. Alexander Calder did many examples of this too.

Biome House: [Geography/Biology] Show students several biome posters from the biology classes. Environments can be tundra, desert, mountains, grasslands, rain forest, etc. Students choose their favorite; learn a bit more about it, and with foam-core, oaktag, or cardboard, create an architectural cottage or home that would fit within that biome.

Pen of Power: [History/World Cultures] Students take and carve an old branch adding feathers and other natural elements to make a shaman's pen. Students should have a discussion about Native American cultures and create the pen with this in mind. After adding a nib, pens can be used to do a drawing, write a poem, or even create a magical spell. See example in book.

Monumental Design: [History] Students create a miniature monument to an historic hero, an event they wish they could re-visit, or a monument to a personal achievement, or personal experience. There are many memorials from which to pull examples. See example in book.

Goal and Obstacle: [Problem Solving] Students create lists of life goals and things that may prevent them from these achievements. These lists are converted into symbols. The students then create a work that shows 1 of each. The Obstacle on the bottom as a base and the achievement above. (This can also be done with a box and doing different things with the inside and outside OR combine with the next project of Expressive Heads)

Expressive Head: [History, Social Studies, Problem Solving] (I use a foam head from eNasco for this project) Students create a blank head form to cover in a variety of materials to illustrate a personal or social issue they care about. Some ideas: Use magazines and cover the head with words, cover head with a map painting and add pins for places you've visited, destroy head and reassemble, empty head and fill with expressive items, alter the head for expressive reasons. See the artist Robert Arneson for examples. List on page 21 may be helpful for topic based sculptures. See example in book.

Lippold Crystals: [Geometry] Look up imagery by the artist Lippold. Students create their own crystals with any linear material. (*I use eNasco acrylic straws, pipe cleaners, and 527 glue.*) Students start simply and add on structures to make their project grow. They should learn about the necessity of structures that are rigid for project strength. Modular sculptures can be used too, so all work can be combined into a monumental work for display. See example in book.

Paper Structures: [Physics/Engineering] Students create the tallest tower possible with 4 large sheets of paper and 2 yards of tape. Structure must stand after teacher blows on it. Paper can also be used to design an amusement park, landscape all in white, a house of their dreams. Cardstock can be used to make modular rectangles, like playing cards and glued to create permanent card-houses.

Environmental Sculptures: [Problem Solving & Engineering] After seeing the work of Andrew Goldsworthy, students create their own environmental sculpture. Students can be broken into smaller groups to make larger structures. Work should be photographed, printed, and displayed.

Word Sculpture: [English/Social Studies] Students take a word (Social issue, personal issue or topic they know well) Like "EARTH" and make each letter look like part of the issue you care about. The "E" could be a factory spewing toxins, the "A" could be a hurricane, the "R" could be melting, etc. A list of expressive words in this book may be helpful for topic-based sculptures.

Gargoyle of Protection: [World Cultures, History] Students create a list of their own phobias, and incorporate a symbol that would repel that phobia into their gargoyle. (Fear of the dark?) Their gargoyle may hold a light, candle OR be created with light colors. Combine with research about gargoyles of Paris—water symbols that were to ward off fire. (Japan uses dolphin symbols)

Revelation Mask: [History/World Cultures] Students create a mask based on a symbol that reveals part of their personality people are not aware of. The Mask is created to reveal the self rather than conceal. Couple this lesson with samples of masks from other cultures or historical periods. Consider a 2-sided mask expressing inner and outer personalities.

Plaster People: [Problem Solving & Construction] After seeing examples of the work of George Segal, students work in groups to make a plaster cast of a student engaged in a school activity. This sculpture should be placed in the school environment. I suggest casting parts each day and assembling parts at the end and stuffing them with paper. Face, back of head, body trunk, arms, legs. You will need tools to cut plaster safely from the body. Models wear OLD clothes as they will be ruined. Casts can be made in multiple 40-minute periods if well planned.

Masterworks: [History] Students reproduce a master painting in 3-D relief with plaster of paris on canvas boards. This can be a great tie-in for an art history unit. Students could also reproduce an artwork on an unusual surface like a chair, or re-do an artwork with an element related to the student's own interest, experiences, or symbol for themselves.

Viral Sculptures/Pollen Sculptures: [Science, Biology] After researching the forms of micro-organisms by either internet, library, or microscopic observation, students re-create their sample in 3-D. Often these may begin with a paper or aluminum foil base and other items added to it. String, cardboard, pipe-cleaners, wire, etc. Once the initial form is complete, students can be encouraged to embellish these forms to go from clinical to artistic. Students should note the name of their source for their form. See example in book.

Talisman: [Archeology/History] Students create a "coin" negative in clay (Oil-based clay is best) then cast plaster into the form. Students can create a coin to commemorate an event, a talisman to protect them from something, a "charm" to do some imaginary magic, or fill it with objects that represent themselves. This lesson can be coupled with a lesson in archeological discoveries of Greek or Roman coins and imperial artifacts. Students can take on the persona of Caesar & create a coin to immortalize themselves and include symbols for their own strengths and points of view.

Structure: [Engineering] In either groups or as individuals students could build a bridge with limited supplies and create a contest to see how much weight that structure could hold. (4 x 24 inch dowels, 12 inches of masking tape, and wood glue) Similarly, students could create towers with limited supplies to see whose is the tallest and can withstand a fan placed on it (Emphasizing strength and height with 4 sheets of 18 x 24 inch paper, scissors and 3 yards of tape.) Also given 50 sheets of copy paper and 3 yards of tape, students create a structure that can hold books 8 inches or more above the surface of a table. Groups can complete to see whose group holds the most textbooks.

Altered Books: [Problem Solving & Recycling] *"Don't Judge a book by its cover."* Find a source for old hard cover books that are being discarded, many libraries have piles of these. Students then alter the book by painting in, cutting out, gluing in and outside the book. If you have too many books, one can be an experiment book to try out techniques, and the second for the actual graded project. Students should complete the worksheet in this book about how they are perceived by others and how they know themselves to be. Then generate symbols for these. The outside of the book should express how they are seen by others, and the inside is what they know about themselves. Encourage students to "code" their work from the worksheet about the expressive qualities of color and shape. In this way they can keep personal information private yet still express themselves.

Puppetry: [Construction, public speaking, writing, literature] Made from non-composite carpet foam, staples, pliers, and hot glue for a muppet-look. Paper mache, felt, socks, and other puppet media would be fine as well. Each student creates a creature that would best express their hidden personality. Students can use a T-Shirt for body if one is needed for a muppet style project. Once the creature is created, students can be grouped together and create their own mini-performance on a topic of teacher choice: Anti-bullying, recreation of a short story from literature, or even lip-syncing to a song. This project, if well done, can be a means to reach out to neighboring schools and the community.

Consumer Products: [Advertising Design] Students examine and break down the elements found on a can of soda, box of cereal, or other consumer product. They create their own consumer product that has the same kinds of elements as their samples. Label, form, logo, directions, imagery, title, subtitle, etc.

3-D Glasses: [Optics, Physics, Recycling, Environmental Sciences] By visiting most movie theatres, one may ask a manager for 3-D glasses often thrown away. Sanitize them for student use with Lysol or another cleaner. Partner with a science teacher to explore the technology of 3-D glasses and polarized plastics. They are pretty cool and do some interesting tricks. Glasses can be redesigned to become super-hero glasses by adding on sculptural elements, paint and craft supplies. They could make glasses they feel have a super power they wish they had. If you add recycled electronic items, they can look rather sci-fi high tech too. They may be painted with a theme of a particular school of art or artist. What would sunglasses look like if they were designed by Picasso, or Van Gogh? What might cubist sunglasses look like?

Idioms: [English, World Cultures] Students research idioms and their meanings from their cultures of origin. They choose one to illustrate as a sculpture in clay or plaster. This can even be done as a painting or drawing project. Show the idiom in its literal meaning, but have a written explanation of the cultural meaning of the idom to share with the class as part of a show-and-tell closure.

Wire Heads: [Self Expression/Problem Solving] Using soft annealed wire, students create a head based on their own face (Symbolically). This is then filled with objects representing things and skills that are "inside" the student. This is best coordinated with the Self Expression Worksheet early in this book to generate ideas. Inner objects can be created or actual objects brought in.

SKETCHBOOK IDEAS: This list is also in student books.

Many of these may be turned into actual projects, but these sketchbook ideas are meant to be done in 1 class period or less as a way to warm up for larger projects. **If you have a student who finishes their work early**, you can direct them to this page in their workbook, circle the one they want to do on their own while others complete their current project. This will keep them meaningfully occupied and on task. I have a ream of copy paper available for these.

Fill a page with scribbles, and then look at them and reveal what can be seen in them. This is similar to looking at clouds and spotting objects in them, but here you color them in.

Rip a random small piece of paper from a magazine and draw it. Enlarge it to fill the page.

Draw the view through a window.

Write your name 30 times, in different sizes and directions, overlapping often to divide the page into many shapes. Color in using colors that express your mood today using the expressive colors and shapes worksheet.

Draw a tree from your imagination then draw a tree from observation. Which looks better to you? Why?

Trace your hand in an interesting position and turn it into an animal. DO NOT MAKE A TURKEY.

Find a common small object and enlarge it to fill your paper.

Draw yourself in a mirror but DO NOT look at the paper while you do it.

Draw a friend or family member with one continuous line. Do not lift the pencil until it is complete.

Find a tree and draw what is seen between the branches without drawing the tree itself.

Find a face in a magazine or photograph, turn it up-side-down and draw it up-side-down too.

Fill a page with shapes, get into every corner, but DO NOT lift your pencil until you are done. Color in using colors that express your personality using the expressive colors and shapes worksheet.

Do a hybrid drawing of 2 unrelated animals as a new animal (lion & fish maybe). Be sure to have examples of both in front of you if possible.

Draw some clouds from observation.

Draw your hand holding a CD. Draw as much of yourself in the mirror as you can see even if it is just a fragment.

Trace a leaf, trace the shadow it makes. Color in as realistically as you can with shadows too!

Trace your hand in an interesting position; fill it with patterns and color that express what you like to do with your hands.

Draw what you have in your pockets right now.

Draw a shoe, position the laces in such a way as to create a hidden face in your show. Draw it realistically but be sure to capture the idea of a face as well.

Take 2 unrelated objects and create a hybrid image of this new object. (Like scissors and a bird)

Half fill a clear glass with water. Place 1 or 2 objects inside that are both in and out of the liquid (like a spoon or chopstick), draw it.

Take a common object that would relate to yourself, then repeat that object to make an animal that you also feel expresses your personality. Feel free to abstract and stretch the objects to make your animal.

Get a new pencil, do a drawing of something around you by holding the very end where the eraser is.

Write your name and a short statement in block letters, maybe a poem or memory, BUT do it with your eyes closed. Color in after you are done.

Using only color and shape, try to do a drawing that represents LOVE without using a heart.

Do a drawing of the feeling of WAR with colors and shapes and NO objects. Try other words.

Try to draw an object from observation as if you were looking at it through a shattered window or mirror.

Draw an object from observation but draw several points of view at the same time, overlapping.

Try to draw a moving object and capture the idea of that movement you observe.

Take a magazine image, cut it in half and paste onto a new paper. (Rubber cement works best) Complete the missing half by hand. Include shadows too.

Take the magazine image left over from the last drawing and paste on another sheet of paper. Complete the missing half in a strange and unexpected way.

Draw a childhood memory.

Using a reference like yourself, a friend, or picture, draw a detailed eye.

Draw the line that separates your lips. Note how dynamic this line really is. Finish by adding your upper and lower lips.

Draw a night scene from observation through a widow.

Gargoyles are meant to protect you and scare away evil spirits. Draw and create your own gargoyle to keep one of your fears away from you. For example, if you have a fear of darkness, your gargoyle might hold a torch or emit light.

Find an un-illustrated poem & create a picture for it.

Draw a solid object from observation, but do it as if it were glass.

Tightly wrap an object with cloth. Be sure the form of the object can still be understood. Draw It.

Fill a page with an image that simulates the texture of rock. Have a rock as reference to look at.

Draw a coin but enlarge it to fill the page. Add shadows and shines to make it look 3-D.

Draw a still life with 5 objects but color them with the opposite colors than they actually are.

Draw the outline of an observed object. Create a negative by coloring highlights, dark shadows, and areas of light.

Set two very differently colored and textured objects side by side, but color & texture one with the colors & textures of its neighbor.

Draw the outlines of two objects and partially overlap the drawings. Color each with a different primary color, where they overlap color with the secondary color they would create.

Color in a whole page with gray, use an eraser to draw. Try to vary the tones you see. Finish by adding very dark tones with heavy pencil. Be sure erasures show.

Draw something as if you were losing your mind.

Create a black and white landscape with one object in color.

Sketch a new way to design the face of a clock.

Write a short poem backwards (Mirror Writing) with big bold overlapping block letters. Color in the spaces created with analogous colors (Neighboring Colors on the color wheel)

Create a cartoon of yourself or a friend.

Draw a portrait of a friend or yourself; color in by signing that person's name over and over. Layer names for shadows like crosshatching.

Draw a self portrait made entirely of objects that represent what interests you.

Create a logo for yourself; be sure that it contains a clue about your personality.

Draw yourself as a monster.

Draw an object from observation above. Color the light side with warm colors (yellow through red) and the shaded side with cool colors like purple, blue, and green.

Put together a group of similarly colored objects. Set them up on a contrasting or opposite color for a still life drawing.

Draw a flag that would represent your family. Try to be symbolic. Use the worksheet in this book on the expressive qualities of shapes and colors.

Set an object in a box. Draw the object in the box; include the inside of the box in your drawing.

Draw an outline of a simple object.
- Draw the object again without lifting your pencil.
- Draw the object again without looking at your hand while you draw. Try to do it with a mostly continuous line.
- Draw the object's outline and shade with crosshatching lines.
- Draw the object again and use scribble lines to create shadow.
- Draw the object again only using dots for color and shadow.

Take a pattered fabric or shirt, drape it over a chair and draw it showing the pattern changes as the fabric folds and drapes.

Draw something from an unusual point of view.

Draw your hand drawing your hand in a funny way. (M.C. Escher did something like this)

Find a small simple, common object. Draw it large and turn it into an architectural design.

Draw your head realistically or as a cartoon. Add a large hole or opening to it and have objects escaping from that hole that tell a story about what goes on in your mind.

Trace an object about the size of this page, onto a page. Turn it into a very different object by how you finish the drawing. A pair of scissors may become a bird. You may add onto the object as you wish, try not to erase much of the original outline.

Cover half of your face with an object, and then create a self portrait.

Draw an original super hero with a power you wish you had.

Draw a stabbed object. (Like a piece of fruit with a pencil stabbed into it) Make the drawing with exaggerated sense of emotion.

Draw someone talking. Fill the background with their words in a creative way. This could be a historical figure or someone around you today.

Draw the *thing* that lives under a child's bed.

Draw something flying that would not normally be able to fly.

Write an expressive word in large fat bubble-letters. Fill in the letters with images that relate the meaning of the word.

Draw an animal based on a photograph of it, BUT only draw it with letters found in its name. It is okay to abstract the letters to make them fit. Use the colors of the animal to finish it.

Design an item of clothing, color and texture it.

Draw the kind of house you would like to live in.

Draw your hand pointed away from you toward an object, draw both your hand and the object. Overlap a bit if you can to add realism and a hint of perspective.

Use candles, burn sticks and draw a still life with home-made charcoal.

Draw a wall with windows, and details of adjacent items like bookshelves, chairs, etc. Then draw an unexpected environment through the window.

Draw yours or a friend's face, divide it into 4 parts, and color each section with symbols for 4 things that are important to that person.

Trace your hand and draw what might be inside if you were an awesome robot.

Paste down half a face from a magazine. Choose an attractive model. Finish the other half of the face as if they were an alien.

If you could design your very own cell phone, what would it look like?

Draw a container, and on the back draw something unexpected that would be inside the container. Hold the page up to the light to see an x-ray view of both.

Design a piece of jewelry and use a symbol from your own cultural background in it.

Draw a piece of foil with a few wrinkles in it.

Place a coin under a page, rub a pencil over the page to create an embossed image. Then draw your hand holding the coin.

Draw a design you think would make a cool tattoo for you. Remember that tattoos are often symbolic of thing important to the person wearing it.

Draw someone's ear from about 6 inches away from them. Be so close you can see every detail.

Using a flashlight, draw an object and its shades and highlights, but light it from an unusual point of view. (Like a face with the light below the chin, or still life lit from below.

Crumple a page, flatten it lightly so the creases are still obvious, then draw the page.

Draw a CD cover for your favorite song.

Draw your home as a castle but include details that are there right now.

Crumple this page, lightly flatten it, and trace the wrinkles making what you can imagine into the creases. This is similar to finding objects in clouds. As you stare, object will become apparent.

Draw something dry as if it was wet.

Have a friend lay down on the floor. Draw their portrait while sitting above their head so their face is up-side-down. Your drawing will be up-side-down as well.

How would you re-design your hand to be better than it is? If you were into basketball, how might it be different? Consider your hobbies and activities.

What might a flower look like on an alien planet?

Design a new cologne bottle for either a great scent, or something very bad.

Willy Wonka remade an environment out of candy, what would you draw an environment out of?

Create a new label for your favorite beverage.

Pick a playing card and do a design based on that card that no linger looks like a playing card. Use repetition and pattern if it helps.

Create a cover for a ridiculous comic book.

Draw something in the room no one notices.

Lay on the floor and look up. Draw part of the room with this unusual perspective.

Put your leg up on the table and draw your leg, shoe and all, in perspective.

When you cross your eyes, you see double. Draw something around you as if you had double vision. Find a creative way to handle overlapped areas.

Do a portrait of a friend, but re-imagining their hair in a way that shows off their personality. Draw the trophy you wish you could win.

Draw the first thing you would buy if you won the lottery.

Draw your hand holding your favorite possession.

Draw what it looks like sitting in the front of your car, and put something unexpected in the rear-view mirror.

Draw something pretty next to something ugly.

Draw a piece of popcorn to fill this page.

Draw something floating in a magical way.

Hold a tube of paper up to your eye and draw your point of view. (If you have glasses, maybe you can tape a small tube to them.)

Stand on something tall and draw your view looking down.

While lying on the floor, draw what you see from that perspective as if you were a bug.

Draw an object that makes noise. Draw what you imagine that noise might look like if it could be seen.

Sit in the back of a bus or car and draw your point of view. Feel free to change the scene through the window or make it realistic.

Draw something lit by a candle.

Draw two objects side by side that should never be put together.

Draw two objects side by side that represent opposite themes: War and peace, good and evil, love and hate…

Make a drawing that expresses a lie either literally, figuratively, or symbolically.

Draw an object as if it were in-side-out.

Draw the surface of a coin with a water droplet on it. If you have a magnifying glass, use it.

Draw your bedroom as if it was inside a container like a teapot, jar, cardboard box…

Ask the closest person to you pick an object in the area, and then draw it.

Place a few objects on a white piece of paper, only draw the shadows.

Draw what you imagine the inside of your stomach looks like after the last meal you ate.

Imagine you ARE your favorite animal. Do a drawing you think that animal would draw if it could or from its point of view.

Draw a fun pattern for a necktie or bow.

Draw an amazing sand castle on the beach.

Write your initials very large and turn it into a drawing of animals, objects, or other subject.

Draw a new and unique sea creature.

Draw a new and unique dinosaur.

Draw a how-to label or poster for something you know how to do. If it is too complicated, illustrate just 1 to 4 steps of the process.

Draw a simple cartoon that illustrates the last time you were embarrassed.

Draw something with wings that normally would not have them.

Do a drawing of a person combined with an animal. The Egyptians did this a lot.

Create an advertisement for yourself as if you were a product in a store.

Create your initials in a very ornate and decorative way, like old illuminated manuscripts.

Remove your socks and shoes and draw your foot. How would you redesign a common road sign? Yield, Stop, No Running, Poison...

Draw yourself as if you were 100 years old.

Draw how you would symbolize the 4 seasons.

Re-imagine the wrapper for your favorite candy bar. Create a new design for it.

Draw a soft object with a steel skin with screws, rivets, and bolts.

Draw a cute animal as if it were Frankenstein's pet.

Draw an animal you consider unappealing, as cute.

Draw an object from observation but re-arrange its parts in an unexpected way.

Draw an advertisement for a product you would not like but make it seem appealing.

Draw two objects side by side but change their scale. For example, you might have a giant ant next to a tiny teacup.

Crumple a picture from a magazine and draw it as you see it.

Design a new kind of chair.

Do a line drawing of your shoe, and color it in the way you think would look interesting.

Life is often full of choices. Draw a portrait of yourself, divide the face in half, and show two potential life choices you will need to make as an adult in the design. (You as a teacher or you as a hairdresser) Use symbols and colors in the portrait to show the possible directions your life might take.

Take a common object and draw it as if it was a skeleton. What would the skeleton of a pear look like?

Design a monument for a common object, like a monument to a thumbtack.

Draw a face card from a deck of cards making you the queen, king, jack, or joker.

Draw what you see reflected in a bowl or plate of water. It will reflect better if the bowl is a dark color.

Draw your home or backyard from an aerial perspective. (From above)

Draw a mysterious doorway.

Design a metal of honor commemorating your greatest achievement in your life so far. If you do not have one you can think of, consider an accomplishment you hope to achieve in the future.

Draw an eating utensil turning into something else.

The Tao of Teaching Art

1. Every project must be designed to incorporate the student's life or experience.
Instead of making a monster, my students might make a gargoyle that would protect them from a specific fear through their choices of symbols, forms, material, and colors. Connect the project to the student experience and they will be invested in the outcome. With this method every project is unique, personal, and expressive.

2. Every project must have a tie-in to core courses.
When we grid—we teach geometry. When we make sculptures—we teach engineering. When we teach color mixing—physics. When we create illustrations for stories—we teach literature. When we review the styles of art from da Vinci to Warhol—we teach history. Ultimately, we teach creative problem solving and divergent thinking skills. Continue this tradition, and share with students that though this is art, it is also geometry, science, history, etc. Your students will succeed at higher levels in school, and you have a job you can defend against cuts.

3. Every student deserves a little one-on-one time.
Sit with students, one-on-one, to learn about their lives and motivations. Students are better motivated by people they feel care about them.

4. Keep it fun. It's art after all.
Avoid overly academic exercises and *crafy kitsch*. Do projects you would have liked to have done when you were a child. Silliness, exploration, imagination, and inventiveness help motivate and engage students.

5. Students should plan work with a sketch, a paragraph, or list, and organize ideas with clear parameters and expectations.
This avoids the use of materials you did not intend, waste, and creates a student-generated plan.

6. Flexibility; be ready to change ideas or methods with the tone of the class.
If students seem unmotivated, it may be an indication that you need to switch gears, re-motivate, or ask questions to understand student hesitation. It may also mean production steps were too large, a sample was too vague, or the project should be taught in smaller increments.

7. Love what you do, do what you love, and the students will follow you anywhere.
Children are emotional tuning forks. They can sense if you are *phoning it in*, faking it, or do not really care. Do projects that excite you; share your passion, yourself, and success will be assured.

8. Be dependable, predictable, and a good example.
Plan, prepare, and be consistent. Students do not have to *like you*, but they need to *respect* you. If your expectations are clear, and your classroom management is evenhanded, they will see you as fair. If you need to correct behavior, speak from the heart, and explain why change needs to happen. Corrections starting with "I" are better motivators than demands beginning with "You."

Assessment: Graded by both the teacher and the student. Only the teacher's grade counts, but if there is a larger difference between the assessments, they can be discussed.

Project Title _______________________________ Date Complete _______________
Short Description ____

Assess a grade of "A, B, C, D or F." You may add + or – if you feel the need.

Student Assessment Below   **Teacher Assessment Below.**

Neatness   _____   Neatness   _____
Completeness   _____   Completeness   _____
Originality   _____   Originality   _____

Following Directions   _____   Following Directions   _____
Meeting Project Goals   _____   Meeting Project Goals   _____   Recorded Grade

----

Project Title _______________________________ Date Complete _______________

Short Description ____

Assess a grade of "A, B, C, D or F." You may add + or – if you feel the need.

Student Assessment Below   **Teacher Assessment Below.**

Neatness   _____   Neatness   _____
Completeness   _____   Completeness   _____
Originality   _____   Originality   _____

Following Directions   _____   Following Directions   _____
Meeting Project Goals   _____   Meeting Project Goals   _____   Recorded Grade

----

Project Title _______________________________ Date Complete _______________

Short Description ____

Assess a grade of "A, B, C, D or F." You may add + or – if you feel the need.

Student Assessment Below   **Teacher Assessment Below.**

Neatness   _____   Neatness   _____
Completeness   _____   Completeness   _____
Originality   _____   Originality   _____

Following Directions   _____   Following Directions   _____
Meeting Project Goals   _____   Meeting Project Goals   _____   Recorded Grade

----

Project Title _______________________________ Date Complete _______________

Short Description ____

Assess a grade of "A, B, C, D or F." You may add + or – if you feel the need.

Student Assessment Below   **Teacher Assessment Below.**

Neatness   _____   Neatness   _____
Completeness   _____   Completeness   _____
Originality   _____   Originality   _____

Following Directions   _____   Following Directions   _____
Meeting Project Goals   _____   Meeting Project Goals   _____   Recorded Grade

Pass-Points   NAME________________ Period___

This pass may be used in 1 of 2 ways and may not be shared with another student...

#1. You may use this pass to have 1 free class where you choose not to participate. If you are caught not participating, you will be requested to hand in this 1 pass. If all of your passes are used up and you are not participating you may receive a ZERO for that day, and/or a detention. You may not distract others from working when you choose not to work or do something other than a class project.

#2. If NOT USED, this pass can add 10 points to any project or test or replace 1 missing homework.

Pass-Points   NAME________________ Period___

This pass may be used in 1 of 2 ways and may not be shared with another student...

#1. You may use this pass to have 1 free class where you choose not to participate. If you are caught not participating, you will be requested to hand in this 1 pass. If all of your passes are used up and you are not participating you may receive a ZERO for that day, and/or a detention. You may not distract others from working when you choose not to work or do something other than a class project.

#2. If NOT USED, this pass can add 10 points to any project or test or replace 1 missing homework.

Pass-Points   NAME________________ Period___

This pass may be used in 1 of 2 ways and may not be shared with another student...

#1. You may use this pass to have 1 free class where you choose not to participate. If you are caught not participating, you will be requested to hand in this 1 pass. If all of your passes are used up and you are not participating you may receive a ZERO for that day, and/or a detention. You may not distract others from working when you choose not to work or do something other than a class project.

#2. If NOT USED, this pass can add 10 points to any project or test or replace 1 missing homework.

Pass-Points   NAME________________ Period___

This pass may be used in 1 of 2 ways and may not be shared with another student...

#1. You may use this pass to have 1 free class where you choose not to participate. If you are caught not participating, you will be requested to hand in this 1 pass. If all of your passes are used up and you are not participating you may receive a ZERO for that day, and/or a detention. You may not distract others from working when you choose not to work or do something other than a class project.

#2. If NOT USED, this pass can add 10 points to any project or test or replace 1 missing homework.

PASS POINTS AUTHENTICATION, DO NOT COPY, ORIGINAL MUST HAVE NAME IN COLOR, ALL OTHERS VOID. PASS POINTS AUTHENTICATION, DO NOT COPY, ORIGINAL MUST HAVE NAME IN COLOR, ALL OTHERS VOID. PASS POINTS AUTHENTICATION, DO NOT COPY, ORIGINAL MUST HAVE NAME IN COLOR, ALL OTHERS VOID. PASS POINTS AUTHENTICATION, DO NOT COPY, ORIGINAL MUST HAVE NAME IN COLOR, ALL OTHERS VOID. PASS POINTS AUTHENTICATION, DO NOT COPY, ORIGINAL MUST HAVE NAME IN COLOR, ALL OTHERS VOID. PASS POINTS AUTHENTICATION, DO NOT COPY, ORIGINAL MUST HAVE NAME IN COLOR, ALL OTHERS VOID. PASS POINTS AUTHENTICATION, DO NOT COPY, ORIGINAL MUST HAVE NAME IN COLOR, ALL OTHERS VOID. PASS POINTS AUTHENTICATION, DO NOT COPY, ORIGINAL MUST HAVE NAME IN COLOR, ALL OTHERS VOID. PASS POINTS AUTHENTICATION, DO NOT COPY, ORIGINAL MUST HAVE NAME IN COLOR, ALL OTHERS VOID. PASS POINTS AUTHENTICATION, DO NOT COPY, ORIGINAL MUST HAVE NAME IN COLOR, ALL OTHERS VOID. PASS POINTS AUTHENTICATION, DO NOT COPY, ORIGINAL MUST HAVE NAME IN COLOR, ALL OTHERS VOID. PASS POINTS AUTHENTICATION, DO NOT COPY, ORIGINAL MUST HAVE NAME IN COLOR, ALL OTHERS VOID. PASS POINTS AUTHENTICATION, DO NOT COPY, ORIGINAL MUST HAVE NAME IN COLOR, ALL OTHERS VOID. PASS POINTS AUTHENTICATION, DO NOT COPY, ORIGINAL MUST HAVE NAME IN COLOR, ALL OTHERS VOID. PASS POINTS AUTHENTICATION, DO NOT COPY, ORIGINAL MUST HAVE NAME IN COLOR, ALL OTHERS VOID. PASS POINTS AUTHENTICATION, DO NOT COPY, ORIGINAL MUST HAVE NAME IN COLOR, ALL OTHERS VOID. PASS POINTS AUTHENTICATION, DO NOT COPY, ORIGINAL MUST HAVE NAME IN COLOR, ALL OTHERS VOID. PASS POINTS AUTHENTICATION, DO NOT COPY, ORIGINAL MUST HAVE NAME IN COLOR, ALL OTHERS VOID. PASS POINTS FORM. ORIGINAL MUST HAVE NAME IN COLOR, ALL OTHERS VOID. PASS POINTS AUTHENTICATION, DO NOT COPY, ORIGINAL MUST HAVE NAME IN COLOR, ALL OTHERS VOID. PASS POINTS AUTHENTICATION, DO NOT COPY, ORIGINAL MUST HAVE NAME IN COLOR, ALL OTHERS VOID. PASS POINTS AUTHENTICATION, DO NOT COPY, ORIGINAL MUST HAVE NAME IN COLOR, ALL OTHERS

Ordering Supplies

These are the supplies I order for 1 year of both sculpture and a general art classes.

I am given a budget of about 6 thousand dollars every year to supply 150 students that meet daily. My classes average about 20 to 25 students for six 50-minute periods daily. Many companies sell the same materials but have very different pricing. Some offer free shipping. Some offer a percentage off the order if it is over $200. Some offer both. It is well worth your time to comparison shop.

A school should generally budget $40 to $50 per student for art. This would be based on the number of students you see on the average day.

The following are supplies I order on a regular basis.

6 reams of 11 x 17 inch drawing paper
3 reams of 18 x 24 inch paper
3 reams of 11 x 17 watercolor paper
1 ream 18 x 24 watercolor paper
100 16 x 20 inch canvas board
20 doz. Sharpie fine point
20 Doz. Sharpie ultra fine point
6 set Sharpie color pack of 24 (2 varieties)
2 gallon acrylic gloss medium
4 cans clear acrylic spray paint

50 doz. Sargent #2 Pencils
3 pencil sharpeners
1 gross erasers
1 six pen set Sakura
24 rulers 12 inch
6 box latex gloves
1 drying rack
2 packages of "Flawboard" 100 pack
12 packs of ¼ inch dowels
6 cases of plaster craft
12 rolls of 5 lb stovepipe wire, 20 gauge
6 rolls of 5 lb stovepipe wire, 16 gauge
12 long nose pliers with cutter
24 jumbo eye needles, 5 inch
4 rolls of aluminum sheet metal (NOT foil)
2 packs of pipe cleaners, multi-color x1000

6 pint of blockout white acrylic paint
6 pint of acrylic paint Mars Black, ***and all colors you may need. Go heavy on primaries***.
24 sets of water color pencils 24 colors
3 tubes "Kiss off" or other stain remover
2 bulk set of 144 brushes rounds & flats
4 rolls craft paper 1000 ft. x 36 in. 2 white/2 brown
20 sheets of 3/16 foamcore
20 sheets ½ in foamcore
12 X-Acto knives
5 packs of X-Acto blades of 100
12 bottles rubber cement
12 bottles 7.5 oz. Elmer's Glue
6 bottles carpenter's glue
527 glue (good for plastics & metal)
4 box glue stick
4 hot glue guns
400 hot glue refills
60 rolls assorted masking tape
10 bags of casting plaster 25 lbs
1 container of Vaseline 12 oz. (inexpensive release agent for plaster)
2 Rube-r-mold kits
10 packs of 1 oz. cups/ 250 cups (lids?)
5 packs 3.25 oz. cups and lids / 250 cups
5 packs 3.25 oz. cups and lids / 250 cups
10 rolls of aluminum foil 12 in. x 200 ft.
10 bottles speedball ink

If there is enough money I would also order metallic acrylic paints & some spray paint.
Order some tools like hammers, hacksaws, blades, hand-held Fiscar drill & 1 set drill bits.

Often what is purchased in one year can be used the next year.
Here is a list of some supplies I recommend.

Craft Sticks / Popsicle Sticks
Junk Brushes (cheap house-painting-like brushes)
Plastic plates
Buckets, sponges, rags
Rubber buckets for plaster work
Disposable aprons
Yarns and string
Nylon kite-type string
Acrylic rods for construction
Scrap or copy paper
Construction paper
Storage bins for wet work
Wood scraps in bulk
Nails, pins and fastening devices
Mirrors, small and or large
Miniature Mannequins
Clips, tacks, binders & folders
Glitter and minimal craft-like items
Speedball pen tips
Clay if you have access to a kiln
Bulk packs of markers, pencils, crayons, oil pastels
Modeling clay (non-hardening)
Drawing boards
Rubbing alcohol
Paint thinner (odorless)

Critique with sample:

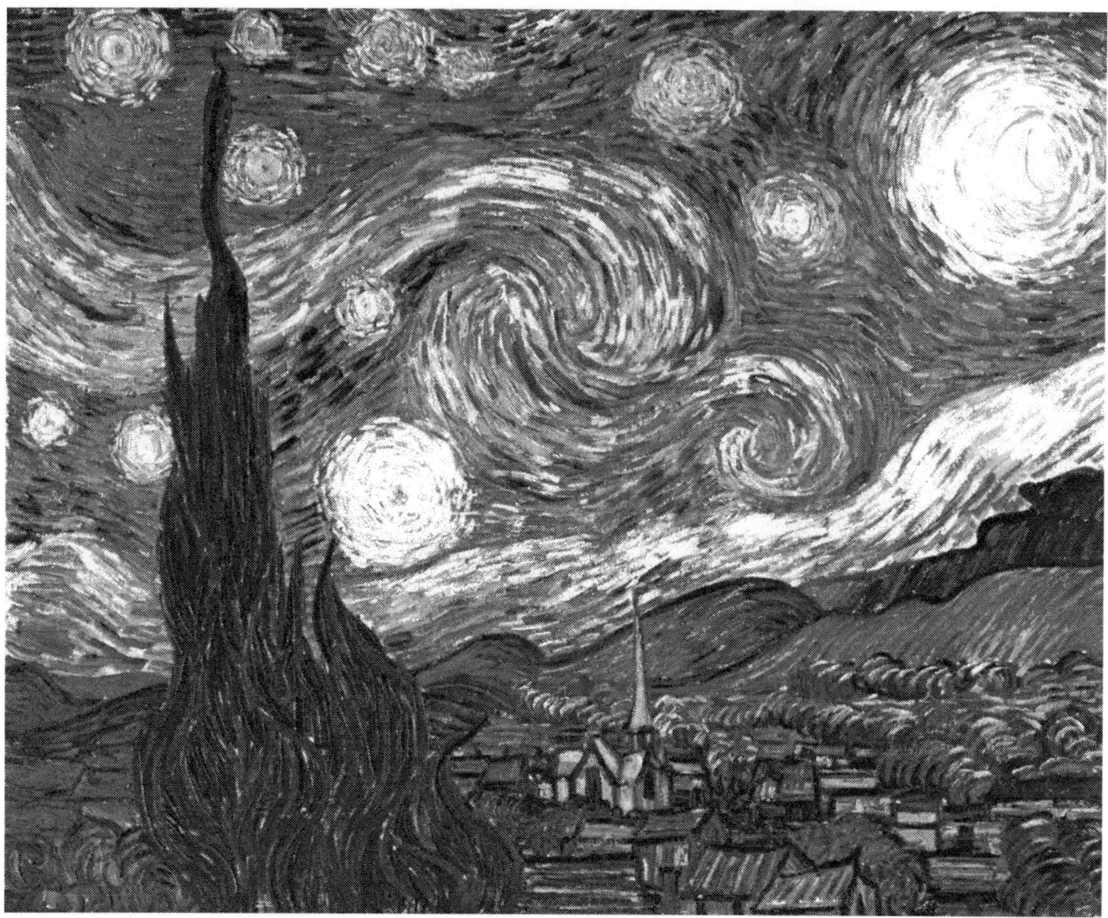

Critique of artwork is by _Vincent van Gogh_ Title/Description: _Starry Night_

From 1 (not showing) to 10 (very strong) rate the following parts of the project:

Neatness = _8_ , Completeness = _9_ , Originality = _10_ , Following directions = _10*_

What art element is the strongest in this project? _Color seems to be the most strong art element_

Evidence: _The use of contrasting color, and bold saturated color makes it stand out_

What art principle is strongest in this project? _Many are, but movement stands out for me._

Evidence: _The sky seems to swirl, the hills are like churning waves, stars seem to twinkle,_

What is most successful about this project? _*Van Gogh set out to try and do a painting of a night sky from observation, so he met his goal. It is a very original idea._

Besides completeness, what could be improved upon in this project: _There are some small portions of the canvas showing between paint strokes. Coloring the canvas first may have hid this._

What can you say about the artist based on their artwork (Be positive): _I feel that the artist wants us to pay attention to the beauty around us, maybe we don't pay attention enough._

THIS PAGE MAY BE PHOTOCOPIED FOR STUDENTS

Critique of artwork is by _____________________ Title/Description: ___________________________________

From 1 (not showing) to 10 (very strong) rate the following parts of the project:

Neatness = _______, Completeness = _______, Originality = _______, Following directions = ______

What art element is the strongest in this project? ____

Evidence: ____

What art principal is strongest in this project? ____

Evidence: ____

What is most successful about this project? ____

____

Besides completeness, what could be improved upon in this project: ____________________________________

____

What can you infer about the artist based on their artwork (Be positive): ________________________________

____

- -

Critique of artwork is by _____________________ Title/Description: ___________________________________

From 1 (not showing) to 10 (very strong) rate the following parts of the project:

Neatness = _______, Completeness = _______, Originality = _______, Following directions = ______

What art element is the strongest in this project? ____

Evidence: ____

What art principal is strongest in this project? ____

Evidence: ____

What is most successful about this project? ____

____

Besides completeness, what could be improved upon in this project: ____________________________________

____

What can you infer about the artist based on their artwork (Be positive): ________________________________

____

THIS PAGE MAY BE PHOTOCOPIED FOR STUDENTS

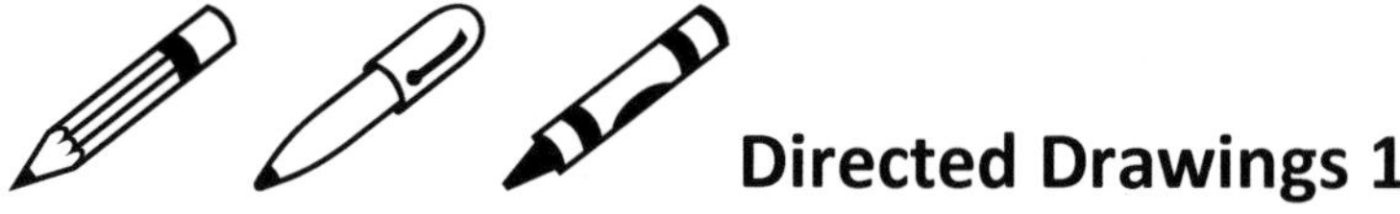 **Directed Drawings 1**

Directed drawings are simple exercises to be completed with any of the prompts below.

Substitute Directions:

Have all students label their papers with their full name and period, then please select one of the drawing prompts below. Check it off as it is assigned so that unused prompts may be used during the next class. Encourage students to do their best and include as much detail as possible. If students finish early, you may select another prompt for them.

[__] Write your name 30 times, in different sizes and directions, overlapping often to divide the page into many shapes. Color in each shape with a different color.

[__] Trace your hand in an interesting position and turn it into an animal, sea creature, or fictional monster. **Do NOT make a turkey.**

[__] Do a drawing of this room with a single line, never lifting your pencil until you are done. It will create a lot of interesting shapes. Use the rest of the class to color it in using only primary and secondary colors (Red, orange, yellow, green, blue, and purple.)

[__] Fold your paper in half to make a card. Design a card for a holiday that is fake. What would a card look like for National Booger Day? How about a Happy Zombie Day? Those are two ideas, now you come up with something completely different and unusual!

[__] Draw the person sitting next to you as if they were an alien. Include details so you can be sure it is them (Like glasses or a pony tail if they have one) then color it in realistically. If you have time include what you see behind them as a background.

Note to sub: Student may use the following materials only:

____

____

____

Storage Directions:

____

____

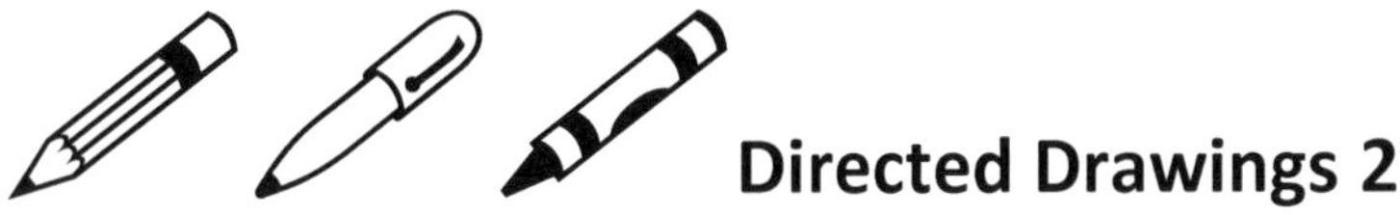 **Directed Drawings 2**

Directed drawings are simple exercises to be completed with any of the prompts below.

Substitute Directions:

Have all students label their papers with their full name and period, then please select one of the drawing prompts below. Check it off as it is assigned so that unused prompts may be used during the next class. Encourage students to do their best and include as much detail as possible. If students finish early, you may select another prompt for them.

[__] Draw a window in the classroom that you can see, either on the main door, or the window on the wall. Draw and color it realistically, and include what you see around it. Then draw something totally unexpected in that window; coral reef, tornado, aliens, dinosaur, zombies?

[__] Write an expressive word in large fat bubble-letters. Fill in the letters with images that relate the meaning of the word. Add color as well. Words like "War" and "Peace" work well, but it is okay to choose a work you can relate to.

[__] Draw something flying that would not normally be able to fly. It can be a living thing like a pig or an object like a strawberry or pair of scissors. It is okay to draw something unusual. If you have time include a background and lots of color.

[__] Draw someone talking. Fill the background with their words in a creative way. Use lots of colors in the words and color in the face. You do not have to using realistic colors.

[__] Draw an original super hero with a power you wish you had. If you have time include what you see behind them as a background.

Note to sub: Student may use the following materials only:

____

____

____

Storage Directions:

____

____

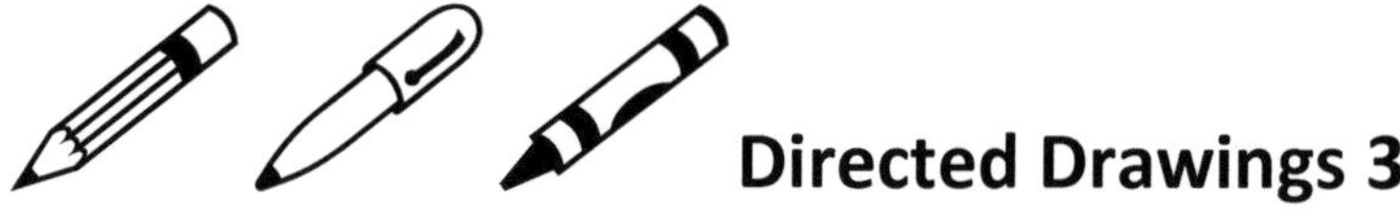 **Directed Drawings 3**

Directed drawings are simple exercises to be completed with any of the prompts below.

Substitute Directions:

Have all students label their papers with their full name and period, then please select one of the drawing prompts below. Check it off as it is assigned so that unused prompts may be used during the next class. Encourage students to do their best and include as much detail as possible. If students finish early, you may select another prompt for them.

[__] Trace your hand and arm on a piece of paper; color it in as realistically as you can. Then draw a cool tattoo on your hand that would have some personal meaning.

[__]Place a coin under your paper, rub a pencil over the page to create an embossed image of the coin. Use the side of the pencil for the best results. Then draw your hand holding the coin. Add as much detail as you can to make your hand look real.

[__] The teacher will put a loosely crumpled paper on your table and turn off all the lights except one. Do a drawing of the paper, adding the shadows as you see them. If your back is to the light, turn so the shadows are obvious on your crumpled paper.

[__] Crumple your drawing paper then lightly flatten it. Stare at the paper a bit, trace the wrinkles to show off what you can see in the creases, and color them in. This is similar to finding objects in clouds. Objects will become apparent because the human brain likes to find patterns.

[__]Do a drawing of someone in the room, but re-imagine their hair in a way that shows off their personality. Add color and a background to finish the drawing.

Note to sub: Student may use the following materials only:

____

____

____

Storage Directions:

____

____

 **Directed Drawings 4**

Directed drawings are simple exercises to be completed with any of the prompts below.

Substitute Directions:

Have all students label their papers with their full name and period, then please select one of the drawing prompts below. Check it off as it is assigned so that unused prompts may be used during the next class. Encourage students to do their best and include as much detail as possible. If students finish early, you may select another prompt for them.

[__] Draw an object that makes noise. Draw what you imagine that noise might look like if it could be seen. Include color and a background if you have time.

[__] Trace your hand, and then draw it as if you had steel skin with screws, rivets, and bolts.

[__]Draw a cute animal as if it were Frankenstein's pet. Include color, textures, and a background to complete the image.

[__] Draw the classroom as if it was part of a haunted house or during a zombie apocalypse. Include details like textures and a background to complete the image.

[__] Life is often full of choices. Draw a portrait of yourself, and divide the face in half. In the design, show the two potential life choices you may need to make as an adult. (You as a teacher or you as a hairdresser.) Use symbols and colors in the portrait to show the possible directions your life might take. Include things in the background to show off the two potential choices.

Note to sub: Student may use the following materials only:

____

____

____

Storage Directions:

____

____

 **Directed Drawings 5**

Directed drawings are simple exercises to be completed with any of the prompts below.

Substitute Directions:

Have all students label their papers with their full name and period, then please select one of the drawing prompts below. Check it off as it is assigned so that unused prompts may be used during the next class. Encourage students to do their best and include as much detail as possible. If students finish early, you may select another prompt for them.

[__] Draw a landscape with a house, car, or man-made object in it. Give the man-made object natural textures like leaves and grass, and give the natural elements mechanical textures found in the object. Be sure to use color to complete your drawing.

[__] Do a portrait from very careful observation but rearrange the parts of the face. Be sure to include a re-arranged background and color to complete your drawing.

[__] Draw your bedroom as if it was inside a container like a teapot, jar, cardboard box, or Something unexpected. Include color and a background to complete your drawing.

[__] Draw an amazing sand castle on the beach. Include color, details, and a background to complete your drawing.

[__] Do a drawing of an animal, either real or imagined, but ONLY use the letters of your name to do it. You may repeat letters, draw them backwards, re-arrange their parts if you must, but only use letters to build the image. Color in your work to complete it.

Note to sub: Student may use the following materials only:

____

____

____

Storage Directions:

____

____

 **Re-Imagine**

Each page has a single common object on it. Add to the image with lines and colors to turn it into something else like this example. The scissor were turned into a beak for a bird, and the pencil drawn so it looks like the bird is holding it.

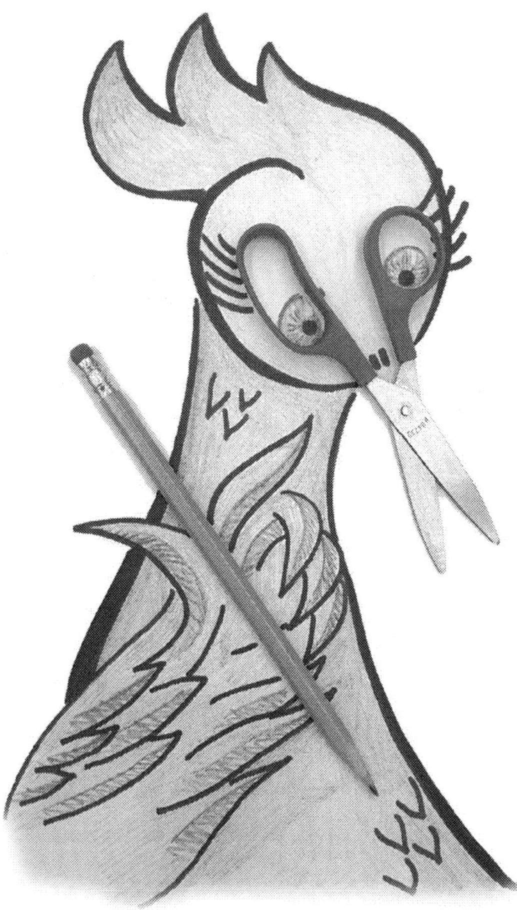

Note to sub: Student may use the following materials only:

____

____

____

Storage Directions:

____

____

This is a whisk. Add to the image and turn it into something else. You may turn the paper in any direction. Can you turn it into a tree or an odd nose for a monster? Use your imagination and surprise your teacher. Be sure to add a background!

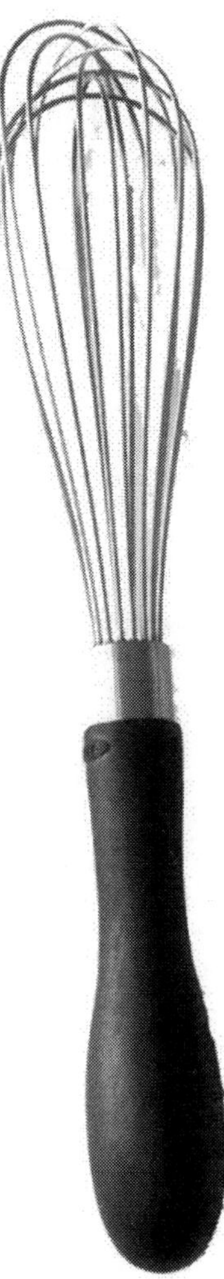

This is a dog. Add to the background and show the unusual place where this dog lives.
You may add to the dog too: wings, horns, extra legs, or whatever. Use your
imagination and surprise your teacher.

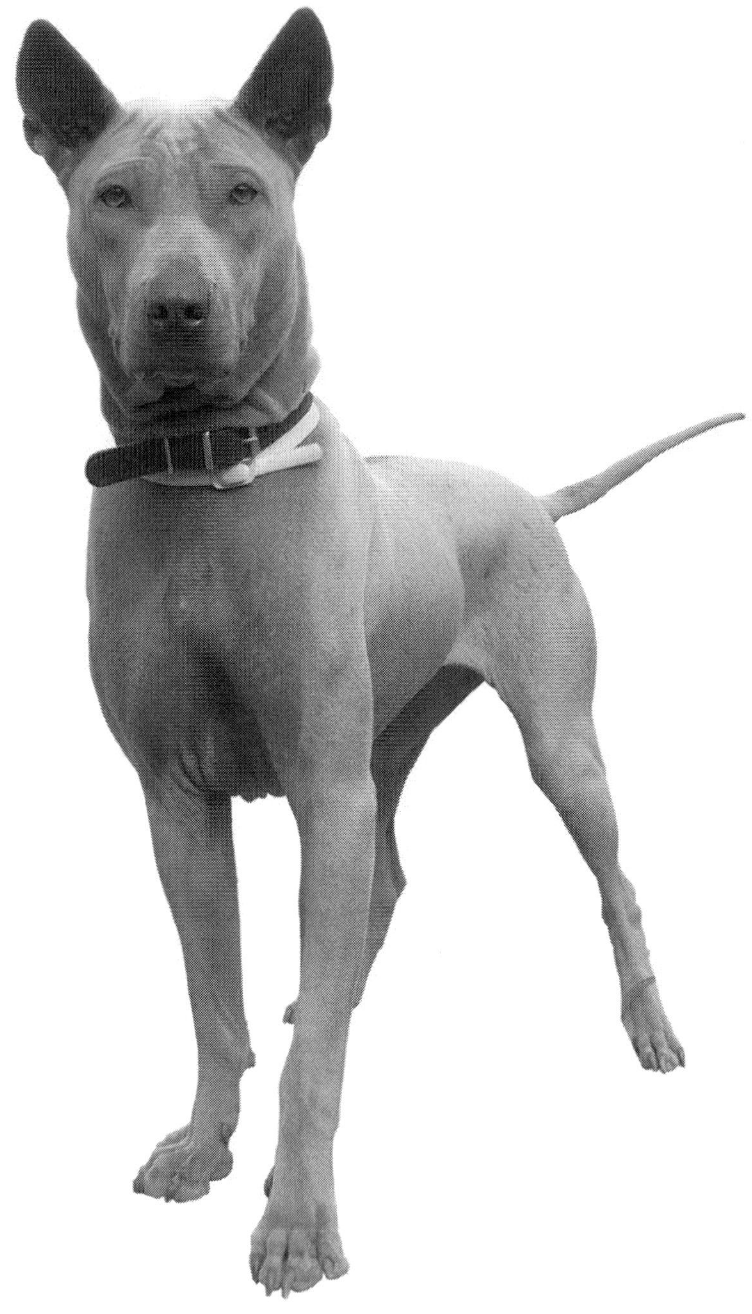

This is a rose. Add to the background and show the unusual place where this rose grows. You may add to the flower by overlapping colors, or adding a little creature on it. Use your imagination and surprise your teacher. Be sure the background is filled in too.

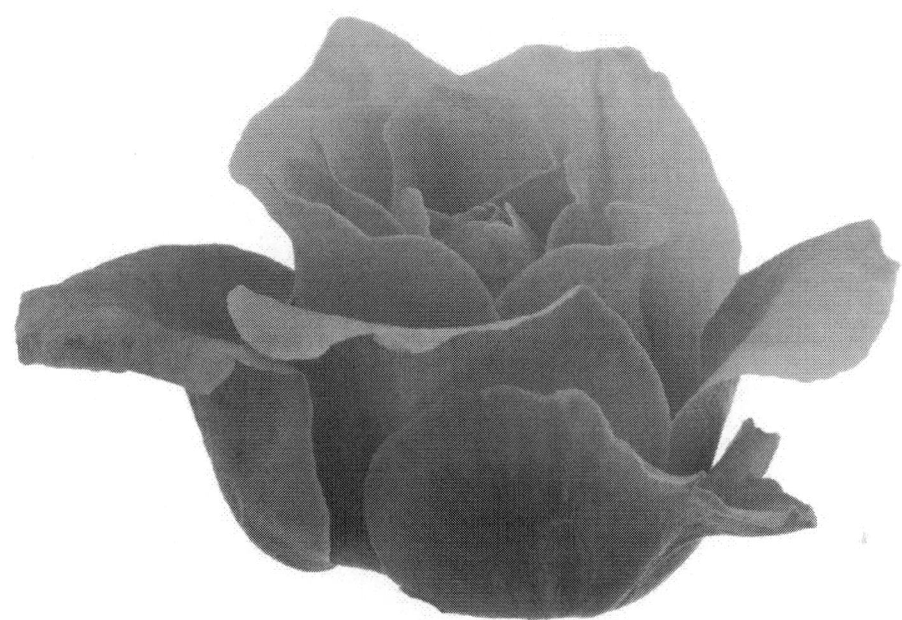

Some Art/Math Answers

1. If your sales tax is 7% then multiply $100 by .07 and the sales tax is $7.
2. Add the above to $100. In this example the amount would be $107.00
3. Retail price is $200. 50% of $200 is $100.
4. Multiply the number of squares in the length by those in the width
5. 70, 70, 166
6. 16 x 14 inches (Remember you have frame on both sides, not one)
7. 216 in^2
8. The ends of rulers are often worn or chipped
9. Multiply the length and height of the wall and divide by 300.
10. Multiply the answer from number 9 by $15.00.
11. Multiply the answer from 10 by your sales tax amount, and add them together.
12. NO: You have to buy the paint, the paper or canvas, the frame, drive the work to the gallery, and all this costs money. Profit is the total money you earned, so you have to subtract (take away) the money it costs to make the art.
13. Rent in New York is almost the highest in the United States. The gallery owner has to pay for lights, heat, rent, taxes, printing invitations, pay to mail things, paying for advertising (commercials) and also has to pay the people who work in the gallery. Running a gallery is very expensive so they need 50% to pay to keep the business open.
14. Multiply the square feet by $5 for the answer.
15. 30 times the number of students. Divide that by 60 for the number of minutes.
16. 12 x 15 inches. Take each number and multiply by 1.5 for the answers.

We are always looking to make improvements, if you spot errors in this edition you wish to make us aware of, or have a lesson you think should be included, please email us directly. For significant help, at our digression, we offer a free copy of the book as a thank you, and note your name as the originator of the material. All submissions become the property of Firehouse Publishing, and the Firehouse Gallery of Bordentown, LLC. Email us directly at: LOVSART@aol.com

Made in United States
Orlando, FL
22 December 2024